STRATEGIC ASSET ALLOCATION

Strategic Asset Allocation

Portfolio Choice for Long-Term Investors

JOHN Y. CAMPBELL
LUIS M. VICEIRA

OXFORD
UNIVERSITY PRESS

OXFORD

UNIVERSITY PRESS

Great Clarendon Street, Oxford OX2 6DP

Oxford University Press is a department of the University of Oxford.
It furthers the University's objective of excellence in research, scholarship,
and education by publishing worldwide in

Oxford New York

Auckland Bangkok Buenos Aires Cape Town Chennai
Dar es Salaam Delhi Hong Kong Istanbul Karachi Kolkata
Kuala Lumpur Madrid Melbourne Mexico City Mumbai Nairobi
São Paulo Shanghai Taipei Tokyo Toronto

Oxford is a registered trade mark of Oxford University Press
in the UK and in certain other countries

Published in the United States
by Oxford University Press Inc., New York

British Library Cataloguing in Publication Data

Data available

Library of Congress Cataloging in Publication Data

Campbell, John Y.
Strategic asset allocation: portfolio choice for long-term investors/
John Y. Campbell, Luis M. Viceira.
p. cm.
Includes bibliographical references.
1. Asset allocation. 2. Portfolio management. 3. Investments. I. Viceira, Luis M.
II. Title.
HG4529.5.C35 2002 332.6—dc21 2001046491
ISBN 0-19-829694-0

5 7 9 10 8 6 4

Typeset by Newgen Imaging Systems (P) Ltd., Chennai, India
Printed in Great Britain
on acid-free paper by
T.J. International Ltd., Padstow, Cornwall

To Alec and Marta

Preface

This book has its origins in John Campbell's graduate class in asset pricing at Harvard University in 1995–6. The course emphasized a simplified approach to the difficult problem of intertemporal asset pricing, in which nonlinear equations are approximated by loglinear equations that capture much of the economics of the problem. Luis Viceira, the teaching fellow for the course, proposed that a similar approach could be used to study the portfolio choice problems of long-term investors. This became the basis of a chapter in Viceira's 1998 Harvard Ph.D. thesis on labor income risk and portfolio choice, published as Viceira (2001), and of a series of joint papers studying various types of risk to investment opportunities: the risk of a changing equity premium, the risks of changing real interest rates and inflation, and the risk of changing volatility (Campbell and Viceira 1999, 2001a; Chacko and Viceira 1999; Campbell, Chan, and Viceira 2001). At the same time, a number of other financial economists realized that portfolio choice theory, long a rather quiet backwater of finance, was again an exciting frontier. Kim and Omberg (1996), Brennan, Schwartz, and Lagnado (1997), Brennan (1998), Balduzzi and Lynch (1999), Brandt (1999), Barberis (2000), and others have developed empirical models of portfolio choice for long-term investors, building on the fundamental insights of Samuelson (1963, 1969), Mossin (1968), Merton (1969, 1971, 1973), Stiglitz (1970), Rubinstein (1976a,b), and Breeden (1979), that have at last fulfilled the empirical promise of that earlier theoretical literature.

In 1999, Campbell delivered three Clarendon Lectures at Oxford summarizing a large part of this research. His first lecture covered the material in Chapters 1–3 of this book; his second lecture presented the material in Chapter 4; and his last lecture discussed material in Chapters 6 and 7. This book further expands the scope of the discussion in an attempt to survey the major themes of the portfolio choice literature in the last few years of the twentieth century.

There has always been a tension in economics between the attempt to describe the optimal choices of fully rational individuals ('positive economics') and the desire to use our models to improve people's imperfect choices ('normative economics'). The desire to improve the world with economics was well expressed by Keynes (1930): 'If economists could manage to get themselves thought of as humble, competent people, on a level with dentists, that would be splendid!' For much of the twentieth century, economists concentrated on improving economic outcomes through government economic policy; Keynes may have imagined the economist as orthodontist, intervening with the painful but effective tools of monetary and fiscal policy. Today dentists spend much of their time giving advice on oral hygiene; similarly, economists can try to provide useful advice to improve the myriad economic decisions that private individuals are asked to make. This book is an attempt at normative economics of this sort.

Of course, optimal portfolio decisions depend on the details of the environment: the financial assets that are available, their expected returns and risks, and the preferences and circumstances of investors. These details become particularly important for long-term investors, who are the subject of this book. Such investors must concern themselves not only with expected returns and risks today, but with the way in which expected returns and risks may change over time. They must also consider their income today and their income prospects for the future. Accordingly, this book emphasizes the statistical analysis of asset returns and of income.

Academic economists are not the only, or even the leading, source of financial advice for long-term investors. A sizeable financial planning industry has arisen to help people save for retirement. This industry is highly sophisticated in some respects (for example in tax planning), but tends to use rules of thumb to guide the trade-off between risk and return. Conservative investors, for example, are advised to hold fewer equities and more bonds than aggressive investors; younger investors are told that it is appropriate for them to take greater equity risk than older investors. Similar rules of thumb are used by the consultants who advise pension funds and endowments. An important purpose of this book is to evaluate such rules of thumb and place them on a firm scientific foundation.

Any book about the principles of investing has a large potential audience. Unfortunately, these principles cannot be explained in detail without mathematical reasoning that many readers would prefer to avoid. We have tried to make the ideas in this book as accessible as possible by explaining them verbally at the beginning and end of each chapter and by using tables and figures to display numerical solutions to particular portfolio choice problems. The introductory Chapter 1 sets the stage for the subsequent analysis, and a verbal summary of our main conclusions can be found at the end of Chapter 7. Chapter 5 contains the highest level of technical detail; this chapter can be skipped without loss of continuity.

A large project of this sort creates tricky issues of notation and terminology. We have tried to minimize notational conflicts across chapters, and in some cases this prevents us from using the most natural notation within each chapter. For example, we use the letter y to denote a bond yield in Chapters 3 and 4, and therefore we use the letter l rather than y to denote labor income in Chapter 6. We also use 'he' and 'his' throughout the book, and intend these words to be gender-neutral. We considered using 'she' and 'her' instead, as we have often done in previous papers, but decided that this was inappropriate given that the empirical results in Chapter 7 are based entirely on male-headed households.

We owe thanks to more people than we can list by name. Dirk Jenter and Josh White provided skilled and tireless research assistance. Lewis Chan was our co-author on the paper (Campbell, Chan, and Viceira 2001) that forms the backbone of Chapter 4. Joao Cocco, Francisco Gomes, and Pascal Maenhout were co-authors of the paper (Campbell *et al.* 2001a) that forms the backbone of Chapter 7. They also wrote with us a paper on the accuracy of the loglinear approximate approach to portfolio choice (Campbell *et al.* 2001b).

We have benefited from the probing questions and insightful comments of these and other students and colleagues, especially David Bates, Geert Bekaert, Michael Brennan, Mark Kritzman, Egil Matsen, Bob Merton, Lars Tyge Nielsen, Rafael Repullo, Mark Rubinstein, Paul Samuelson, Paul Soderlind, Jessica Wachter, and Motohiro Yogo. John Campbell's partners at Arrowstreet Capital, notably John Capeci, Bruce Clarke, and Peter Rathjens, have constantly challenged us to relate our academic work to the concerns of institutional investors and the asset managers who serve them.

The hospitality of Andrew Glyn, on behalf of Corpus Christi College, and Andrew Schuller, on behalf of Oxford University Press, made John Campbell's visit to Oxford particularly enjoyable and productive. Campbell is also grateful for the financial support of the National Science Foundation and the hospitality and financial support of the Sloan School of Management at MIT, through the Fischer Black Visiting Professorship in Finance, during academic year 1998–9. Luis Viceira thanks the Banco de España and the Division of Research of the Harvard Business School for their financial support.

We acknowledge Michael Brennan, Eduardo Schwartz, and Ronald Lagnado (1997) for coining the phrase 'strategic asset allocation' to contrast with 'tactical asset allocation', an industry term for short-term shifts in portfolio weights in response to market conditions. We have borrowed their term for the title of this book. We also thank Ed Keon for suggesting the title of Section 3.3. We particularly thank Bob Shiller for his encouragement and advice. Last but not least, we are deeply grateful to our families for supporting us in this and many other endeavors.

J.Y.C.
L.M.V.

Contents

List of Figures   xiii
List of Tables   xiv

1. Introduction   1

2. Myopic Portfolio Choice   17
   2.1. *Short-Term Portfolio Choice*   18
   2.2. *Myopic Long-Term Portfolio Choice*   31
   2.3. *Conclusion*   46

3. Who Should Buy Long-Term Bonds?   48
   3.1. *Long-Term Portfolio Choice in a Model*
        with Constant Variances and Risk Premia   50
   3.2. *A Model of the Term Structure of Interest Rates*   62
   3.3. *Conclusion: Bonds, James, Bonds*   86

4. Is the Stock Market Safer for Long-Term Investors?   88
   4.1. *Long-Term Portfolio Choice in a VAR Model*   90
   4.2. *Stock and Bond Market Risk in*
        Historical US Data   101
   4.3. *Conclusion*   117

5. Strategic Asset Allocation in Continuous Time   120
   5.1. *The Dynamic Programming Approach*   121
   5.2. *The Martingale Approach*   133
   5.3. *Recursive Utility in Continuous Time*   143
   5.4. *Should Long-Term Investors Hedge Volatility Risk?*   147
   5.5. *Parameter Uncertainty and Portfolio Choice*   154
   5.6. *Conclusion*   160

xii   *Contents*

6. Human Wealth and Financial Wealth   162
    6.1. *Single-Period Models with Labor Income*   167
    6.2. *Labor Income, Precautionary Savings, and*
         Long-Horizon Portfolio Choice   182
    6.3. *Conclusion*   193

7. Investing over the Life Cycle   195
    7.1. *What Do We Know about Household*
         Asset Allocation?   197
    7.2. *A Life-Cycle Model of Portfolio Choice*   202
    7.3. *Conclusion*   219

References   226
Author Index   241
Subject Index   249

List of Figures

1.1. Mean–standard deviation diagram   2
2.1. Concave utility of wealth   22
2.2. Epstein–Zin utility   44
3.1. Fitted real and nominal yields and inflation, 1952–1999   77
3.2. Optimal and myopic allocations to nominal
   bonds and equity, 1952–1999   81
3.3. Optimal and myopic allocations to nominal
   bonds and equity, 1983–1999   83
4.1. Alternative portfolio rules   99
4.2. Variability of multi-period asset returns   109
4.3. Optimal allocations to stocks and
   nominal bonds in annual VAR   111
5.1. Effect of persistence on portfolio demand   152
5.2. Effect of correlation on portfolio demand   153
6.1. Portfolio allocation to stocks plotted against the
   standard deviation of log labor income growth   192
6.2. Target wealth–income ratio plotted against
   the standard deviation of labor income growth   193
7.1. Labor income profiles   209
7.2. Consumption, income, and wealth   212
7.3. Liquid wealth, stocks, and Treasury bills   213

List of Tables

1.1. The asset allocation puzzle of Canner *et al.* (1997)　5
3.1. Term structure model estimation　71
3.2. Sample and implied moments of the term structure　74
3.3. Optimal allocations to equities and long-term bonds　78
4.1. Sample statistics for asset returns　104
4.2. VAR estimation results: annual sample, 1890–1998　105
5.1. Stochastic volatility model estimation　148
5.2. Mean optimal percentage allocation to stocks and percentage hedging demand over myopic demand　151
6.1. Optimal percentage allocation to stocks of employed and retired investors　188
6.2. Optimal long-run holdings of financial wealth relative to income　190
7.1. Baseline parameters　210
7.2. Variance decomposition of labor income　215
7.3. Regression of permanent aggregate shock on lagged excess stock returns　217
7.4. Life-cycle profiles　218

1

Introduction

One of the most important decisions many people face is the choice of a portfolio of assets for retirement savings. These assets may be held as a supplement to defined-benefit public or private pension plans; or they may be accumulated in a defined-contribution pension plan, as the major source of retirement income. In either case, a dizzying array of assets is available.

Consider for example the increasing set of choices offered by TIAA–CREF, the principal pension organization for university employees in the United States. Until 1988, the two available choices were TIAA, a traditional nominal annuity, and CREF, an actively managed equity fund. Funds could readily be moved from CREF to TIAA, but the reverse transfer was difficult and could be accomplished only gradually. In 1988 it became possible to move funds between two CREF accounts, a money market fund and an equity fund. Since then other choices have been added: a bond fund and a socially responsible stock fund in 1990, a global equity fund in 1992, equity index and growth funds in 1994, a real estate fund in 1995, and an inflation-indexed bond fund in 1997. Retirement savings can easily be moved among these funds, each of which represents a broad class of assets with a different profile of returns.

Institutional investors also face complex decisions. Some institutions invest on behalf of their clients, but others, such as foundations and university endowments, are similar to individuals in that they seek to finance a long-term stream of discretionary spending. The investment options for these institutions have also expanded enormously since the days when a portfolio of government bonds was the norm.

Mean–variance analysis
What does financial economics have to say about these investment decisions? Modern finance theory is often thought to have started with the mean–variance analysis of Markowitz (1952); this

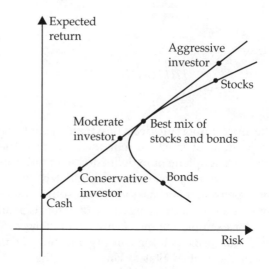

Figure 1.1. Mean–standard deviation diagram.

makes portfolio choice theory the original subject of modern finance. Markowitz showed how investors should pick assets if they care only about the mean and variance—or equivalently the mean and standard deviation—of portfolio returns over a single period.

The results of his analysis are shown in the classic mean–standard deviation diagram, Figure 1.1. (A much more careful mathematical explanation can be found in the next chapter.) For simplicity the figure considers three assets: stocks, bonds, and cash (not literally currency, but a short-term money market fund). The vertical axis shows expected return, and the horizontal axis shows risk as measured by standard deviation. Stocks are shown as offering a high mean return and a high standard deviation, bonds a lower mean and lower standard deviation. Cash has a lower mean return again, but is riskless over one period, so it is plotted on the vertical zero-risk axis. (In the presence of inflation risk, nominal money market investments are not literally riskless in real terms, but this short-term inflation risk is small enough that it is conventional to ignore it. We follow this convention here and return to the issue in the next chapter.)

The curved line in Figure 1.1 shows the set of means and standard deviations that can be achieved by combining stocks and bonds in a risky portfolio. When cash is added to a portfolio of risky assets, the set of means and standard deviations that can be achieved is a straight line on the diagram connecting cash to the risky portfolio. An investor who cares only about the mean and standard deviation of his portfolio will choose a point on the straight line illustrated in the figure, that is tangent to the curved line. This straight line, the mean–variance efficient frontier, offers the highest mean return for any given standard deviation. The point where the straight line touches the curved line is a 'tangency portfolio' of risky assets, marked in the figure as 'Best mix of stocks and bonds'.

The striking conclusion of this analysis is that all investors who care only about mean and standard deviation will hold the same portfolio of risky assets, the unique best mix of stocks and bonds. Conservative investors will combine this portfolio with cash to achieve a point on the mean–variance efficient frontier that is low down and to the left; moderate investors will reduce their cash holdings, moving up and to the right; aggressive investors may even borrow to leverage their holdings of the tangency portfolio, reaching a point on the straight line that is even riskier than the tangency portfolio. But none of these investors should alter the relative proportions of risky assets in the tangency portfolio. This result is the mutual fund theorem of Tobin (1958).

Financial planning advice
Financial planners have traditionally resisted the simple investment advice embodied in Figure 1.1. This resistance may to some extent be self-serving; as Peter Bernstein points out in his 1992 book *Capital Ideas*, many financial planners and advisors justify their fees by emphasizing the need for each investor to build a portfolio reflecting his or her unique personal situation. Bernstein calls this the 'interior decorator fallacy', the view that portfolios should reflect personal characteristics in the same way that interior decor reflects personal taste.

There are however many legitimate reasons why different portfolios of risky assets might be appropriate for different investors. The complexity of the tax code creates many differences across investors, not only in their tax brackets but also in their opportunities for sheltering income from taxation. Beyond this, investors differ in their investment horizons: some may have relatively short-term objectives, others may be saving to make college tuition payments in the medium term, yet others may be saving for retirement or to ensure the well-being of their heirs. Investors also differ in the characteristics of their labor income: young investors may expect many years of income, which may be relatively safe for some and risky for others, while older investors may need to finance the bulk of their consumption from accumulated financial wealth. Investors often have illiquid assets such as family businesses, restricted stock options granted by their employer, or real estate.[1] We shall argue in this book that the traditional academic analysis of portfolio choice needs to be modified to handle long investment horizons, labor income, and illiquid assets. The modified theory explains several of the patterns that we see in conventional financial planning advice.

One strong pattern is that financial planners typically encourage young investors, with a long investment horizon, to take more risk than older investors. The single-period mean–variance analysis illustrated in Figure 1.1 assumes a short investment horizon. In this book we shall explore the conditions under which a long investment horizon does indeed justify greater risk-taking.

A second pattern in financial planning advice is that conservative investors are typically encouraged to hold more bonds, relative to stocks, than aggressive investors, contrary to the constant bond–stock ratio illustrated in Figure 1.1. Canner, Mankiw, and Weil (1997) call this the *asset allocation puzzle*. Table 1.1, which reproduces Table 1 from Canner *et al.*'s article, illustrates the puzzle. The table summarizes model portfolios recommended by four different investment advisors in the early 1990s: Fidelity, Merrill Lynch, the financial journalist Jane Bryant Quinn, and the *New York Times*. While the portfolios differ in their details, in every case the recommended ratio of bonds to stocks is

---

[1] Perhaps some of these differences underlie the PaineWebber advertisement that ran in the *New Yorker* and other magazines in 1998: 'If our clients were all the same, their *portfolios* would be too. *They say* the research has been sifted. The numbers have been crunched. The analysts have spoken: Behold! The ideal portfolio. *We say* building a portfolio is not "one size fits all". It begins with knowing you—how you feel about money, how much risk you can tolerate, your hopes for your family, and for your future. By starting with the human element, our Financial Advisors can do something a black box can't do—take the benefits of what PaineWebber has to offer and create an investment plan unique to you.'

Table 1.1. The Asset Allocation Puzzle of Canner *et al.* (1997)

Advisor and investor type	% of portfolio			Ratio of bonds to stocks
	Cash	Bonds	Stocks	
(A) Fidelity				
Conservative	50	30	20	1.50
Moderate	20	40	40	1.00
Aggressive	5	30	65	0.46
(B) Merrill Lynch				
Conservative	20	35	45	0.78
Moderate	5	40	55	0.73
Aggressive	5	20	75	0.27
(C) Jane Bryant Quinn				
Conservative	50	30	20	1.50
Moderate	10	40	50	0.80
Aggressive	0	0	100	0.00
(D) New York Times				
Conservative	20	40	40	1.00
Moderate	10	30	60	0.50
Aggressive	0	20	80	0.25

higher for moderate investors than for aggressive investors, and higher again for conservative investors.

One possible explanation for this pattern of advice is that aggressive investors are unable to borrow at the riskless interest rate, and thus cannot reach the upper right portion of the straight line in Figure 1.1. In this situation, aggressive investors should move along the curved line, increasing their allocation to stocks and reducing their allocation to bonds. The difficulty with this explanation is that it only applies after the constraint on borrowing has started to bind on investors, that is, once cash holdings have been reduced to zero; but the bond–stock ratio in Canner *et al.*'s Table 1 varies even when cash holdings are positive.[2]

---

[2] Elton and Gruber (2000) reconcile the asset allocations in Table 1.1 with mean–variance analysis by arguing that short-term investments are risky in real terms, short sales are restricted, and 5% of the portfolio should be held in cash as a special liquidity reserve. One problem with their analysis is that much of the variability in short-term real returns is predictable, as we show in Chapter 3; thus, it does not

Long-term portfolios

This book argues that it is possible to make sense of both the asset allocation puzzle and the tendency of financial planners to recommend riskier portfolios to young investors. The key is to recognize that optimal portfolios for long-term investors need not be the same as for short-term investors. Long-term investors, who value wealth not for its own sake but for the standard of living that it can support, may judge risks very differently from short-term investors. Cash, for example, is risky in the long term even though it is safe in the short term, because cash holdings must be reinvested in the future at unknown real interest rates. Inflation-indexed bonds, on the other hand, provide a known stream of long-term real payments even though their capital value is uncertain in the short term. There is considerable evidence that stocks, too, can support a stable standard of living more successfully than their short-term price variability would indicate. For these reasons, a long-term investor may be willing to hold more stocks and bonds, and less cash, than a short-term investor would do; and a conservative long-term investor may hold a portfolio that is dominated by bonds rather than cash.

Labor income is also important for long-term investors. One can think of working investors as implicitly holding an asset—human wealth—whose dividends equal labor income. This asset is non-tradable, so investors cannot sell it; but they can adjust their financial asset holdings to take account of their implicit holdings of human wealth. For most investors, human wealth is sufficiently stable in value to tilt financial portfolios towards greater holdings of risky assets.

At a theoretical level, these points have been understood for many years. Samuelson (1963, 1969), Mossin (1968), Merton (1969), and Fama (1970) first described the restrictive conditions under which long-horizon investors should make the same decisions as short-horizon investors. Modigliani and Sutch (1966) asserted that long-term bonds are safe assets for long-term investors, and Stiglitz (1970) and Rubinstein (1976a,b) built

represent risk to a short-term investor. Note that for advisors other than Merrill Lynch, the stock–bond ratio in Table 1.1 varies at cash holdings that are considerably greater than 5%, so a 5% liquidity reserve by itself does not resolve the asset allocation puzzle.

rigorous theoretical models that validate and illustrate this point. Mayers (1972) and Fama and Schwert (1977b) asked how human wealth influences portfolio choice. The seminal work of Merton (1971, 1973) provided a general framework for understanding the portfolio demands of long-term investors when investment opportunities vary over time. Rubinstein (1976b) and Breeden (1979) showed how Merton's results could be interpreted in terms of consumption risk, an idea that has had major influence in macroeconomics through the work of Lucas (1978), Grossman and Shiller (1981), Shiller (1982), Hansen and Singleton (1983), Mehra and Prescott (1985), and others.

Until recently, however, empirical work on long-term portfolio choice has lagged far behind the theoretical literature. Perhaps for this reason, there has been very slow diffusion of understanding from the academic literature to institutional investors, asset managers, financial planners, and households. Most MBA courses, for example, still teach mean–variance analysis as if it were a universally accepted framework for portfolio choice.

One reason for the slow development of the field has been the difficulty of solving Merton's intertemporal model. Closed-form solutions to the model have been available only in a few special cases, in which it turns out that long-term portfolios should be the same as short-term portfolios. Recently this situation has begun to change as a result of several related developments. First, computing power and numerical methods have advanced to the point at which realistic multi-period portfolio choice problems can be solved numerically using discrete-state approximations.[3] Second, financial theorists have discovered some new closed-form solutions to the Merton model.[4] Third, approximate

---

[3] Balduzzi and Lynch (1999), Barberis (2000), Brennan, Schwartz, and Lagnado (1997, 1999), Cocco, Gomes, and Maenhout (1998), and Lynch (2001) are important examples of this style of work.

[4] In a continuous-time model with a constant riskless interest rate and a single risky asset whose expected return follows a mean-reverting (Ornstein–Uhlenbeck) process, for example, the model can be solved if long-lived investors have power utility defined over terminal wealth, or if investors have power utility defined over consumption and the innovation to the expected asset return is perfectly correlated with the innovation to the unexpected return, making the asset market effectively complete, or if the investor has Epstein–Zin utility with intertemporal elasticity of substitution equal to one. We discuss these results in detail in Ch. 5.

analytical solutions have been developed (Campbell and Viceira 1999, 2001a). These solutions are based on perturbations of known exact solutions, so they are accurate in a neighborhood of those solutions. They offer analytical insights into portfolio choice in models that fall outside the still limited class that can be solved exactly. This book offers examples of all three approaches to long-term portfolio choice, but the major emphasis is on approximate analytical solution methods and on the development of empirical models that can be used by practitioners as well as academics.

Utility theory and behavioral finance

Throughout the book, we derive portfolio decisions using standard finance models of preferences. We assume that investors derive utility from consumption, which in turn is supported by financial wealth (and possibly labor income). The utility function takes a standard form in which relative risk aversion is constant.[5] Our contributions are in modelling the financial environment, and developing the link between that environment and portfolio choice, rather than in modelling investor preferences.

Some investment practitioners are uncomfortable with the academic use of utility functions. However, investor preferences—in particular impatience and aversion to risk—do influence optimal portfolios. Students of portfolio choice have no alternative but to model preferences, no matter how hard that task may be. We regard utility functions as a convenient way to capture intuitive notions such as the distinction between conservative and aggressive investors. While it may be hard to interpret numbers such as the coefficient of relative risk aversion in the abstract, our experience is that these numbers are easy to use and to understand in the context of specific empirical models.

---

[5] We do allow the elasticity of intertemporal substitution to differ from the coefficient of relative risk aversion, following Epstein and Zin (1989), while assuming that both parameters are constant. Also, in Ch. 6 we briefly discuss models in which utility is derived from the difference between consumption and a subsistence level. Such models imply that relative risk aversion is constant if consumption and the subsistence level both increase in proportion, but is decreasing if consumption increases relative to the subsistence level. Gollier and Zeckhauser (1997) and Ross (1999) explore horizon effects in models where utility is defined over terminal wealth and can take a general form.

Recently there has been great interest in the field of behavioral finance, which postulates that some investors have non-standard preferences. Often these preferences are modelled using experimental evidence from psychology. The prospect theory of Kahneman and Tversky (1979), for example, models utility as depending on wealth relative to a reference point; the utility function has a kink at the reference point, and different patterns of curvature above and below this point. The theory of mental accounting (Thaler 1985) goes further by suggesting that investors care directly about the values of individual stocks in their portfolios rather than their total wealth. These and many other behavioral models are surveyed by Shiller (1999).

We regard behavioral finance as a promising research area with the potential to explain some types of investor behavior and possibly some patterns in asset pricing. However, we do not believe that it provides a sound basis for a normative theory of asset allocation. First, the experimental evidence that motivates many behavioral models is based on individuals' reactions to risks that are necessarily small. It is impossible to design an experiment that subjects individuals to the large risks they face when saving over a lifetime. Standard theory probably applies better to large risks, with potentially serious consequences for lifetime well-being, than to small risks in an experimental setting.[6] Second, even if behavioral finance describes how investors actually do behave, it may not describe how they should behave. That is, investors may abandon their behavioral biases once they have the benefit of financial education and financial planning advice.[7]

More specifically, we believe that any normative model should judge a portfolio by its total value, rather than by the values of

[6] Consistent with this view, Bowman, Minehart, and Rabin (1999) embed small-scale behavioral elements in a more standard large-scale model of preferences.

[7] There is also some recent work in decision theory that develops axiomatic foundations for models with reference points (Gul 1991). Such models have been applied to equilibrium asset pricing problems by Epstein and Zin (1990) and Bekaert, Hodrick, and Marshall (1997b), and to portfolio choice problems by Ang, Bekaert, and Liu (2000). It is conceivable, but in our view unlikely, that such models will displace the constant relative risk-averse model used in this book as the standard paradigm of finance theory. We believe that a more promising approach is to incorporate reference points within the constant relative risk-averse paradigm by modelling subsistence levels in the manner discussed in Ch. 6.

the individual assets it contains, and should ultimately be based on the standard of living that the portfolio supports. That is, both wealth and expected asset returns are relevant for an investor because these variables determine the consumption that the investor can afford. This normative use of standard finance theory does not contradict behavioral finance as a positive description of investor behavior; in fact, the motivation for a normative analysis is much stronger if investors are subject to behavioral biases than if they are already successfully making optimal portfolio decisions.

The equity premium puzzle
Our thesis in this book is that long-term portfolio choice theory can be implemented empirically to deliver specific quantitative advice about asset allocation. To illustrate the potential of the theory, we solve for the portfolios that are implied by particular preference parameters, together with particular beliefs about the stochastic processes driving asset returns and income. Although our framework can be used by investors with arbitrary beliefs, for illustrative purposes we want to assume beliefs that are reasonable given historical data. A natural approach is to estimate a parametric model for asset returns on historical data, and then to use the estimated parameters to calculate optimal portfolios. In Chapter 3 we use an affine term structure model in this way, in Chapter 4 we use a vector autoregression, and in Chapter 5 we use a stochastic volatility model.

This approach runs into difficulties when we compute the optimal holdings of equities. Historical average returns on US equities have been extraordinarily high relative to returns on bills or bonds, and equities are correspondingly attractive to investors who believe that these returns will continue in the future. Investors with low or moderate risk aversion will hold highly leveraged equity portfolios if they are permitted to do so, and their consumption will be extremely volatile. Only the most conservative investors will shy away from equity risk, given historically based beliefs about stock returns. Many of the considerations we emphasize in this book, such as mean-reversion in stock returns (Chapter 4) and the need to take account of labor income (Chapters 6 and 7), only increase investors' enthusiasm for stocks. Factors that might dampen this enthusiasm, such as volatility risk and uncertainty about average returns (Chapter 5), appear to be somewhat less important empirically.

This raises the question of how such high average stock returns can be consistent with equilibrium in the stock market. Why don't enthusiastic investors bid up the prices of stocks so that their average returns fall to more reasonable levels? In the asset pricing literature, this issue is known as the *equity premium puzzle.* Mehra and Prescott (1985) first identified high average stock returns as a puzzle, building on the theoretical work of Rubinstein (1976b), Lucas (1978), Breeden (1979), and Grossman and Shiller (1981). Economists have worked intensively on the puzzle for over 15 years but have not agreed on an explanation.[8] Certainly the factors discussed in this book tend to exacerbate the puzzle rather than solve it, as pointed out by Campbell (1996).

One reasonable response to the equity premium puzzle is that historical US data are a misleading guide to future stock returns. Perhaps the twentieth century was an unusually lucky period in which favorable shocks produced stock returns that were well above the true long-run average. Economists such as Blanchard (1993), Campbell and Shiller (2001), Fama and French (2000), and Jagannathan, McGrattan, and Scherbina (2001) have all argued that average stock returns are likely to be lower in the future than they have been in the past.

We do not try to settle the issue in this book; it is something that each investor must decide for himself. Instead, we illustrate alternative responses to the puzzle. In Chapters 3, 4, and 5 we use historically estimated parameters without modification. In Chapters 6 and 7, by contrast, we assume a fixed equity premium of 4%, considerably below the historical average but still large enough to make equities an attractive asset class for long-term investors.

Limitations of the book
This book has several limitations that should be acknowledged at the outset. First, we provide an analysis of asset allocation rather than a complete analysis of portfolio choice. That is, we work with broad asset classes such as cash, equities, inflation-indexed

---

[8] Kocherlakota (1996) and Campbell (1999) survey the enormous literature on the equity premium puzzle.

bonds, and nominal bonds, and we say nothing about the choice of individual assets within these broad classes. This is not because the choice of individual assets is unimportant—in fact, the benefits of diversification are enormous—but because we have nothing to add to the traditional mean–variance analysis on this subject.

In effect, we assume that investors have already formed diversified portfolios within each asset class and face a final decision about the amounts to invest in each portfolio. Thus, our results can help individual investors allocate their retirement savings among broadly diversified mutual funds, but not investors trying to pick individual stocks. Similarly, our results are relevant for pension funds and endowments determining their strategic policy portfolios, but are not directly relevant for active asset managers who are judged on their short-term performance relative to a benchmark index within their asset class.

A second limitation is that we do not consider international issues. In our empirical work, we adopt a traditional closed-economy perspective and look at US data to measure the returns on asset classes. Our models could be applied without difficulty to an integrated global economy, in which each asset class contains asset from different countries. We do not explore models with international state variables such as real exchange rates.

Third, for most of the book we assume that investors know with certainty the parameters of the process generating asset returns, including the means, variances, and covariances of returns and the evolution of these moments over time. As we have already discussed, either we can assume that these parameters equal historically estimated values (as we do in Chapters 3, 4, and 5) or we can assume arbitrary parameters reflecting beliefs that the future will differ from the past (as we do in Chapters 6 and 7). It is more challenging to incorporate parameter uncertainty into the asset allocation decision. If an investor anticipates that he will learn by observing asset market data, changing his beliefs in response to returns, this introduces a new type of intertemporal hedging demand into the portfolio decision. We provide a very brief introduction to the literature on optimal learning in Chapter 5, but can do no more than scratch the surface of this important topic.

Fourth, we assume that assets can be traded without cost. Transaction costs are extremely important for investment strategies that require frequent trading, but are less critical for the long-term asset allocation decisions that are the subject of this book.

Fifth, we ignore taxation. Our results apply directly to tax-exempt investors such as endowments or foundations. In a setting where each asset class return has a given tax rate, which is not affected by the length of time the asset class is held, our results apply to taxable investors if we model after-tax returns rather than pre-tax returns. It is much more difficult to handle taxes like the capital gains tax, whose burden depends on whether an asset is held or sold.[9]

Sixth, we have nothing to say about housing. For many individuals this is an important asset that plays multiple roles: it is a large component of wealth, a fixed commitment that is costly to reverse, and a source of housing services and tax benefits. Real estate is equally important in the portfolios of many institutional investors.

Finally, we present a series of partial models rather than a single integrated model that captures all the important aspects of strategic asset allocation. In the first part of the book, for example, we consider time-varying investment opportunities but ignore labor income, while in the last two chapters we assume fixed investment opportunities and concentrate our efforts on realistically modelling labor income. We follow this approach both because it delivers the clearest insights about each aspect of strategic asset allocation, and because the academic literature has not yet developed a reliable, generally accepted model of the complete portfolio problem.

For all these reasons, our book is no substitute for traditional financial planning advice. Nor do we provide cookbook formulas for optimal portfolio weights. Instead, we try to explain carefully what it means to have a long investment horizon. Our objective is to provide a rigorous, empirically relevant framework that

[9] Constantinides (1983, 1984) discusses optimal investment, strategies for taxable investors in the presence of capital gains taxes. Constantinides derives restrictive conditions under which portfolio choice is unaffected by such taxes. Dammon, Spatt, and Zhang (2001) discuss capital gains taxes in a life-cycle model.

long-term investors can use to understand the trade-off of risk and return.

Organization of the book
The rest of the book is organized as follows. Chapter 2 first reviews the traditional mean–variance analysis, showing how it can be founded on utility theory. The chapter argues that the benchmark model of utility should assume that relative risk aversion is independent of wealth. With this assumption, there are well-known conditions under which long-term investors should invest myopically, choosing the same portfolios as short-term investors. Chapter 2 explains these conditions, due originally to Merton (1969) and Samuelson (1969). Myopic portfolio choice is optimal if investors have no labor income and investment opportunities are constant over time. If investors have relative risk aversion equal to one, then myopic portfolio choice is optimal even if investment opportunities are time-varying. Although these conditions are simple, they are widely misunderstood, and the chapter makes an effort to address fallacies that commonly arise in popular discussion.

Legitimate arguments for horizon effects on portfolio choice depend on violations of the Merton–Samuelson conditions. Chapters 3–7 explore such violations. Chapter 3 argues that investment opportunities are not constant because real interest rates move over time. Even if expected excess returns on risky assets over safe assets are constant, time variation in real interest rates is enough to generate large differences between optimal portfolios for long-term and short-term investors. The chapter shows that conservative long-term investors should hold portfolios that consist largely of long-term bonds. These bonds should be inflation-indexed if possible; however, nominal bonds may be adequate substitutes for inflation-indexed bonds if inflation risk is modest, as it has been in the United States since the early 1980s.

The assumption of constant risk premia in Chapter 3 implies that optimal portfolios are constant over time for both short-term and long-term investors. Chapter 4 allows for time variation in the expected excess returns on stocks and bonds. This generates time variation in optimal portfolios: Both short-term and long-term investors should seek to 'time the markets', holding more risky assets at times when the rewards for doing so are high.

But in addition, long-term investors with relative risk aversion greater than one should increase their average holdings of risky assets whose returns are negatively correlated with the rewards for risk-bearing; for example, they should increase their average allocation to stocks because the stock market appears to mean-revert, doing relatively poorly after price increases and relatively well after price declines. These findings are an empirical development of Merton's (1973) theoretical concept of intertemporal hedging by long-term investors.

Chapter 5 seeks to relate the results of Chapters 3 and 4 more closely to the extensive theoretical literature set in continuous time. Explicit solutions for optimal portfolios are provided in Chapters 3 and 4 by the use of loglinear approximations to discrete-time Euler equations and budget constraints. Chapter 5 clarifies the conditions under which such approximate solutions hold exactly, and shows how equivalent approximations can be used in continuous time. This chapter also explores optimal portfolio choice in the presence of time-varying stock market risk and parameter uncertainty. Chapter 5 is the most technically demanding chapter in the book, and less mathematical readers can skip it without loss of continuity.

Chapters 6 and 7 introduce labor income into the long-term portfolio choice problem. Chapter 6 discusses the effect of human wealth—a claim to a stream of labor income—on the optimal allocation of financial wealth by investors with constant relative risk aversion. Drawing on an important paper by Bodie, Merton, and Samuelson (1992), this chapter first uses a stylized two-period model to show that exogenous labor income reduces the aversion to financial risk by reducing the proportional sensitivity of consumption to asset returns. If investors can flexibly adjust their labor supply, varying their labor income endogenously in response to circumstances, their aversion to financial risk is further reduced. This chapter also considers the possibility that investors have subsistence levels—required minimum levels of consumption—and that they derive utility only from consumption that exceeds subsistence needs. The chapter shows that subsistence levels work like negative labor income, subtracting utility-generating resources from financial wealth in the same way that labor income adds resources. Finally, the chapter extends the analysis to a stylized long-horizon model in which employed investors have an exogenous probability of retirement each period.

Chapter 7 embeds labor income in a life-cycle model and asks how investors should adjust their portfolios as they age. The chapter shows that typical households should be willing to invest heavily in risky financial assets in early adulthood, but should scale back their financial risk-taking in late middle age. This conclusion is consistent with the typical advice of financial planners. The chapter also shows that different households can have very different risk properties of their labor income, and that this has large effects on optimal portfolio allocations. Self-employed, college-educated households, for example, have labor income that is particularly volatile and highly correlated with stock returns; these households should be cautious about equity investments.

Chapter 7 also reviews the existing empirical evidence on how households actually do invest over the life cycle. The evidence is fragmentary, and it is clear that household investment strategies are extraordinarily diverse; but a few patterns do appear consistent with the normative recommendations of the life-cycle model. For example, there is some tendency for household risk exposure to decline with age in later years, and wealthy households that own private businesses tend to own fewer publicly traded equities than other wealthy households. The chapter ends by drawing general conclusions that summarize the message of this book.

2

Myopic Portfolio Choice

In this chapter, we review the theory of portfolio choice for short-term investors and explain the special cases in which long-term investors should make the same choices as short-term investors. In these special cases the investment horizon is irrelevant; portfolio choice is said to be myopic because investors ignore what might happen beyond the immediate next period. Throughout the chapter, we assume that investors have financial wealth but no labor income.

The results in this chapter are well known to financial economists. Our contribution is merely to summarize the wisdom of the economics profession. We try to do so in a way that is as accessible as possible, given the inherent complexity of the interaction between time and uncertainty.

Section 2.1 discusses optimal portfolio choice for short-term investors. We begin in Section 2.1.1 with the classic mean–variance analysis of Markowitz (1952), assuming that investors care directly about the mean and variance of portfolio returns over one period. Then in Section 2.1.2 we derive similar results assuming that investors have a utility function defined over wealth at the end of one period. We discuss alternative assumptions that can be made about utility, arguing that there are good reasons to prefer scale-independent utility functions in which relative risk aversion does not depend on wealth. The simplest scale-independent utility function is power utility, and we show how to derive portfolio results analogous to those of the mean–variance analysis, assuming power utility and lognormally distributed returns.

In Section 2.2 we derive conditions under which the same portfolio choice is optimal for long-term investors. We first assume in Section 2.2.1 that investors have power utility defined over wealth many periods ahead. We show that, if investors can rebalance their portfolios each period, they should invest myopically if asset returns are independent and identically distributed (IID) over time or if utility takes the log form. Log utility is the special case of power utility in which both the coefficient of relative risk aversion and the elasticity of intertemporal substitution in consumption equal one.

The conditions for myopic portfolio choice are quite simple and can be derived without the use of advanced mathematics. Nonetheless, these conditions are widely misunderstood, and one often sees specious arguments that there should be horizon effects even when the conditions hold. In Section 2.2.2 we try to expose the fallacies in these arguments.

In Section 2.2.3 we consider investors who have power utility defined over consumption and show that portfolio choice will be myopic under the same conditions as before. Finally, in Section 2.2.4 we introduce a generalization of power utility, Epstein–Zin utility, which allows us to distinguish between the coefficient of risk aversion and the elasticity of intertemporal substitution in consumption. Power utility links these concepts tightly together, making one the reciprocal of the other, but they are different concepts which play quite different roles in the analysis. We show that portfolio choice is myopic if relative risk aversion equals one, regardless of the value of the elasticity of intertemporal substitution in consumption. Epstein–Zin utility will be used extensively in the rest of the book.

Throughout the chapter there is a strong emphasis on the difference between simple returns and log returns, and on the adjustments that are needed to translate from one type of return to the other. Elementary treatments of portfolio choice often gloss over this difference, but it is central to the theory of portfolio choice for long-term investors.

2.1. SHORT-TERM PORTFOLIO CHOICE

2.1.1. *Mean–variance analysis*

Choosing the weight on a single risky asset

Consider the following classic portfolio choice problem. Two assets are available to an investor at time t. One is riskless, with simple return $R_{f,t+1}$ from time t to time $t+1$, and the other is risky. The risky asset has simple return R_{t+1} from time t to time $t+1$, with conditional mean $E_t R_{t+1}$ and conditional variance σ_t^2. Note the timing convention that returns are given time subscripts for the date at which they are realized; the risk-free interest rate is realized at $t+1$ but is known one period in advance at time t. The conditional mean and conditional variance are the mean and variance conditional on the investor's information at time t; thus they are written with t subscripts.

The investor puts a share α_t of his portfolio into the risky asset. Then the portfolio return is

$$R_{p,t+1} = \alpha_t R_{t+1} + (1 - \alpha_t)R_{f,t+1} = R_{f,t+1} + \alpha_t(R_{t+1} - R_{f,t+1}).$$
(2.1)

The mean portfolio return is $E_t R_{p,t+1} = R_{f,t+1} + \alpha_t(E_t R_{t+1} - R_{f,t+1})$, while the variance of the portfolio return is $\sigma_{pt}^2 = \alpha_t^2 \sigma_t^2$.

The investor prefers a high mean and a low variance of portfolio returns. We assume that the investor trades off mean and variance in a linear fashion. That is, he maximizes a linear combination of mean and variance, with a positive weight on mean and a negative weight on variance:

$$\max_{\alpha_t}\left(E_t R_{p,t+1} - \frac{k}{2}\sigma_{pt}^2 \right).$$
(2.2)

Substituting in the mean and variance of portfolio returns, and subtracting $R_{f,t+1}$ (which does not change the maximization problem), this can be rewritten as

$$\max_{\alpha_t} \alpha_t(E_t R_{t+1} - R_{f,t+1}) - \frac{k}{2}\alpha_t^2\sigma_t^2.$$
(2.3)

The solution to this maximization problem is

$$\alpha_t = \frac{E_t R_{t+1} - R_{f,t+1}}{k\sigma_t^2}.$$
(2.4)

The portfolio share in the risky asset should equal the expected excess return, or risk premium, divided by conditional variance times the coefficient k that represents aversion to variance. We will see similar expressions frequently in this book.

A useful concept in portfolio analysis is the Sharpe ratio S_t (Sharpe 1966), defined as the ratio of mean excess return to standard deviation:

$$S_t = \frac{E_t R_{t+1} - R_{f,t+1}}{\sigma_t}. \tag{2.5}$$

The portfolio solution can be rewritten as

$$\alpha_t = \frac{S_t}{k\sigma_t}. \tag{2.6}$$

The mean excess return on the portfolio is S_t^2/k and the variance of the portfolio is S_t^2/k^2, so the ratio of mean to variance is $1/k$. The standard deviation of the portfolio is S_t/k, so the Sharpe ratio of the portfolio is S_t. In this simple model, all portfolios have the same Sharpe ratio because they all contain the same risky asset in greater or smaller amount.

Mean–variance analysis with many risky assets
These results extend straightforwardly to the case where there are many risky assets. We define the portfolio return in the same manner as before, except that we use boldface letters to denote vectors and matrices. Thus, $\mathbf{R}_{t+1}$ is now a vector of risky returns with N elements. It has a mean vector $E_t\mathbf{R}_{t+1}$ and a variance–covariance matrix $\mathbf{\Sigma}_t$. Also, $\boldsymbol{\alpha}_t$ is now a vector of allocations to the risky assets. The maximization problem (2.3) now becomes

$$\max_{\boldsymbol{\alpha}_t} \boldsymbol{\alpha}_t'(E_t\mathbf{R}_{t+1} - R_{f,t+1}\iota) - \frac{k}{2}\boldsymbol{\alpha}_t'\mathbf{\Sigma}_t\boldsymbol{\alpha}_t. \tag{2.7}$$

Here ι is a vector of ones, and $(E_t\mathbf{R}_{t+1} - R_{f,t+1}\iota)$ is the vector of excess returns on the N risky assets over the riskless interest rate. The variance of the portfolio return is $\boldsymbol{\alpha}_t'\mathbf{\Sigma}_t\boldsymbol{\alpha}_t$.

The solution to this maximization problem is

$$\boldsymbol{\alpha}_t = \frac{1}{k}\mathbf{\Sigma}_t^{-1}(E_t\mathbf{R}_{t+1} - R_{f,t+1}\iota). \tag{2.8}$$

This is a straightforward generalization of the solution with a single risky asset. The single excess return is replaced by a vector of excess returns, and the reciprocal of variance is replaced by $\mathbf{\Sigma}_t^{-1}$, the inverse of the variance–covariance matrix of returns.

The investor's preferences enter the solution (2.8) only through the scalar term $1/k$. Thus, investors differ only in the overall scale of their risky asset portfolio, not in the composition of that portfolio. Conservative investors with a high k hold more of the riskless asset and less of all risky assets, but they do not change the relative proportions of their risky assets, which are determined by the vector $\Sigma_t^{-1}(E_t\mathbf{R}_{t+1} - R_{f,t+1}\iota)$. This is the mutual fund theorem of Tobin (1958), as illustrated in Figure 1.1.

The results also extend straightforwardly to the case where there is no completely riskless asset. We can still define a benchmark asset with return $R_{0,t+1}$, and define excess returns relative to this benchmark return. The variance of the portfolio return is $\text{Var}_t(R_{0,t+1}) + \alpha_t'\Sigma_t\alpha_t + 2\alpha_t'\sigma_{0t}$, where Σ_t is now defined to be the conditional variance–covariance matrix of excess returns over the benchmark asset, and σ_{0t} is a vector containing the covariances of the excess returns on the other assets with the benchmark return.[1]

With no riskless asset, the solution becomes

$$\alpha_t = \frac{1}{k}\Sigma_t^{-1}(E_t\mathbf{R}_{t+1} - R_{0,t+1}\iota) - \Sigma_t^{-1}\sigma_{0t}. \qquad (2.9)$$

This has almost the same form as before, except that the relation between portfolio weights and average excess returns is now linear rather than proportional. The intercept is the minimum-variance portfolio of all assets, $-\Sigma_t^{-1}\sigma_{0t}$, which does not place 100% weight in the benchmark asset if the benchmark asset is risky. It is no longer true that all investors hold risky assets in the same proportions; instead, they hold some combination of two risky mutual funds, whose proportions are given by the two terms on the right-hand side of (2.9). If the benchmark asset has low risk, however, as is the case empirically for Treasury bills and other short-term debt instruments, then there is little difference between the solution (2.9) and the riskless-asset solution (2.8).

---

[1] We use a boldface lower-case sigma for σ_{0t} rather than an upper-case sigma, to emphasize the fact that this is a vector rather than a matrix. Throughout the book we will use a boldface lower-case sigma, with a suitable subscript, to denote a vector of covariances between excess returns and the subscripted variable. Abusing this notation slightly, we will also write σ_t^2 for the vector of excess-return variances.

2.1.2. Specifying utility of wealth

Basics of utility theory

So far we have assumed that investors care directly about the mean and variance of portfolio returns. Similar results are available if we assume instead that investors have utility defined over wealth at the end of the period.[2] In this case we redefine the maximization problem as

$$\max E_t U(W_{t+1}) \tag{2.10}$$

subject to

$$W_{t+1} = (1 + R_{p,t+1})W_t. \tag{2.11}$$

Here $U(W_{t+1})$ is a standard concave utility function, as illustrated in Figure 2.1. The curvature of the utility function implies that the investor is averse to risk. Consider for example an investor with initial wealth W_t who is offered a risky gamble that will either add or subtract an amount G to wealth, with equal probabilities of the two outcomes. If the investor turns down the

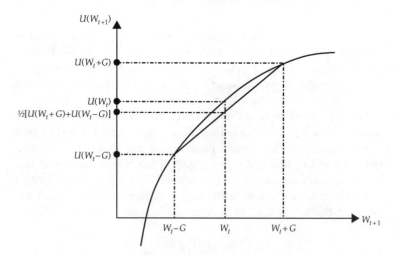

Figure 2.1. Concave utility of wealth.

[2] For textbook expositions of utility theory, see Gollier (2001), Green, Whinston, and Mas-Colell (1995), or Ingersoll (1987). Arrow (1970) is a classic early treatment.

gamble, wealth is certain and utility is $U(W_t)$. If the investor accepts the gamble, there is a one-half chance that wealth will go up to $W_t + G$ and a one-half chance that it will fall to $W_t - G$. Expected utility is $(1/2)U(W_t + G) + (1/2)U(W_t - G)$, which is less than $U(W_t)$ because of the curvature of the utility function. Thus, the investor turns down the gamble; it offers only risk without any accompanying reward, and is unattractive to a risk-averse investor.

The degree of curvature of the utility function determines the intensity of the investor's risk aversion. Curvature can be measured by the second derivative of the utility function with respect to wealth, scaled by the first derivative to eliminate any dependence of the measure of curvature on the arbitrary units in which utility is measured. The *coefficient of absolute risk aversion* is then defined as

$$ARA(W) = -\frac{U''(W)}{U'(W)}, \tag{2.12}$$

where U' indicates the first derivative and U'' the second derivative of the utility function. The *coefficient of relative risk aversion* is defined as

$$RRA(W) = WA(W) = -\frac{WU''(W)}{U'(W)}. \tag{2.13}$$

The reciprocals of these measures are called *absolute and relative risk tolerance*.

Classic results of Pratt (1964) say that for small gambles the coefficient of absolute risk aversion determines the absolute dollar amount that an investor is willing to pay to avoid a gamble of a given absolute size. It is commonly thought that absolute risk aversion should decrease, or at least should not increase, with wealth. Introspection suggests that a billionaire will be relatively unconcerned with a risk that might worry a poor person, and will pay less to avoid such a risk.

The coefficient of relative risk aversion determines the fraction of wealth that an investor will pay to avoid a gamble of a given size relative to wealth. A plausible benchmark model makes relative risk aversion independent of wealth. In this case people at all levels of wealth make the same decisions, when both the risks they face and the costs of avoiding them are expressed as fractions of wealth.

The long-run behavior of the economy suggests that relative risk aversion cannot depend strongly on wealth. Per capita consumption and wealth have increased greatly over the past two centuries. Since financial risks are multiplicative, this means that the absolute scale of financial risks has also increased while the relative scale is unchanged. Interest rates and risk premia do not show any evidence of long-term trends in response to this long-term growth; this implies that investors are willing to pay almost the same relative costs to avoid given relative risks as they did when they were much poorer, which is possible only if relative risk aversion is almost independent of wealth.

The form of the utility function

Tractable models of portfolio choice require assumptions about the form of the utility function, and possibly distributional assumptions about asset returns. Three alternative sets of assumptions produce simple results that are consistent with those of mean–variance analysis:

1. Investors have quadratic utility defined over wealth. In this case, $U(W_{t+1}) = aW_{t+1} - bW_{t+1}^2$. Under this assumption, maximizing expected utility, as in (2.10), is equivalent to maximizing a linear combination of mean and variance, as in (2.2). No distributional assumptions are needed on asset returns. Quadratic utility implies that absolute risk aversion and relative risk aversion are increasing in wealth.

2. Investors have exponential utility, $U(W_{t+1}) = -\exp(-\theta W_{t+1})$, and asset returns are normally distributed. Exponential utility implies that absolute risk aversion is a constant θ, while relative risk aversion increases in wealth.

3. Investors have power utility, $U(W_{t+1}) = (W_{t+1}^{1-\gamma} - 1)/(1 - \gamma)$, and asset returns are lognormally distributed. Power utility implies that absolute risk aversion is declining in wealth, while relative risk aversion is a constant γ. The limit as γ approaches one is log utility: $U(W_{t+1}) = \log(W_{t+1})$.

We have already argued that absolute risk aversion should decline, or at the very least should not increase, with wealth. This rules out the assumption of quadratic utility and favors power utility over exponential utility. Power utility's property of constant relative risk aversion is inherently attractive and is required to explain the stability of financial variables in the face of secular economic growth.

The choice between exponential and power utility also implies distributional assumptions on returns. Exponential utility produces simple results if asset returns are normally distributed, while power utility produces simple results if asset returns are lognormal (that is, if the logarithms of gross asset returns are normal).

The assumption of normal returns is appealing for some purposes, but it is inappropriate for the study of long-term portfolio choice because it cannot hold at more than one time horizon. If returns are normally distributed at a monthly frequency, then two-month returns are not normal because they are the product of two successive normal returns, and sums of normals, but not products of normals, are themselves normal. The assumption of lognormal returns, on the other hand, can hold at every time horizon since products of lognormal random variables are themselves lognormal. Also, lognormal random variables can never be negative, so the assumption of lognormality is consistent with the limited liability feature of most financial assets.

The assumption of lognormal returns runs into another difficulty, however. It does not carry over straightforwardly from individual assets to portfolios. A portfolio is a linear combination of individual assets; if each asset return is lognormal, the portfolio return is a weighted average of lognormals which is not itself lognormal.

This difficulty can be avoided by considering short time intervals. As the time interval shrinks, the non-lognormality of the portfolio return diminishes, and it disappears altogether in the limit of continuous time. In this and the next few chapters we use a discrete-time approximation to the relation between the log return on a portfolio and the log returns on individual assets. The approximation becomes more accurate as the time interval shrinks. In Chapter 5 we develop explicit models set in continuous time.

2.1.3. A lognormal model with power utility

We now develop portfolio choice results under the assumption that investors have power utility and that asset returns are lognormal. We repeatedly apply a key result about the expectation of a lognormal random variable X:

$$\log E_t X_{t+1} = E_t \log X_{t+1} + \tfrac{1}{2}\text{Var}_t \log X_{t+1} = E_t x_{t+1} + \tfrac{1}{2}\sigma_{xt}^2.$$

$$(2.14)$$

Here and throughout the book, the notation 'log' refers to the natural logarithm, and lower-case letters are used to denote the logs of the corresponding upper-case letters. Equation (2.14) can be understood intuitively by reference to Figure 2.1. The log is a concave function like the utility function illustrated in Figure 2.1. Thus, the mean of the log of a random variable X is smaller than the log of the mean, and the difference is increasing in the variability of X. The equation quantifies this difference for the special case in which $\log X$ is normally distributed.

We begin by assuming that the return on an investor's portfolio is lognormal, and hence that next-period wealth is lognormal. We then go on to ask whether this is consistent with lognormality of the returns on underlying assets. Under the assumption of power utility, (2.10) can be written as

$$\max \frac{E_t W_{t+1}^{1-\gamma}}{(1-\gamma)}. \qquad (2.15)$$

Maximizing this expectation is equivalent to maximizing the log of the expectation, and the scale factor $1/(1-\gamma)$ can be omitted since it does not affect the solution. If next-period wealth is lognormal, we can apply (2.14) to rewrite the objective as

$$\max \log E_t W_{t+1}^{1-\gamma} = (1-\gamma)E_t w_{t+1} + \tfrac{1}{2}(1-\gamma)^2\sigma_{wt}^2. \qquad (2.16)$$

The budget constraint (2.11) can be rewritten in log form as

$$w_{t+1} = r_{p,t+1} + w_t, \qquad (2.17)$$

where $r_{p,t+1} = \log(1+R_{p,t+1})$ is the log return on the portfolio, the natural logarithm of the gross simple return, also known as the continuously compounded portfolio return. Dividing (2.16) by $(1-\gamma)$ and using (2.17), we restate the problem as

$$\max E_t r_{p,t+1} + \tfrac{1}{2}(1-\gamma)\sigma_{pt}^2, \qquad (2.18)$$

where σ_{pt}^2 is the conditional variance of the log portfolio return.

To understand this equation, it is helpful to note that

$$E_t r_{p,t+1} + \sigma_{pt}^2/2 = \log E_t(1 + R_{p,t+1}) \tag{2.19}$$

because the portfolio return is assumed to be lognormal. Thus, (2.18) can be rewritten as

$$\max \log E_t(1 + R_{p,t+1}) - \frac{\gamma}{2}\sigma_{pt}^2. \tag{2.20}$$

Just as in the mean–variance analysis, the investor trades off mean against variance in the portfolio return. The relevant mean return is the mean simple return, or arithmetic mean return, and the investor trades the log of this mean linearly against the variance of the log return. The coefficient of relative risk aversion, γ, plays the same role as the parameter k played in the mean–variance analysis.

Equation (2.18) shows that the case $\gamma = 1$ plays a special role in the analysis. When $\gamma = 1$, the investor has log utility and chooses the portfolio with the highest available log return (sometimes known as the 'growth-optimal' portfolio). When $\gamma > 1$, the investor seeks a safer portfolio by penalizing the variance of log returns; when $\gamma < 1$, the investor actually seeks a riskier portfolio, because a higher variance, with the same mean log return, corresponds to a higher mean simple return. The case $\gamma = 1$ is the boundary where these two opposing considerations exactly cancel one another out. This case plays an important role throughout the book.

Approximation of the portfolio return

To proceed further, we need to relate the log portfolio return to the log returns on underlying assets. Consider first the simple case where there are two assets, one risky and one riskless. Then from (2.1) the simple return on the portfolio is a linear combination of the simple returns on the risky and riskless assets. The log return on the portfolio is the log of this linear combination, which is not the same as a linear combination of logs.

Over short time intervals, however, we can use a Taylor approximation of the nonlinear function relating log individual-asset returns to log portfolio returns. Full details are given in Campbell and Viceira (2001b). The resulting expression is

$$r_{p,t+1} - r_{f,t+1} = \alpha_t(r_{t+1} - r_{f,t+1}) + \tfrac{1}{2}\alpha_t(1 - \alpha_t)\sigma_t^2. \quad (2.21)$$

The difference between the log portfolio return and a linear combination of log individual-asset returns is given by $\alpha_t(1 - \alpha_t)\sigma_t^2/2$. The difference disappears if the portfolio weight in the risky asset is zero (for then the log portfolio return is just the log riskless return), or if the weight in the risky asset is one (for then the log portfolio return is just the log risky return). When $0 < \alpha_t < 1$, the portfolio is a weighted average of the individual assets and the term $\alpha_t(1 - \alpha_t)\sigma_t^2/2$ is positive. This positive term reflects the fact that the log of an average is greater than an average of logs as illustrated in Figure 2.1.

Another way to understand (2.21) is to rewrite it as

$$r_{p,t+1} - r_{f,t+1} + \frac{\sigma_{pt}^2}{2} = \alpha_t\left(r_{t+1} - r_{f,t+1} + \frac{\sigma_t^2}{2}\right), \quad (2.22)$$

using the fact that $\sigma_{pt}^2 = \alpha_t^2\sigma_t^2$. If one takes expectations of this equation, one finds that the mean of the simple excess portfolio return is linearly related to the mean of the simple excess return on the risky asset, as required by (2.1).

The approximation in (2.21) can be justified rigorously by considering shorter and shorter time intervals. As the time interval shrinks, the higher-order terms that are neglected in (2.21) become negligible relative to those that are included. In the limit of continuous time with continuous paths (diffusions) for asset prices, (2.21) is exact and can be derived using Itô's lemma. We discuss the continuous-time approach in more detail in Chapter 5.

One important property of the approximate portfolio return is that it rules out the possibility of bankruptcy, even when the investor holds a short position ($\alpha_t < 0$) or a leveraged position in the risky asset financed by borrowing ($\alpha_t > 1$). The log portfolio return is always finite, no matter what the returns on the underlying assets, and thus it is never possible to exhaust wealth completely. Continuous-time diffusion models also have this property; in such models portfolios are rebalanced over such short time intervals that losses can always be stemmed by rebalancing before they lead to bankruptcy. In many applications it is reasonable to exclude the possibility of bankruptcy, but this approach may not be suitable when it implies optimal portfolios with extremely high leverage.

The approximation (2.21) generalizes straightforwardly to the case where there are many risky assets, jointly lognormally distributed with conditional variance–covariance matrix of log returns Σ_t. We write σ_t^2 for the vector containing the diagonal elements of Σ_t, the variances of asset returns. The approximation to the portfolio return becomes

$$r_{p,t+1} - r_{f,t+1} = \alpha_t'(\mathbf{r}_{t+1} - r_{f,t+1}\iota) + \tfrac{1}{2}\alpha_t'\sigma_t^2 - \tfrac{1}{2}\alpha_t'\Sigma_t\alpha_t. \qquad (2.23)$$

This approximation holds in exactly the same form if we replace the riskless return $r_{f,t+1}$ with a risky benchmark return $r_{0,t+1}$, except that in this case the vector σ_t^2 and the matrix Σ_t must contain variances and covariances of *excess* returns on the other risky assets over the benchmark return, rather than variances and covariances of total returns on these assets. (Excess and total returns have the same variances and covariances only when they are measured relative to a riskless return.)

Solution of the model
In a two-asset model, (2.21) implies that the mean excess portfolio return is $E_t r_{p,t+1} - r_{f,t+1} = \alpha_t(E_t r_{t+1} - r_{f,t+1}) + \tfrac{1}{2}\alpha_t(1 - \alpha_t)\sigma_t^2$, while the variance of the portfolio return is $\alpha_t^2\sigma_t^2$. Substituting into the objective function (2.18), the problem becomes

$$\max \alpha_t(E_t r_{t+1} - r_{f,t+1}) + \tfrac{1}{2}\alpha_t(1 - \alpha_t)\sigma_t^2 + \tfrac{1}{2}(1 - \gamma)\alpha_t^2\sigma_t^2.$$

$$(2.24)$$

The solution is

$$\alpha_t = \frac{E_t r_{t+1} - r_{f,t+1} + \sigma_t^2/2}{\gamma\sigma_t^2}. \qquad (2.25)$$

This equation is the equivalent, in a lognormal model with power utility, of the mean–variance solution (2.4). The top line is the expected excess log return on the risky asset, with the addition of one-half the variance to convert from log returns to simple returns that are ultimately of concern to the investor. (The formula for the expectation of lognormal random variables implies that $E_t r_{t+1} - r_{f,t+1} + \sigma_t^2/2 = \log E_t(1 + R_{t+1})/(1 + R_{ft})$.) The bottom line is the coefficient of relative risk aversion times the variance of the risky asset return. Thus, just as in a simple mean–variance model, the optimal portfolio weight is the risk premium divided by risk aversion times variance.

In a model with many risky assets, the solution for the vector of optimal portfolio weights is

$$\boldsymbol{\alpha}_t = \frac{1}{\gamma} \boldsymbol{\Sigma}_t^{-1} (E_t \mathbf{r}_{t+1} - r_{f,t+1} \boldsymbol{\iota} + \sigma_t^2/2). \tag{2.26}$$

This solution is the equivalent of the multiple-asset mean–variance solution (2.8). Like the mean–variance solution, it has the property that the coefficient of relative risk aversion affects only the overall scale of the risky asset position and not its composition. Thus, a version of Tobin's mutual fund theorem holds in the lognormal model with power utility.

If there is no truly riskless asset, and we work instead with a risky benchmark return $r_{0,t+1}$, then the solution becomes

$$\boldsymbol{\alpha}_t = \frac{1}{\gamma} \boldsymbol{\Sigma}_t^{-1} (E_t \mathbf{r}_{t+1} - r_{0,t+1} \boldsymbol{\iota} + \sigma_t^2/2) + \left(1 - \frac{1}{\gamma}\right)(-\boldsymbol{\Sigma}_t^{-1} \boldsymbol{\sigma}_{0t}),$$
$$\tag{2.27}$$

where $\boldsymbol{\sigma}_{0t}$ is the vector of covariances of excess log returns with the benchmark log return. Just as in the simple mean–variance analysis (2.9), covariances with the benchmark affect the optimal portfolio weights. The investor favors assets with positive covariances because, for given expected log returns, they increase the expected simple return on the portfolio; but the investor dislikes such assets because they increase the risk of the portfolio. The two effects cancel when $\gamma = 1$; in this case the solution takes exactly the same form whether the benchmark asset is riskless or risky. As γ increases, the investor becomes more conservative and the optimal portfolio approaches the minimum-variance portfolio $-\boldsymbol{\Sigma}_t^{-1} \boldsymbol{\sigma}_{0t}$.

2.2. MYOPIC LONG-TERM PORTFOLIO CHOICE

2.2.1. *Power utility of wealth*

So far we have assumed that the investor has a short investment horizon and cares only about the distribution of wealth at the end of the next period. Alternatively, we can assume that the investor cares about the distribution of wealth K periods from now, so that the utility function is $U(W_{t+K})$ rather than $U(W_{t+1})$. We continue to assume that all wealth is reinvested, so the budget constraint takes the form

$$\begin{aligned} W_{t+K} &= (1 + R_{pK,t+K})W_t \\ &= (1 + R_{p,t+1})(1 + R_{p,t+2}) \cdots (1 + R_{p,t+K})W_t. \end{aligned} \quad (2.28)$$

Here the notation $(1 + R_{pK,t+K})$ indicates that the portfolio return is measured over K periods, from t to $t + K$. This K-period return is just the product of K successive one-period returns. Note that this is a cumulative return; to calculate an annualized return one would take the Kth root if the base period is a year, the $(K/4)$th root if the base period is a quarter, and in general the (K/S)th root if there are S base periods in a year. Taking logs, the cumulative log return over K periods is just a sum of K successive one-period returns:

$$r_{pK,t+K} = r_{p,t+1} + \cdots + r_{p,t+K}. \quad (2.29)$$

The annualized log return can be found by dividing by (K/S) if there are S base periods in a year.

The long-term investor's optimal portfolio depends not only on his objective, but also on what he is allowed to do each period. In particular, it depends on whether he is allowed to rebalance his portfolio each period, or must choose an allocation at time t without any possibility of asset sales or purchases between t and the horizon $t + K$.

Myopic portfolio choice without rebalancing
We first assume that rebalancing is not possible between t and $t + K$, so that the long-term investor must evaluate K-period returns in the same manner that the short-term investor evaluates

single-period returns. We continue to assume that utility takes the power form and that asset returns are conditionally lognormally distributed. For simplicity, we return to the case where there is a single risky asset.

We now make a highly restrictive additional assumption: that all asset returns are independent and identically distributed (IID) over time. This implies that the log riskless rate is a constant r_f and the log K-period riskless return is Kr_f; the mean log return on the risky asset is a constant Er and the mean log K-period return on the risky asset is KEr; the variance of the log return on the risky asset is a constant σ^2 and the risky asset return is serially uncorrelated, so the variance of the log K-period return on the risky asset is just $K\sigma^2$:

$$\text{Var}_t r_{K,t+K} = \text{Var}_t r_{t+1} + \cdots + \text{Var}_t r_{t+K} = K\sigma^2. \tag{2.30}$$

Here the first equality follows from the absence of serial correlation in risky returns, and the second follows from the constant variance of the risky return.

With IID returns, the mapping from single-period log returns to K-period log returns is straightforward. All means and variances for individual assets are scaled up by the same factor K. If we can apply the same approximation (2.21) relating individual asset returns to the portfolio return, this implies that the previous short-term portfolio solution is still optimal for a long-term investor. Intuitively, the optimal portfolio weight on a risky asset is the mean excess log return, plus one-half the log variance to convert from mean log to mean simple return, divided by risk aversion times variance. If both the mean and the variance are multiplied by K, this solution does not change. The argument can be readily extended to the case with multiple risky assets. Both the short-term investor and the long-term investor perceive the same mean–variance diagram, merely scaled up or down by a factor K; thus, they choose the same point on the diagram, which is to say that they choose the same portfolio.

The weakness in this argument is the assumption that the approximate budget constraint (2.21) applies to a long holding period. Recall that this budget constraint holds exactly in continuous time, and is an accurate approximation over short discrete time intervals; but the quality of the approximation deteriorates if it is applied over long holding periods. For this reason, an exact solution to the long-term portfolio choice problem without rebalancing does involve some horizon effects, even if risky returns are IID. In practice, however, these horizon effects are small.[3]

Myopic portfolio choice with rebalancing

The assumption that a long-horizon investor cannot rebalance his portfolio is superficially appealing because it makes the long-horizon problem formally analogous to the short-horizon problem. Unfortunately, it creates a technical difficulty because it invalidates the use of the loglinear budget constraint (2.21). More seriously, this assumption does not describe reality. Investors with long horizons are free to trade assets at any time, and financial intermediaries exist to rebalance portfolios on behalf of investors who find this task costly to execute. (This is the purpose of so-called lifestyle mutual funds.) There is no inherent connection between the investment horizon and the frequency with which portfolios can be rebalanced. Accordingly, we now assume that the long-term investor can rebalance his portfolio every period, and we continue to use this assumption throughout the rest of the book.

Classic results of Samuelson (1969) and Merton (1969, 1971) give two sets of conditions under which the long-term investor acts myopically, choosing the same portfolio as a short-term investor. First, portfolio choice will be myopic if the investor has power utility and returns are IID. This result was originally derived using dynamic programming, but here we give a simple intuitive argument.

We first recall that, with constant relative risk aversion, portfolio choice does not depend on wealth, and hence does not depend on past returns. Next, we note that if returns are IID no new information arrives between one period and the next, so there is no reason for portfolio choice to change over time in a random fashion. We can therefore restrict attention to deterministic portfolio rules in which the risky asset share α_t may depend

---

[3] Barberis (2000) plots portfolio allocation against horizon for a portfolio choice problem without rebalancing. These plots appear horizontal in the IID case; that is, the horizon effects caused by deterioration of the approximation (2.21) are not visible to the naked eye.

on time. We also note that K-period returns are lognormal if single-period returns are lognormal and IID. This means that the power utility investor chooses a portfolio on the basis of the mean and variance of the K-period log portfolio return.

The K-period log return is just the sum of successive single-period log returns. For simplicity, consider an example in which $K = 2$. Then we can write

$$r_{p2,t+2} - 2r_f = (r_{p,t+1} - r_f) + (r_{p,t+2} - r_f)$$
$$= \alpha_t(r_{t+1} - r_f) + \tfrac{1}{2}\alpha_t(1 - \alpha_t)\sigma^2$$
$$+ \alpha_{t+1}(r_{t+2} - r_f) + \tfrac{1}{2}\alpha_{t+1}(1 - \alpha_{t+1})\sigma^2, \quad (2.31)$$

where we are allowing α_t and α_{t+1} to be different because the investor can freely rebalance his portfolio each period. The conditional variance of the two-period log return is

$$\text{Var}_t(r_{p2,t+2}) = (\alpha_t^2 + \alpha_{t+1}^2)\sigma^2, \quad (2.32)$$

since both α_t and α_{t+1} are deterministic and hence are known at time t. The mean two-period log return, adjusted by adding one-half the variance of the two-period return, is

$$E_t(r_{p2,t+2}) + \tfrac{1}{2}\text{Var}_t(r_{p,2,t+2}) = 2r_f + (\alpha_t + \alpha_{t+1})(Er - r_f + \sigma^2/2). \quad (2.33)$$

The objective of a two-period investor with power utility can be written as

$$\max E_t(r_{p,2,t+2}) + \tfrac{1}{2}\text{Var}_t(r_{p,2,t+2}) - \tfrac{\gamma}{2}\text{Var}_t(r_{p,2,t+2}). \quad (2.34)$$

Thus, the investor with $\gamma > 0$ will always prefer a lower variance of log returns for a given variance-adjusted mean. But from (2.33), the variance-adjusted mean depends only on the sum $(\alpha_t + \alpha_{t+1})$. The investor can fix this sum and adjust the individual shares, α_t and α_{t+1}, to minimize the variance. Since variance depends on the sum of squares $(\alpha_t^2 + \alpha_{t+1}^2)$, this is accomplished by setting $\alpha_t = \alpha_{t+1}$, a constant portfolio rule.

Once we know that the portfolio rule is constant, we also know that it must be the same as the optimal rule for a short-term investor. The reason is that in the last period before the horizon the long-term investor has become a short-term investor and will choose the optimal short-term portfolio.

This argument for myopic portfolio choice straightforwardly extends to any long horizon K. It can be related to a puzzle posed by Mark Kritzman (2000) in his book *Puzzles of Finance*. In a chapter entitled 'Half Stocks All the Time or All Stocks Half the Time?' Kritzman points out that these two strategies have the same expected simple return, but the latter strategy is riskier; thus, a risk-averse investor should always prefer the former. This is precisely the effect that underlies the argument for a constant portfolio rule.

The second Samuelson–Merton condition for myopic portfolio choice is that the investor has log utility. In this case portfolio choice will be myopic even if asset returns are not IID. The argument here is particularly simple. Recall that the log utility investor chooses a portfolio that maximizes the expected log return. Equation (2.29) shows that the K-period log return is just the sum of one-period log returns. Since the portfolio can be chosen freely each period, the sum is maximized by maximizing each of its elements separately, that is by choosing, each period, the portfolio that is optimal for a one-period log utility investor.

2.2.2. Fallacies of long-term portfolio choice

Although the conditions for myopic portfolio choice are simple, and their logic can be understood without resort to advanced mathematics, there has been much confusion about these issues over the years. One source of confusion is the common tendency to measure risk in units of standard deviation rather than variance and to work with mean–standard deviation diagrams (like Figure 1.1) rather than mean–variance diagrams. With IID returns, the variance of a cumulative risky return is proportional to the investment horizon K, but the standard deviation is proportional to the square root of K. (If returns are annualized, the variance is constant but the standard deviation shrinks in proportion to the square root of K.) Thus, the Sharpe ratio of any risky investment, its mean excess return divided by its standard deviation, grows with the square root of K.

It is tempting to calculate long-horizon Sharpe ratios, observe that they are large, and conclude that lengthening the investment horizon somehow reduces risk in a manner analogous to the effect of diversifying a portfolio across uncorrelated risky assets. But this 'time diversification' argument is a fallacy. Sharpe ratios cannot be compared across different investment horizons: they must always be measured over a common time interval.

A related fallacy is to argue that there is a single best long-term portfolio for all investors, regardless of their preferences. The proposed portfolio is the 'growth-optimal' portfolio that max-imizes the expected log return. As the investment horizon increases, this portfolio outperforms any other portfolio with higher and higher probability. In the limit, the probability that it outperforms goes to one. To understand this property of the growth-optimal portfolio, note that the difference between the cumulative growth-optimal log return and the log return on any other portfolio is a normally distributed random variable. Write the mean of this difference as $\mu(K)$ and the standard deviation as $\sigma(K)$. The mean $\mu(K)$ is positive because the growth-optimal log return has the highest mean of any available portfolio strategy. The probability that the difference is positive is $\Phi(\mu(K)/\sigma(K))$, where $\Phi(\cdot)$ denotes the cumulative distribution function of the standard normal random variable. As the investment horizon K increases, the ratio $\mu(K)/\sigma(K)$ grows with $\sqrt{K}$, so $\Phi(\mu(K)/\sigma(K))$ goes to one.

The fallacy is the claim that this property of the growth-optimal portfolio makes it the best portfolio for all long-term investors. It is, of course, the best portfolio for an investor with log utility, but investors with higher risk aversion should hold more con-servative portfolios. Even though the growth-optimal portfolio will almost always outperform such conservative portfolios over long horizons, the loss when it does underperform is larger at long horizons, and this possibility is heavily weighted by con-servative investors. This point was forcefully made by Samuelson (1979) in an article entitled 'Why We Should Not Make Mean Log of Wealth Big though Years to Act Are Long'. The last paragraph of the article reads as follows: 'No need to say more. I've made my point. And, save for the last word, have done so in prose of but one syllable' (p. 306). A more recent popular discussion of the fallacy, which is easier to read because it allows itself a wider selection of words, is in Kritzman (2000, chapter 3).

2.2.3. *Power utility of consumption*

The assumption that investors care only about wealth at a single horizon is analytically convenient but empirically troublesome. Most investors, whether they are individuals saving for retirement or institutions such as universities that are living off endowment income, are concerned not with the level of wealth for its own sake, but with the standard of living that their wealth can support. In other words, they consume out of wealth and derive utility from consumption rather than wealth.

In this section we assume that utility is defined over a stream of consumption. Once we make this assumption, the horizon plays a much smaller role in the analysis; it still defines a terminal date, but conditions at each intermediate date are also important. If the terminal date is distant, intermediate conditions dominate the solution, which will not depend sensitively on the exact choice of terminal date. In fact, we can let the terminal date go to infinity and work with an attractively simple infinite-horizon model in which portfolio choice depends on preferences and state variables, but not on time. We can vary the effective investment horizon by varying the time discount factor that determines the relative weights investors place on the near-term future versus the distant future. This is our mode of analysis until the last chapter of the book, where we present an explicit life-cycle model with a finite horizon.

We first assume that investors have time-separable power utility, defined over consumption:

$$\max E_t \sum_{i=0}^{\infty} \delta^i U(C_{t+i}) = E_t \sum_{i=0}^{\infty} \delta^i \frac{C_{t+i}^{1-\gamma} - 1}{1 - \gamma}. \tag{2.35}$$

Here δ is the time discount factor. When δ is large, investors place a relatively high weight on the distant future. As δ shrinks, they place more and more weight on the near future; in the limit, as δ approaches zero, they behave like single-period investors. Investors face the intertemporal budget constraint that wealth next period equals the portfolio return times reinvested wealth, that is, wealth today less what is subtracted for consumption:

$$W_{t+1} = (1 + R_{p,t+1})(W_t - C_t). \tag{2.36}$$

This objective function and budget constraint imply the following first-order condition, or *Euler equation*, for optimal consumption choice:

$$U'(C_t) = E_t\left[\delta U'(C_{t+1})(1 + R_{i,t+1})\right], \tag{2.37}$$

where $(1 + R_{i,t+1})$ denotes any available return, for example the riskless return $(1 + R_{f,t+1})$, the risky return $(1 + R_{t+1})$, or the portfolio return $(1 + R_{p,t+1})$. Equation (2.37) says that at the optimum, the marginal cost of saving an extra dollar for one period must equal the marginal benefit. The marginal cost is the marginal utility of a dollar of consumption, $U'(C_t)$. The marginal benefit is the expectation of the payoff if the dollar is invested in an available asset for one period, $(1 + R_{i,t+1})$, times the marginal utility of an extra dollar of consumption next period, $U'(C_{t+1})$, discounted back to the present at rate δ.

We can divide (2.37) through by $U'(C_t)$ and use the power utility condition that $U'(C_t) = C_t^{-\gamma}$ to rewrite it as

$$1 = E_t\left[\delta\left(\frac{C_{t+1}}{C_t}\right)^{-\gamma}(1 + R_{i,t+1})\right]. \tag{2.38}$$

In the case where the return is riskless, $R_{i,t+1} = R_{f,t+1}$, it is known at time t and thus can be brought outside the expectations operator; we have

$$\frac{1}{(1 + R_{f,t+1})} = E_t\left[\delta\left(\frac{C_{t+1}}{C_t}\right)^{-\gamma}\right]. \tag{2.39}$$

The term $\delta(C_{t+1}/C_t)^{-\gamma}$ that appears in these expressions is known as the 'stochastic discount factor' or SDF because it can be used to discount expected payoffs on any assets to find their prices. The consumption of any investor who is able to freely trade in the financial markets can be used as an SDF. It is conventional to write the SDF as M_{t+1}, so that (2.38) and (2.39) become

$$1 = E_t[M_{t+1}(1 + R_{i,t+1})] \tag{2.40}$$

and

$$\frac{1}{(1 + R_{f,t+1})} = E_t[M_{t+1}]. \tag{2.41}$$

With power utility, $M_{t+1} = \delta(C_{t+1}/C_t)^{-\gamma}$. Different forms of utility will imply different relationships between M_{t+1} and consumption, but (2.40) and (2.41) will still hold.

The field of asset pricing asks how the properties of the SDF explain the properties of asset returns, and how the SDF is determined by the general equilibrium of the economy. Representative-agent asset pricing models, for example, relate the SDF to the properties of aggregate consumption and the preferences of a representative investor who consumes aggregate consumption. In this book we take a partial equilibrium perspective and seek to explain the properties of optimal consumption and portfolio choice given asset returns. The discrete-time SDF methodology was pioneered by Rubinstein (1976b), Grossman and Shiller (1981), and Shiller (1982), and extended by Hansen and Jagannathan (1991) and Cochrane and Hansen (1992). Campbell (2000) and Cochrane (2001) survey the SDF methodology.

A lognormal consumption-based model
The natural way to proceed, given our earlier discussion, is to assume that asset returns and consumption are jointly lognormal and to work with loglinear versions of these equations. Hansen and Singleton (1983) introduced this approach. The log form of the riskless-rate Euler equation (2.39) can be written as

$$E_t[\Delta c_{t+1}] = \frac{\log \delta}{\gamma} + \frac{1}{\gamma} r_{f,t+1} + \frac{\gamma}{2} \sigma_{ct}^2, \tag{2.42}$$

where Δ is the first-difference operator and $c_{t+1} \equiv \log(C_{t+1})$ so Δc_{t+1} is consumption growth. The three terms on the right-hand side of (2.42) correspond to three forces acting on consumption. First, a patient investor with a high time discount factor δ is inherently willing to postpone consumption. Second, a high interest rate gives an investor an incentive to postpone consumption. Postponing consumption means raising consumption in the future relative to consumption today, tilting the consumption path upwards. However, diminishing marginal utility of consumption limits the investor's willingness to tolerate any deviation from a flat consumption path. The investor's willingness to tilt consumption in response to incentives is known as the *elasticity of intertemporal substitution in consumption* (EIS). In a model with power utility, the EIS equals the reciprocal of risk aversion, $1/\gamma$. Thus, with a high γ the investor is extremely unwilling to tilt consumption and the planned consumption growth rate will change only slightly with the time discount factor and the riskless interest rate. The third term on the right-hand side of (2.42) represents the effect of consumption uncertainty. A risk-averse investor with power utility will respond to uncertainty by increasing precautionary saving, again tilting the consumption path upwards.

It is also possible to write expected consumption growth in terms of the expected portfolio return. The first term on the right-hand side of (2.42) is unchanged by doing this, the second term becomes $(1/\gamma)E_t r_{p,t+1}$, and the third term involves the variances and covariances of the portfolio return and consumption growth. This alternative representation is more convenient for some purposes and will be used in our analysis of Epstein–Zin utility in the next section.

The Euler equation for power utility can also be used to describe the risk premium on a single risky asset over the riskless interest rate. The log form of the general Euler equation (2.38), less γ times (2.42), is

$$E_t r_{t+1} - r_{f,t+1} + \frac{\sigma_t^2}{2} = \gamma \, \text{Cov}_t(r_{t+1}, \Delta c_{t+1}), \qquad (2.43)$$

where we have dropped the subscript i because we are assuming that there is only a single risky asset. In equilibrium, the expected excess return on the risky asset must equal risk aversion γ times the covariance of the asset return with consumption growth. A similar equation describes each risky asset's risk premium in a model with multiple risky assets. In asset pricing theory, this equation is used to explain assets' risk premia and is known as the *consumption capital asset pricing model* or CCAPM (Breeden 1979; Hansen and Singleton 1983). Here we take the risky asset return as given and seek consumption and portfolio rules that will make (2.43) hold.

A constant consumption–wealth ratio

A difficulty with the lognormal consumption-based model is that the intertemporal budget constraint (2.36) is not generally loglinear because consumption is *subtracted* from wealth before *multiplying* by the portfolio return. The combination of subtraction and multiplication creates an intractable nonlinearity.

In later chapters of this book, following Campbell (1993), we will approach this problem by approximating the budget constraint. For now, however, we assume that the consumption–wealth ratio is constant, in which case the budget constraint becomes loglinear. We solve the model under this assumption and then seek conditions that justify the assumption. A constant consumption–wealth ratio can be written as

$$\frac{C_t}{W_t} = b, \tag{2.44}$$

and the budget constraint (2.36) can then be written in log form as

$$
\begin{aligned}
\Delta w_{t+1} &= r_{p,t+1} + \log(1 - b) \\
&= r_{f,t+1} + \alpha_t(r_{t+1} - r_{f,t+1}) + \tfrac{1}{2}\alpha_t(1 - \alpha_t)\sigma_t^2 \\
&\quad + \log(1 - b),
\end{aligned} \tag{2.45}
$$

where the second equality substitutes in from (2.21).

The constant consumption–wealth ratio (2.44) also implies that the growth rate of consumption equals the growth rate of wealth, so the terms in consumption in (2.42) and (2.43) can be rewritten in terms of wealth. The formula for a single risky asset's expected excess return, (2.43), becomes

$$\mathrm{E}_t r_{t+1} - r_{f,t+1} + \sigma_t^2/2 = \gamma \operatorname{Cov}_t(r_{t+1}, \Delta w_{t+1}) = \gamma \alpha_t \sigma_t^2, \tag{2.46}$$

where the second equality follows from (2.45). Solving this equation for α_t, we once again obtain the myopic solution (2.25):

$$\alpha_t = \frac{\mathrm{E}_t r_{t+1} - r_{f,t+1} + \sigma_t^2/2}{\gamma \sigma_t^2}.$$

It is straightforward to show that the myopic solution for multiple risky assets, (2.27), is equally valid for a long-term investor with a constant consumption–wealth ratio.

In a model with power utility, then, the assumption that the consumption–wealth ratio is constant immediately leads to the conclusion that portfolio choice is myopic. Under what conditions can this assumption be justified? The answer to this question is by now familiar. First, if returns are IID, there are no changes over time in investment opportunities that might induce changes in consumption relative to wealth. The scale independence of the power utility function implies that consumption is a constant fraction of wealth in this case. Second, if risk aversion $\gamma = 1$, consumption is again a constant fraction of wealth. The intuition for this result is that changing investment opportunities have opposing effects on consumption relative to wealth. An improved investment opportunity, say a higher riskless interest rate, raises the amount that can be consumed each period without depleting wealth. This *income effect* tends to increase consumption relative to wealth. On the other hand, an improved investment opportunity creates an incentive to postpone consumption to the future. This *substitution effect* tends to decrease consumption relative to wealth. In the power utility model, the log-utility case $\gamma = 1$ is the case where income and substitution effects exactly cancel out, so that the consumption–wealth ratio is always constant regardless of any fluctuations in investment opportunities.

To prove these statements, one can use the budget constraint (2.45) to find the conditional mean and variance of wealth, and substitute into (2.42). The resulting equation can be solved for a constant b if asset returns are IID or if $\gamma = 1$. Intuitively, (2.42) says that expected consumption growth should move $1/\gamma$ for one with the expected return. This is consistent with a constant consumption–wealth ratio if the expected return is constant, or if expected consumption growth adjusts one for one with the expected return so that the desired changes in consumption growth can be financed just by the variation in the expected return itself, without any need for savings adjustments.

2.2.4. *Epstein–Zin utility*

Despite the many attractive features of the power utility model, it does have one highly restrictive feature. Power utility implies that the consumer's elasticity of intertemporal substitution, ψ, is the reciprocal of the coefficient of relative risk aversion, γ. Yet it is not clear that these two concepts should be linked so tightly. Risk aversion describes the consumer's reluctance to substitute consumption across states of the world and is meaningful even in an atemporal setting, whereas the elasticity of intertemporal substitution describes the consumer's willingness to substitute consumption over time and is meaningful even in a deterministic setting.

Epstein and Zin (1989, 1991) and Weil (1989) use the theoretical framework of Kreps and Porteus (1978) to develop a more flexible version of the basic power utility model. The Epstein–Zin model retains the desirable scale independence of power utility but breaks the link between the parameters γ and ψ. This added flexibility is extremely helpful in developing a clear understanding of intertemporal portfolio choice. In particular, we shall see in later chapters that risk aversion is the chief determinant of portfolio choice. The elasticity of intertemporal substitution has a major effect on consumption decisions, but only a secondary effect on portfolio decisions.

The Epstein–Zin objective function is defined recursively by

$$U_t = \left[(1 - \delta)C_t^{(1-\gamma)/\theta} + \delta(E_t U_{t+1}^{1-\gamma})^{1/\theta} \right]^{\theta/(1-\gamma)}, \tag{2.47}$$

where $\theta \equiv (1 - \gamma)/(1 - 1/\psi)$. When $\gamma = 1/\psi$, the parameter $\theta = 1$ and the recursion (2.47) becomes linear; it can then be solved forward to yield the familiar time-separable power utility model.

The Epstein–Zin model can be understood by reference to Figure 2.2. The horizontal axis shows the elasticity of intertemporal substitution, ψ, while the vertical axis shows the coefficient of relative risk aversion, γ. The set of points with unit elasticity of intertemporal substitution is drawn as a vertical line, while the set of points with unit relative risk aversion is drawn as a horizontal line. The set of points with power utility is drawn as the hyperbola $\gamma = 1/\psi$. Log utility is the point where all three lines cross; it has $\gamma = \psi = 1$.

The nonlinear recursion (2.47) does not look at all easy to work with. Fortunately Epstein and Zin have shown, using dynamic programming arguments, that, if the intertemporal budget constraint takes the form (2.36) (that is, if the investor finances consumption entirely from financial wealth and does not receive labor income), then there is a Euler equation of the form

$$1 = E_t \left\{ \left[\delta \left(\frac{C_{t+1}}{C_t} \right)^{-1/\psi} \right]^{\theta} \left[\frac{1}{(1 + R_{p,t+1})} \right]^{1-\theta} (1 + R_{i,t+1}) \right\}, \tag{2.48}$$

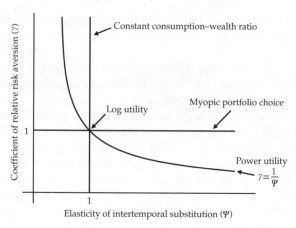

Figure 2.2. Epstein–Zin utility

where as before $(1 + R_{i,t+1})$ is the gross return on any available asset, including the riskless asset and the portfolio itself.

Equation (2.48) simplifies somewhat if we set $(1 + R_{i,t+1}) = (1 + R_{p,t+1})$. If the portfolio return and consumption are jointly lognormal, we then find that expected consumption growth equals

$$E_t(\Delta c_{t+1}) = \psi \log \delta + \psi E_t r_{p,t+1} + \frac{\theta}{2\psi} \text{Var}_t(\Delta c_{t+1} - \psi r_{p,t+1}).$$

(2.49)

Expected consumption growth is determined by time preference, the expected portfolio return, and the effects of uncertainty summarized in the variance term. Note that the elasticity of intertemporal substitution ψ, and not the coefficient of relative risk aversion γ, determines the response of expected consumption growth to variations in the expected return. Randomness in future consumption growth, relative to portfolio returns, increases precautionary savings and lowers current consumption if $\theta > 0$ (a condition satisfied by power utility for which $\theta = 1$), but reduces precautionary savings and increases current consumption if $\theta < 0$.

When there is a single risky asset, the premium on the risky asset over the safe asset is

$$E_t r_{t+1} - r_{f,t+1} + \frac{\sigma_t^2}{2} = \theta \frac{\text{Cov}_t(r_{t+1}, \Delta c_{t+1})}{\psi}$$
$$+ (1 - \theta)\text{Cov}_t(r_{t+1}, r_{p,t+1}). \qquad (2.50)$$

The expected excess return on the risky asset is a weighted average of the risky asset's covariance with consumption growth (divided by the elasticity of intertemporal substitution ψ) and the asset's covariance with the portfolio return. The weights are θ and $1 - \theta$, respectively.

A similar equation holds for each risky asset in a model with multiple risky assets and no short-term riskless asset. In vector notation, we have

$$E_t(\mathbf{r}_{t+1} - r_{0,t+1}\boldsymbol{\iota}) + \frac{\sigma_t^2}{2} = \frac{\theta}{\psi}\boldsymbol{\sigma}_{ct} + (1 - \theta)\boldsymbol{\sigma}_{pt} - \boldsymbol{\sigma}_{0t}, \qquad (2.51)$$

where as before $r_{0,t+1}$ is the total return on the risky benchmark asset, σ_t^2 is the vector of excess-return variances, $\boldsymbol{\sigma}_{ct}$ is the vector of excess-return covariances with consumption growth, $\boldsymbol{\sigma}_{pt}$ is the vector of excess-return covariances with the total return on the portfolio, and $\boldsymbol{\sigma}_{0t}$ is the vector of excess-return covariances with the total return on the benchmark asset. In an asset pricing context, this equation explains any asset's risk premium by reference to both its consumption covariance (the consumption capital asset pricing model) and its covariance with the investor's overall portfolio (the traditional CAPM). In the power utility case, $\theta = 1$ and we have a pure consumption CAPM.

The familiar conditions for myopic portfolio choice follow immediately from (2.50). If asset returns are IID, then consumption is a constant fraction of wealth, and covariance with consumption growth equals covariance with portfolio return. In this case, the right-hand side of (2.50) can be rewritten as $(\theta/\psi + 1 - \theta)\text{Cov}_t(r_{t+1}, r_{p,t+1}) = \gamma \text{Cov}_t(r_{t+1}, r_{p,t+1})$, which implies the myopic portfolio rule.

Alternatively, if relative risk aversion $\gamma = 1$, then $\theta = 0$ and the right-hand side of (2.50) is just $\text{Cov}_t(r_{t+1}, r_{p,t+1})$, which again implies the myopic portfolio rule. This derivation makes it clear that what is required for myopic portfolio choice is unit relative risk aversion, not a unit EIS. Log utility is the special case where both relative risk aversion and the elasticity of intertemporal substitution EIS equal one.

The case of a unit EIS requires careful handling in this model. As ψ approaches one, θ approaches positive or negative infinity. Equation (2.49) can be satisfied only if $\text{Var}_t(\Delta c_{t+1} - r_{p,t+1}) = 0$, which implies a constant consumption–wealth ratio. To analyze portfolio choice in this case, one must take appropriate limits of the terms on the right-hand side of (2.50). Giovannini and Weil (1989) have conducted this analysis and have shown that the model with $\psi = 1$ does not have myopic portfolio choice unless $\gamma = 1$ (in which case we have log utility). The constancy of the consumption–wealth ratio in the unit EIS model makes this a particularly tractable specification. (This is also true in a continuous-time setting, as shown by Schroder and Skiadas 1999.) In the next three chapters we will use the unit EIS case as a benchmark case in which we can get exact solutions, and around which we can construct approximate solutions.

Finally, Epstein and Zin have also shown that the maximized utility function or value function per unit wealth, $V_t \equiv U_t/W_t$, is related to consumption per unit wealth C_t/W_t by the expression

$$V_t = (1 - \delta)^{-\psi/(1-\psi)} \left(\frac{C_t}{W_t} \right)^{1/(1-\psi)}. \tag{2.52}$$

Two special cases are worth noting. First, as ψ approaches one, the exponents in (2.52) increase without limit. The value function has a finite limit, however, because the ratio C_t/W_t approaches $(1 - \delta)$ as shown by Giovannini and Weil (1989). Second, as ψ approaches zero, V_t approaches C_t/W_t. A consumer who is extremely reluctant to substitute intertemporally consumes the annuity value of wealth each period, and this consumer's utility per dollar is the annuity value of the dollar.

2.3. CONCLUSION

Does the investment horizon affect portfolio choice? In this chapter we have shown that it may not. We have assumed that investors' relative risk aversion does not depend systematically on their wealth, an assumption that is required to explain the stability of interest rates and asset returns through two centuries of economic growth. Under this assumption, the investment horizon is irrelevant for investors who have only financial wealth and who face constant investment opportunities. Even if investment opportunities are time-varying, the investment horizon is still irrelevant for investors whose relative risk aversion equals one. Such investors should behave myopically, choosing the portfolio that has the best short-term characteristics. Popular arguments to the contrary, such as the claim that long-term investors can afford to take greater risk because they have 'time to ride out the ups and downs of the market', are simply wrong under these conditions.

Legitimate arguments for horizon effects on portfolio choice depend on violations of the conditions for myopic portfolio choice discussed in this chapter. In our view there is strong empirical evidence that these conditions fail in various ways. The rest of the book is devoted to an exploration of portfolio choice in the presence of such failures.

3

Who Should Buy Long-Term Bonds?

In Chapter 2 we explored the conditions under which optimal portfolio choice is myopic. We now begin to develop a theory of long-term portfolio choice when these conditions fail. We start by considering one particularly important source of variation in investment opportunities: time variation in the short-term real interest rate. In this chapter we allow the real interest rate to change over time, but we fix all the moments of excess returns on risky assets; that is, we assume constant risk premia and constant variances and covariances of returns. In Chapter 4 we allow risk premia to vary as well, and in Chapter 5 we consider time-varying volatility.

We devote special attention in this chapter to long-term bonds. We first consider inflation-indexed bonds, whose payments are fixed in real terms. An inflation-indexed bond would be an uninteresting asset if the short-term real interest rate were constant, for then the bond would have a constant real price and would be a perfect substitute for a short-term real bill. Once the real interest rate varies over time, however, the price of an inflation-indexed bond moves with the real interest rate and the bond becomes risky from the point of view of a short-term investor. At the same time, short-term investments become risky from the point of view of a long-term investor, because they have to be rolled over in the future at uncertain real interest rates. An inflation-indexed bond is the safe asset for a long-term investor, because it supports a stable standard of living in the long term. Thus, real interest rate variation drives a wedge between the risk perceptions of a short-term investor and those of a long-term investor. Optimal portfolio choice is no longer myopic.

We also consider nominal bonds, whose payments are fixed in nominal rather than real terms. The prices of these bonds vary both with real interest rates and with expected inflation. If inflation risk is modest, then nominal bonds behave much like inflation-indexed bonds; in an environment with high inflation risk, however, long-term nominal bonds are risky even from the point of view of long-term investors.

Throughout this and the next two chapters, we consider an investor who has only financial wealth and no labor income, deferring a consideration of labor income to Chapter 6. We assume that the investor cares not about wealth for its own sake but about the consumption stream that can be financed by wealth. To keep the analysis simple, we assume that the investor is infinitely lived; we can vary the effective investment horizon by varying the investor's rate of time preference and thus varying the relative importance of the near future and the distant future. We assume that the investor has the Epstein–Zin preferences developed in Section 2.2.4, with constant relative risk aversion γ and a constant elasticity of intertemporal substitution ψ that need not be related to one another.

The key problem in solving an intertemporal model of this sort is that the investor's intertemporal budget constraint is nonlinear. In Section 3.1.1 we approach this problem by taking a loglinear approximation of the budget constraint, as first proposed by Campbell (1993). The approximation is exact if the consumption–wealth ratio is constant (as it will be if ψ equals one) and is accurate if the consumption–wealth ratio is not too variable (as it will be if ψ is not too far from one). In Section 3.1.2 we use the approximate budget constraint to substitute consumption out of the Euler equations of the Epstein–Zin model, giving an expression relating assets' risk premia to their covariances with current portfolio returns and revisions in expected future portfolio returns.

Section 3.1.3 applies these methods to the portfolio problem, assuming that all the random variables that are relevant for investors are lognormally distributed with constant variances and covariances. This assumption is not innocuous in the context of portfolio choice theory, because it requires both that the investor's portfolio return has a constant variance and that the returns on individual assets have constant variances and a constant covariance with the portfolio. These conditions are consistent with one another only if the composition of the portfolio is constant, which in turn is optimal—given constant variances— only if the expected excess returns on all assets are constant.

Expected asset returns can change over time, but they must move in parallel with the riskless interest rate.

Using this assumption, we derive an explicit expression for the portfolio weight on a single risky asset. When the investor has risk aversion greater than one, the demand for the risky asset is affected not only by the asset's risk premium in relation to its variance, but also by its covariance with revisions in expected future interest rates. An asset whose value increases when interest rates fall is a desirable hedge against declines in interest rates that would otherwise reduce the income generated by the portfolio. This is the intertemporal hedging effect first explored by Merton (1973).

Section 3.1.4 develops this idea further. Long-term bond prices move inversely with interest rates, so they are good intertemporal hedges. As the investor's risk aversion increases, the optimal portfolio approaches an inflation-indexed perpetuity or consol that pays one unit of real consumption for ever. In an important sense this asset is the riskless asset for a long-term investor; even though it may have an unstable capital value in the short term, it finances a riskless consumption stream over the long term. Section 3.1.5 generalizes the analysis to the case where there are multiple risky assets and there may be no short-term riskless asset. This also allows us to find the optimal portfolio even when the investor faces borrowing and short-sales constraints.

In Section 3.2 we develop a more specific model and fit it to historical interest rate data from the United States. We specify the model in Section 3.2.1, present empirical estimates in Section 3.2.2, and derive the implied optimal portfolios in Section 3.2.3. Section 3.3 concludes.

3.1. LONG-TERM PORTFOLIO CHOICE IN A MODEL WITH CONSTANT VARIANCES AND RISK PREMIA

3.1.1. *Approximation of the intertemporal budget constraint*

Recall that the intertemporal budget constraint, in a model with consumption at every date, is

$$W_{t+1} = (1 + R_{p,t+1})(W_t - C_t). \tag{3.1}$$

A central problem in the theory of intertemporal portfolio choice is that this budget constraint is nonlinear because consumption is subtracted from wealth before the portfolio return multiplies the remainder. In other words, only reinvested wealth earns the portfolio return and not all wealth is reinvested.

In the last chapter we concentrated on models in which the consumption–wealth ratio is constant. In this case, reinvested wealth $(W_t - C_t)$ is a constant fraction of total wealth, and (3.1) can be rewritten in loglinear form.

We now develop an alternative approach to the problem of nonlinearity. Following Campbell (1993), we approximate the budget constraint around the mean of the consumption–wealth ratio. We first divide (3.1) by W_t to get

$$\frac{W_{t+1}}{W_t} = (1 + R_{p,t+1})\left(1 - \frac{C_t}{W_t}\right). \tag{3.2}$$

Taking logs, this becomes

$$\Delta w_{t+1} = r_{p,t+1} + \log(1 - \exp(c_t - w_t)). \tag{3.3}$$

The second term on the right-hand side of (3.3) is a nonlinear function of the log consumption–wealth ratio. If that ratio is not too variable, this can be well approximated using a first-order Taylor expansion around its mean. Details are given in Campbell and Viceira (2001b). The resulting expression is

$$\Delta w_{t+1} = k + r_{p,t+1} + \left(1 - \frac{1}{\rho}\right)(c_t - w_t), \tag{3.4}$$

where k and ρ are parameters of linearization. The parameter ρ is defined by $\rho \equiv 1 - \exp(\overline{c - w})$. When the consumption–wealth ratio is constant, then ρ can be interpreted as $(W - C)/W$, the ratio of reinvested wealth to total wealth. The parameter k is defined by the messy expression $k \equiv \log(\rho) + (1 - \rho)\log(1 - \rho)/\rho$.

It is helpful to derive a long-term version of this budget constraint. To do this, we can use the trivial equality

$$\Delta w_{t+1} = \Delta c_{t+1} + (c_t - w_t) - (c_{t+1} - w_{t+1}). \tag{3.5}$$

Equating the left-hand sides of (3.4) and (3.5), we obtain a difference equation in the log consumption–wealth ratio. We can solve forward, assuming that $\lim_{j\to\infty} \rho^j(c_{t+j} - w_{t+j}) = 0$ (a condition that will hold, for example, if the consumption–wealth ratio is stationary), to get

$$c_t - w_t = \sum_{j=1}^{\infty} \rho^j(r_{p,t+j} - \Delta c_{t+j}) + \frac{\rho k}{1 - \rho}. \tag{3.6}$$

This equation says that a high consumption–wealth ratio today must be followed either by high returns on invested wealth or by low consumption growth. That is, high consumption today will deplete wealth and hence future consumption possibilities unless it is offset by high investment returns. This follows simply from the intertemporal budget constraint; there is no model of optimal behavior in (3.6).

Equation (3.6) holds ex post, but it also holds ex ante; if one takes expectations of (3.6) at time t, the left-hand side is unchanged, and the right-hand side becomes an expected discounted value:

$$c_t - w_t = \mathrm{E}_t \sum_{j=1}^{\infty} \rho^j(r_{p,t+j} - \Delta c_{t+j}) + \frac{\rho k}{1 - \rho}. \tag{3.7}$$

Equation (3.7) describes not only rational expectations, but also irrational expectations that satisfy the accounting identity (3.6). It can be substituted into (3.4) and (3.5) to obtain

$$c_{t+1} - \mathrm{E}_t c_{t+1} = (\mathrm{E}_{t+1} - \mathrm{E}_t) \sum_{j=0}^{\infty} \rho^j r_{p,t+1+j}$$

$$- (\mathrm{E}_{t+1} - \mathrm{E}_t) \sum_{j=1}^{\infty} \rho^j \Delta c_{t+1+j}. \tag{3.8}$$

This says that an upward surprise in consumption today must correspond to a positive unexpected return on wealth today (the first term in the first sum on the right-hand side of the equation), to upward revisions in expectations of future returns (the remaining terms in the first sum), or to downward revisions in expected future consumption growth (the second sum on the right-hand side, which starts one period ahead). The last two terms might be called 'news' about future dividends and returns.

These formulas are analogous to expressions developed by Campbell and Shiller (1988) and Campbell (1991) relating dividends, stock prices, and stock returns. Wealth can be thought of as an asset that pays consumption as its dividend. This insight applies both to an individual's wealth and consumption and to aggregate wealth and consumption; thus the assumption commonly made in empirical finance research, that an aggregate stock index is a good proxy for the market portfolio of aggregate wealth, is equivalent to the assumption of Lucas (1978) and Mehra and Prescott (1985) that stocks are priced as if they pay dividends equal to the aggregate consumption of the economy.

3.1.2. Substituting out consumption

We have shown that the consumption–wealth ratio can be related to expected future returns and consumption growth. The next step is to substitute expected consumption growth out of the model. For this purpose we can use the Euler equation for Epstein–Zin utility under lognormality, (2.49):

$$E_t(\Delta c_{t+1}) = \psi \log \delta + \psi E_t r_{p,t+1}$$
$$+ \frac{\theta}{2\psi} \operatorname{Var}_t(\Delta c_{t+1} - \psi r_{p,t+1}).$$

If consumption and the portfolio return are not only lognormal but also homoskedastic, then the variance term in (2.49) is constant and we can rewrite as

$$E_t(\Delta c_{t+1}) = \mu + \psi E_t r_{p,t+1}, \tag{3.9}$$

where the intercept μ includes not only the pure rate of time preference but also the effects of risk on consumption.

Substituting (3.9) into (3.7), we find

$$c_t - w_t = (1 - \psi) E_t \sum_{j=1}^{\infty} \rho^j r_{p,t+j} + \frac{\rho(k - \mu)}{1 - \rho}. \tag{3.10}$$

The log consumption–wealth ratio depends on the expected discounted value of all future portfolio returns, with positive sign if $\psi < 1$ and negative sign if $\psi > 1$. There are opposing income and substitution effects of an increased portfolio return. On the one hand, if the portfolio return is higher, consumption can be higher in all periods for any value of wealth; this is the positive income effect of the portfolio return on consumption. On the other hand, if the portfolio return is higher, there is a greater incentive to delay consumption, cutting consumption today in order to exploit more favorable investment opportunities; this is the negative substitution effect of the portfolio return on consumption. The income effect dominates if $\psi < 1$ and the substitution effect dominates if $\psi > 1$. If $\psi = 1$, the two effects cancel and the consumption–wealth ratio is constant as previously noted.

Equation (3.10) allows us to rewrite (3.8) as

$$c_{t+1} - E_t c_{t+1} = r_{p,t+1} - E_t r_{p,t+1}$$

$$+ (1 - \psi)(E_{t+1} - E_t) \sum_{j=1}^{\infty} p^j r_{p,t+1+j}. \qquad (3.11)$$

The innovation in consumption is the surprise component of the portfolio return, which has a one-for-one effect because of the scale independence of the utility function, plus $(1 - \psi)$ times the revision in expectations of future returns. If $\psi < 1$, a positive surprise about future returns increases consumption today through the dominant income effect; if $\psi > 1$, a positive surprise about future returns reduces consumption today through the dominant substitution effect.

Earlier we assumed that consumption and the portfolio return are jointly lognormal and homoskedastic. We can now see what is required to justify this assumption. According to (3.11), we need log portfolio returns and revisions in expectations of future log portfolio returns to be normal and homoskedastic, as they will be for example in a linear time-series model for log returns and other state variables.

Recall that, under Epstein–Zin utility with a single risky asset, the premium on the risky asset over the safe asset is given by (2.50):

$$E_t r_{t+1} - r_{f,t+1} + \frac{\sigma_t^2}{2} = \theta \frac{\text{Cov}_t(r_{t+1}, \Delta c_{t+1})}{\psi}$$

$$+ (1 - \theta)\, \text{Cov}_t(r_{t+1}, r_{p,t+1}).$$

Although we are assuming that conditional variances and covariances are constant over time, we retain their time subscripts to make it clear that they are calculated conditional on time t information. Equation (3.11) implies that the covariance with consumption that appears in this expression can be replaced by the covariance with the portfolio return, plus $(1 - \psi)$ times the covariance with revised expectations about future returns. Using the relation between the parameters θ, γ, and ψ, we find that

$$E_t r_{t+1} - r_{f,t+1} + \frac{\sigma_t^2}{2} = \gamma \operatorname{Cov}_t(r_{t+1}, r_{p,t+1})$$

$$+ (\gamma - 1) \operatorname{Cov}_t \left(r_{t+1}, (E_{t+1} - E_t) \sum_{j=1}^{\infty} p^j r_{p,t+1+j} \right).$$

(3.12)

Campbell (1993) derived this equation, and Campbell (1996) used it in an asset pricing context, asking whether the capital asset pricing model (CAPM), as extended by the second term on the right-hand side of (3.12), could explain the pattern of risk premia in US financial markets.

This analysis shows that under Epstein–Zin utility there is an elegant separation of the elasticity of intertemporal substitution ψ and the coefficient of relative risk aversion γ. Given the log-linearization coefficient ρ, only the parameter ψ appears in (3.10) and (3.11) relating consumption to returns, and only the parameter γ appears in (3.12) relating the risk premium to the second moments of asset returns. A caveat is that in general the log-linerization parameter ρ itself depends on both ψ and γ; however, we shall see that this dependence is empirically weak and does not seriously undermine the separation of ψ and γ.

3.1.3. *Application to portfolio choice*

So far we have assumed only that consumption and the optimal portfolio are jointly lognormal with constant variances. In order to apply (3.12) in a model of portfolio choice, we need to make the further assumption that the available individual assets have constant variances and risk premia. This implies that variation in the expected portfolio return is due entirely to variation in the riskless interest rate, so the revisions in expected future portfolio returns in (3.12) are equivalent to revisions in expected future riskless interest rates:

$$(E_{t+1} - E_t) \sum_{j=1}^{\infty} \rho^j r_{p,t+1+j} = (E_{t+1} - E_t) \sum_{j=1}^{\infty} \rho^j r_{f,t+1+j}.$$

It also implies that optimal portfolio weights are constant, reconciling the assumptions of constant variances for both individual assets and the portfolio return.

In a model with a single risky asset, we have $\text{Cov}_t(r_{t+1}, r_{p,t+1}) = \alpha_t \sigma_t^2$. Substituting into (3.12) and rearranging, we find that the optimal portfolio weight on the risky asset is a constant α given by

$$\alpha = \frac{1}{\gamma} \frac{E_t r_{t+1} - r_{f,t+1} + \sigma_t^2/2}{\sigma_t^2}$$

$$+ \left(1 - \frac{1}{\gamma}\right) \frac{\text{Cov}_t\left[r_{t+1}, - (E_{t+1} - E_t) \sum_{j=1}^{\infty} \rho^j r_{f,t+1+j}\right]}{\sigma_t^2}. \quad (3.13)$$

The demand for the risky asset is a weighted average of two desirable attributes. The first attribute is the asset's risk premium, relative to its variance, and the second is the asset's covariance with reductions in expected future interest rates, again relative to its variance. The first attribute determines myopic demand for the asset, while the second determines intertemporal hedging demand. The weight on the first attribute is relative risk tolerance $(1/\gamma)$, which becomes negligible as γ increases. A highly conservative investor does not buy the risky asset for its risk premium. The weight on the second attribute is $1 - (1/\gamma)$, which is zero for a myopic investor with $\gamma = 1$ but approaches one as γ increases. A highly conservative investor holds the risky asset only if it covaries with declines in interest rates, compensating the portfolio for the reduction in income that occurs when interest rates fall.

A variant of (3.13) was derived by Restoy (1992). Using (3.10), Restoy noted that revisions in expected future portfolio returns are proportional to surprises in the log consumption–wealth

ratio, $(E_{t+1} - E_t) \sum_{j=1}^{\infty} \rho^j r_{p,t+1+j} = (E_{t+1} - E_t)(c_{t+1} - w_{t+1})/(1 - \psi)$.
Hence we can write

$$\alpha = \frac{1}{\gamma} \frac{E_t r_{t+1} - r_{f,t+1} + \sigma_t^2/2}{\sigma_t^2} \qquad (3.14)$$
$$+ \left(1 - \frac{1}{\gamma}\right)\left(\frac{1}{1 - \psi}\right)\frac{\text{Cov}_t[r_{t+1}, -(c_{t+1} - w_{t+1})]}{\sigma_t^2}.$$

This equation shows that the intertemporal component of asset demand works through covariance of the risky asset with the consumption–wealth ratio. However, it can be misleading, because it suggests that the parameter ψ plays a role in asset demand while in fact ψ cancels out of the previous equation.

A third transformation of (3.13) uses the Epstein–Zin result (2.52) relating the value function per unit wealth to the consumption–wealth ratio. Taking logs of (2.52), the second term in (3.14) can be restated in terms of the covariance of the risky asset return with the value function,

$$\alpha - \frac{1}{\gamma} \frac{E_t r_{t+1} - r_{f,t+1} + \sigma_t^2/2}{\sigma_t^2} + \left(1 - \frac{1}{\gamma}\right)\frac{\text{Cov}_t(r_{t+1}, -v_{t+1})}{\sigma_t^2}.$$
$$(3.15)$$

This shows that the intertemporal component of asset demand is determined by the covariance of the risky asset return with the investor's utility per unit wealth, which varies over time with investment opportunities.

One can use these three equations to understand the intellectual history of research on long-term portfolio choice. Merton (1971, 1973) introduced the concept of intertemporal hedging demand for risky assets. He worked with the indirect utility or value function defined over wealth and state variables; thus, his approach was similar in spirit to (3.15). Rubinstein (1976b) and Breeden (1979) first used covariance with consumption as a measure of risk for long-term investors; their approach was similar to (3.14). Neither author derived an explicit solution comparable to (3.13), relating portfolio demands to covariances of assets with exogenous variables. Equation (3.13) depends on specific assumptions, but it can be used to obtain general insights. Note in particular that intertemporal hedging demand in (3.13) depends on the discounted present value of all future interest rates; thus, portfolio choice of long-term investors is affected far more strongly by persistent variations in investment opportunities than by transitory variations.

3.1.4. What is the riskless asset?

The identity of the riskless asset is a fundamental issue in finance. It is conventional to think of the riskless asset as an asset that has a stable capital value in the short term, such as a Treasury bill or a money market fund. Such an asset has a known return over one period and will be held by an infinitely conservative short-term investor.

For a long-term investor, however, a strategy of rolling over Treasury bills is not necessarily safe because maturing bills must be reinvested at unknown future real interest rates. Over thirty years ago, Modigliani and Sutch (1966, pp. 183–4) made this point particularly clearly:

Suppose a person has an n period habitat; that is, he has funds which he will not need for n periods and which, therefore, he intends to keep invested in bonds for n periods. If he invests in n period bonds, he will know exactly the outcome of his investments as measured by the terminal value of his wealth.... If, however, he stays short, his outcome is uncertain.... Thus, if he has risk aversion, he will prefer to stay long.

Modigliani and Sutch's assumption, that an investor cares only about wealth at a single future date, is somewhat artificial. However, a similar insight applies to a long-term investor of the sort modelled in this book, who cares about the stream of consumption or standard of living that can be supported by wealth. This point was first made by Stiglitz (1970) and Rubinstein (1976b).

To show the result in the context of our model, we consider what happens to portfolio choice as the coefficient of relative risk aversion increases. In this case relative risk tolerance $(1/\gamma)$ goes to zero, so (3.13) approaches

$$\alpha_t = \frac{\mathrm{Cov}_t[r_{t+1}, - (E_{t+1} - E_t) \sum_{j=1}^{\infty} \rho^j r_{f,t+1+j}]}{\sigma_t^2}. \tag{3.16}$$

Now consider the pricing of an inflation-indexed perpetuity or *consol*, that pays one unit of consumption each period for ever. Campbell, Lo, and MacKinlay (1997, p. 408), following Shiller (1979), show that a loglinear approximation to the log yield y_{ct} on a real consol is

$$y_{ct} = \mu_c + (1 - \rho_c)\mathrm{E}_t \sum_{j=0}^{\infty} \rho_c^j r_{f,t+1+j}. \tag{3.17}$$

Here μ_c is a constant that captures any risk premium on the consol, and ρ_c is a loglinearization parameter defined as $\rho_c \equiv 1 - \exp[\mathrm{E}(-p_{ct})]$, where p_{ct} is the log 'cum-dividend' price of the consol including its current coupon.[1] Also, the consol return is given by

$$
\begin{aligned}
r_{c,t+1} &= \frac{1}{1 - \rho_c} y_{ct} - \frac{\rho_c}{1 - \rho_c} y_{c,t+1} \\
&= r_{f,t+1} + \mu_c - (\mathrm{E}_{t+1} - \mathrm{E}_t) \sum_{j=1}^{\infty} \rho_c^j r_{f,t+1+j}.
\end{aligned}
\tag{3.18}
$$

Thus, the consol return has the property that its variance σ_t^2 equals the negative of its covariance with revisions in expected future interest rates. If a consol is the risky asset, $\alpha = 1$ in (3.16), implying that an infinitely risk-averse investor puts all his wealth in an inflation-indexed consol. In this sense the consol, and not the short-term safe asset, is the riskless asset for a long-term investor.

The above argument assumes that $\rho = \rho_c$. These two constants are indeed the same for an individual who is infinitely reluctant to substitute consumption intertemporally ($\psi = 0$). Such an individual consumes the annuity value of wealth, the consumption stream that can be sustained indefinitely by the initial level of wealth. But the annuity value of a real consol is just its dividend

---

[1] Campbell, Lo, and MacKinlay work with expected future returns on the perpetuity, but in the current model with constant risk premia these equal the riskless interest rate plus a constant. Also, Campbell, Lo, and MacKinlay give an alternative definition of ρ_c in relation to the 'ex-dividend' price of the consol excluding its current coupon. This is more natural in a bond pricing context, but less convenient here, because the form of the budget constraint implies that we are measuring wealth inclusive of current consumption, that is, on a 'cum-dividend' basis.

of one. Thus, for this investor $C/W = 1/P_c$, which implies $E(c - w) = E(-p_c)$, and thus, from the definitions of the loglinerization parameters, $\rho = \rho_c$. The infinitely risk-averse investor who is infinitely reluctant to substitute intertemporally holds a real consol that finances a riskless consumption stream over the infinite future.

3.1.5. Generalizing the solution

The above analysis generalizes straightforwardly to the case where there are multiple risky assets, with or without a short-term riskless asset. As in the previous chapter, we write the variance–covariance matrix of excess risky asset returns as Σ_t and the vector of excess-return variances, the main diagonal of Σ_t, as σ_t^2. We also define a vector σ_{ht} that contains the covariances of each risky asset return with declines in expected future interest rates:

$$\sigma_{ht} \equiv \text{Cov}_t\left(\mathbf{r}_{t+1}, -(E_{t+1} - E_t)\sum_{j=1}^{\infty} \rho^j r_{f,t+1+j} \right). \tag{3.19}$$

The use of the letter h here is intended to evoke Merton's concept of intertemporal hedging demand.

If a short-term riskless asset exists, we have

$$\alpha_t = \frac{1}{\gamma}\Sigma_t^{-1}(E_t\mathbf{r}_{t+1} - r_{f,t+1}\iota + \sigma_t^2/2) + \left(1 - \frac{1}{\gamma}\right)\Sigma_t^{-1}\sigma_{ht}. \tag{3.20}$$

Just as before, the vector of risky asset allocations is a weighted average of a myopic term and a hedging term, where the weights are determined by relative risk tolerance. As risk aversion increases, risk tolerance declines and all weight shifts to the hedging term. If there is no short-term riskless asset, then the solution is augmented by an intercept, just as in the myopic case (2.27). The intercept can be combined with the intertemporal hedging term to write

$$\alpha_t = \frac{1}{\gamma}\Sigma_t^{-1}(E_t\mathbf{r}_{t+1} - r_{f,t+1}\iota + \sigma_t^2/2) + \left(1 - \frac{1}{\gamma}\right)\Sigma_t^{-1}(\sigma_{ht} - \sigma_{0t}),$$

$$\tag{3.21}$$

where σ_{0t} is the vector of covariances of each risky asset's excess return over the benchmark with the benchmark return itself. In practice, as we have noted earlier, the adjustment for benchmark covariances tends to be small when a short-term asset is used as the benchmark.

It is tempting to relate these solutions to the inflation-indexed consol introduced in the previous section. If the loglinearization parameter ρ is fixed and equal to ρ_c, then the vector σ_{ht} is equal to a vector σ_{ct} containing covariances of each risky asset return with the inflation-indexed consol return. In this case we can give a regression interpretation to the hedging term in (3.20). $\Sigma_t^{-1}\sigma_{ct}$ is the vector of population regression coefficients from a multiple regression of an inflation-indexed consol return onto the set of risky asset returns. If an inflation-indexed consol is in the set of available risky assets, then this vector will place zero weight on all risky assets except the inflation-indexed consol itself. If an inflation-indexed consol is not available, then the optimal hedging portfolio will be that combination of the risky assets that best approximates the return on an inflation-indexed consol in a regression sense.

The problem with this interpretation is that the loglinearization parameter ρ depends on preferences, and will not exactly equal ρ_c unless the investor is infinitely risk-averse and infinitely unwilling to substitute consumption intertemporally $(1/\gamma = \psi = 0)$. For all other preferences, $\rho \neq \rho_c$ and thus $\sigma_{ht} \neq \sigma_{ct}$, although the differences are small empirically. In the case where $\psi = 1$, we know that $\rho = \delta$, the time discount factor. If $\psi \neq 1$, we must solve for ρ numerically. We do this using a recursive procedure. We take an initial value of ρ, solve (3.21) for the optimal portfolio, solve for the corresponding optimal consumption–wealth ratio using (3.10), use this consumption–wealth ratio to calculate a new value for ρ, and repeat until convergence. In practice, these calculations are extremely rapid and straightforward.

We can also allow for borrowing and short-sales constraints. Unconstrained portfolio allocations are often highly leveraged; but this permits the possibility of bankruptcy in a discrete-time model, and many investors are constrained in their use of leverage. Because the unconstrained optimal portfolio policy is constant over time, we can impose constraints using results in Teplá (2000). Following Cvitanić and Karatzas (1992), Teplá shows that standard results in static portfolio choice with borrowing and short-sales constraints extend to intertemporal models whose unconstrained optimal portfolio policies are constant over time. The optimal portfolio allocations under borrowing constraints are the unconstrained allocations with a higher short-term interest rate, and the optimal portfolio allocations under short-sales constraints are found by reducing the dimensionality of the asset space until the optimal unconstrained allocations imply no short sales. These and all other results given in this section are explained in detail in Campbell and Viceira (2001b).

3.2. A MODEL OF THE TERM STRUCTURE OF INTEREST RATES

3.2.1. Specification of the model

Our analysis of portfolio choice with constant risk premia gives a special role to long-term bonds. The riskless asset for a long-term investor is an inflation-indexed consol. If this asset is available, it will play some role in the optimal portfolio of any investor who has relative risk aversion greater than one. If an inflation-indexed consol is not available, a conservative investor will hold assets that are good proxies for it.

In order to go further, we need to use an explicit model of the term structure of interest rate to derive quantitative predictions for investors' holdings of Treasury bills, long-term bonds, and equities. Following Campbell and Viceira (2001a), we now present such a model. The model is set in discrete time; it has two factors, one real and one nominal, with lognormal distributions and constant variances. This is the simplest term structure model that allows us to distinguish between real and nominal bonds. The real part of the model is a discrete-time version of the well-known Vasicek (1977) continuous-time model.

Because bonds have deterministic payoffs, they can be priced by writing down a time-series model for the stochastic discount factor (SDF) M_{t+1}. The SDF determines the prices of all assets in the economy, as discussed in Section 2.2.3, but the link is particularly direct with bonds since we do not have to model their payoffs. A more detailed explanation of this type of model is given by Campbell, Lo, and MacKinlay (1997, chapter 11) and Campbell (2000).

We first take logs and work with $m_{t+1} \equiv \log(M_{t+1})$. We break the negative of the log SDF into its conditional expectation at time t, x_t, and a shock realized at time $t + 1$, $v_{m,t+1}$:

$$-m_{t+1} = x_t + v_{m,t+1}. \tag{3.22}$$

We assume that x_t follows a first-order autoregressive (AR(1)) process,

$$x_{t+1} = (1 - \phi_x)\mu_x + \phi_x x_t + \varepsilon_{x,t+1}, \tag{3.23}$$

and we allow the innovations to the log SDF to be correlated with innovations to its conditional expectation:

$$v_{m,t+1} = \beta_{mx}\varepsilon_{x,t+1} + \varepsilon_{m,t+1}. \tag{3.24}$$

Here the underlying shocks $\varepsilon_{x,t+1}$ and $\varepsilon_{m,t+1}$ are assumed to be uncorrelated with one another. Each is serially uncorrelated, normally distributed, and has a constant variance. Thus, the SDF in this model is lognormally distributed.

The term structure of real interest rates
The economic meaning of these assumptions can best be appreciated by working out their implications for the term structure of real interest rates. There is a direct link between the SDF and the return, or equivalently the price or yield, on a one-period inflation-indexed bond. We first recall from (2.41) that $1/(1 + R_{f,t+1}) = E_t(M_{t+1})$. Taking logs and reversing signs, this implies that $r_{f,t+1} = -\log E_t(M_{t+1})$: the log riskless return is the negative of the log expected SDF.

In a term structure context, the log riskless return is the log return on a one-period inflation-indexed bond, which equals the log yield on that bond at the end of the previous period, or equivalently the negative of the log price of the bond at the end of the previous period: $r_{f,t+1} = r_{1,t+1} = y_{1t} = -p_{1t}$. Putting these results together, we have

$$-p_{1t} = y_{1t} = -\log E_t(M_{t+1}) = E_t(-m_{t+1}) - \tfrac{1}{2}\mathrm{Var}_t(m_{t+1}), \tag{3.25}$$

where the second equality follows from the assumed lognormality of the SDF. Substituting in from (3.22)–(3.24), we have

$$-p_{1t} = y_{1t} = x_t - \tfrac{1}{2}(\beta_{mx}^2 \sigma_x^2 + \sigma_m^2), \tag{3.26}$$

where $\sigma_x^2 \equiv \mathrm{Var}_t(\varepsilon_{x,t+1})$ and $\sigma_m^2 \equiv \mathrm{Var}_t(\varepsilon_{m,t+1})$. The short-term real interest rate equals the state variable x_t adjusted by a constant, so it follows an AR(1) process with persistence ϕ_x.

Longer-term inflation-indexed bonds can be priced recursively. A two-period bond today will become a one-period bond tomorrow, when its price will be described by (3.26). Thus, one can solve for its log price, or equivalently its log yield, and then for the log prices and yields of all longer-maturity bonds. The solution for the negative of the log price of an n-period inflation-indexed zero-coupon bond, $-p_{nt}$, which equals maturity n times the log yield on the bond, ny_{nt}, is given by

$$-p_{nt} = ny_{nt} = A_n + B_n x_t, \tag{3.27}$$

where A_n and B_n are functions of bond maturity n but not of time t.

A recursive expression for the coefficient A_n is given in Campbell and Viceira (2001b). More important for our present discussion, the coefficient B_n is given by

$$B_n = 1 + \phi_x B_{n-1} = \frac{1 - \phi_x^n}{1 - \phi_x}. \tag{3.28}$$

To understand this equation, note that the expectations hypothesis of the term structure holds in this model. Thus, the log bond yield is a constant plus an average of expected future real interest rates over the next n periods, and n times the log bond yield is a constant plus a sum of expected future real interest rates. Since the real interest rate follows an AR(1) process with persistence coefficient ϕ_x, the expected real interest rate k periods ahead is a constant plus ϕ_x^k times the real interest rate today. Summing up over n periods gives (3.28).

The one-period log return on an n-period inflation-indexed zero-coupon bond is just the change in its price ($p_{n-1,t+1} - p_{nt}$).

Combining this expression with (3.27) and (3.28), the excess return over the one-period log interest rate is

$$r_{n,t+1} - r_{1,t+1} = -\tfrac{1}{2}B_{n-1}^2\sigma_x^2 - \beta_{mx}B_{n-1}\sigma_x^2 - B_{n-1}\varepsilon_{x,t+1}, \quad (3.29)$$

so the n-period bond return is driven only by real interest rate shocks $\varepsilon_{x,t+1}$, with a sensitivity B_{n-1}. Because the real part of our model has only a single factor, yields and prices of inflation-indexed bonds of all maturities react only to the short-term real interest rate and thus are perfectly correlated with one another. The variance of the n-period bond return is $\sigma_{nt}^2 = B_{n-1}^2\sigma_x^2$, and the risk premium is

$$E_t\left(r_{n,t+1} - r_{1,t+1}\right) + \frac{\sigma_{nt}^2}{2} = -\beta_{mx}B_{n-1}\sigma_x^2. \quad (3.30)$$

The risk premium on the long-term bond, or term premium, is determined by the conditional covariance of the excess bond return with the log SDF. In our homoskedastic model the conditional covariance is constant through time but dependent on the bond maturity; thus, the term premium is constant as postulated by the expectations hypothesis of the term structure. Since $\beta_{n-1} > 0$, the term premium has the opposite sign to β_{mx}. With a positive β_{mx}, long-term inflation-indexed bonds pay off when the SDF or, equivalently, the marginal utility of consumption for a representative investor is high, that is when wealth is most desirable. In equilibrium, these bonds have a negative term premium and the real yield curve is on average downward-sloping. With a negative β_{mx}, on the other hand, long-term inflation-indexed bonds pay off when the marginal utility of consumption for a representative investor is low, and so in equilibrium they have a positive term premium. In this case the real yield curve is on average upward-sloping.

Equation (3.30) implies that the Sharpe ratio for inflation-indexed bonds is $-\beta_{mx}\sigma_x$, which is independent of bond maturity. The invariance of the Sharpe ratio to bond maturity follows from the single-factor structure of the real sector of the model. The ratio of the risk premium to the variance of the excess return, which determines a myopic investor's allocation to long-term bonds, is $-\beta_{mx}/B_{n-1}$. This does depend on bond maturity, but not on the volatility of the real interest rate.

The optimal portfolio of inflation-indexed bonds
If only inflation-indexed bonds are available to the investor, the real sector of the model is all we need to derive an explicit solution to the portfolio problem. Because all long-term inflation-indexed bonds are perfectly correlated, we can consider without loss of generality the choice between two assets: a single-period inflation-indexed bond, and an n-period inflation-indexed bond. Using (3.29) to calculate the terms in (3.13), we find that the optimal portfolio weight on the n-period bond is

$$\alpha_n = \frac{1}{\gamma}\left(\frac{-\beta_{mx}}{B_{n-1}}\right) + \left(1 - \frac{1}{\gamma}\right)\left(\frac{1}{B_{n-1}}\right)\left(\frac{\rho}{1 - \rho\phi_x}\right). \tag{3.31}$$

As before, the first term in this equation represents myopic demand, while the second term represents intertemporal hedging demand.

This solution has several interesting properties. First, the variance of real interest rate shocks, σ_x^2, does not directly affect the portfolio weight α_n because, given the parameterization of our model, it moves the variance of returns and the risk premium in proportion to one another. Interest rate variance can affect the solution only indirectly, through the loglinearization parameter ρ. Empirically, we find that ρ changes very little when the parameters of the model change, so the indirect effect through ρ is quantitatively negligible.

Second, the interest rate sensitivity of the optimal portfolio is given by $\alpha_n B_{n-1}$, and this does not depend on the bond maturity n. Two assets are enough to complete the market with respect to real interest rate risk, and thus the investor can use any two inflation-indexed bonds to construct a portfolio with the optimal level of interest rate sensitivity. If only short-maturity bonds with a low sensitivity are available, the investor can compensate by holding more of them or even leveraging his position; if only long-maturity bonds with a high sensitivity are available, the investor can compensate by holding fewer of them.

Third, the intertemporal hedging demand, the second term in (3.31), is increasing in the persistence of interest rate shocks ϕ_x. This is because, as shown in the general solution (3.13), hedging demand is determined by the covariance of the risky asset return with the discounted value of all future interest rates. A major theme of this book is that persistent shocks to investment opportunities are much more important for portfolio choice than are transitory shocks to investment opportunities.

Fourth, as risk aversion increases and the elasticity of intertemporal substitution declines, the limit of (3.31) is a portfolio that is equivalent to an inflation-indexed consol. In this model an inflation-indexed consol has interest rate sensitivity $-\rho_c/(1-\rho_c\phi_x)$, and $\rho = \rho_c$ when $1/\gamma = \psi = 0$. This is a special case of the general point made in Section 3.1.4.

Equation (3.31) is appealingly simple, but it lacks realism because it does not allow investors to hold nominal bonds or equities. In order to go further, we need to augment the model to include such assets.

The term structure of nominal interest rates
In order to price nominal bonds, we must model the process driving inflation. We assume that this process has the same form that we have already assumed for the SDF. That is, realized log inflation π_{t+1} equals expected log inflation z_t plus an inflation shock, and expected inflation follows an AR(1) process:

$$\pi_{t+1} = z_t + v_{\pi,t+1}, \tag{3.32}$$

$$z_{t+1} = (1 - \phi_z)\mu_z + \phi_z z_t + v_{z,t+1}. \tag{3.33}$$

We assume that the shocks to realized and expected inflation, $v_{\pi,t+1}$ and $v_{z,t+1}$, can be correlated with each other and with the real shocks to the model:

$$v_{z,t+1} = \beta_{zx}\varepsilon_{x,t+1} + \beta_{zm}\varepsilon_{m,t+1} + \varepsilon_{z,t+1}, \tag{3.34}$$

$$v_{\pi,t+1} = \beta_{\pi x}\varepsilon_{x,t+1} + \beta_{\pi m}\varepsilon_{m,t+1} + \beta_{\pi z}\varepsilon_{z,t+1} + \varepsilon_{\pi,t+1}. \tag{3.35}$$

The model is driven by four normally distributed, white-noise shocks, $\varepsilon_{m,t+1}, \varepsilon_{\pi,t+1}, \varepsilon_{x,t+1}$, and $\varepsilon_{z,t+1}$, that determine the innovations to the log SDF, the log inflation rate, and their conditional means. These shocks are cross-sectionally uncorrelated, with variances $\sigma_m^2, \sigma_\pi^2, \sigma_x^2$, and σ_z^2. It is important to note that z_{t+1}, the expected inflation rate, is affected by both a pure expected-inflation shock $\varepsilon_{z,t+1}$ and the shocks to the expected and unexpected log SDF $\varepsilon_{x,t+1}$ and $\varepsilon_{m,t+1}$. That is, innovations to expected inflation can be correlated with innovations in the log SDF, and hence with innovations in the short-term real interest rate. These correlations mean that nominal interest rates need not move one-for-one with expected inflation—that is, the Fisher hypothesis need not hold—and nominal bond prices can include an inflation risk premium as well as a real term premium.

We have written the model with a self-contained real sector (3.22)–(3.24) and a nominal sector (3.32)–(3.35) that is affected by shocks to the real sector. But this is merely a matter of notational convenience. Our model is a reduced-form rather than a structural model, so it captures correlations among shocks to real and nominal interest rates but does not have anything to say about the true underlying sources of these shocks.

The pricing of nominal bonds follows the same steps as the pricing of indexed bonds. The log price of an n-period nominal zero-coupon bond, $p_{nt}^{\$}$, is a linear combination of x_t and z_t whose coefficients are time-invariant, though they vary with the maturity of the bond:

$$-p_{nt}^{\$} = n y_{nt}^{\$} = A_n^{\$} + B_{1n}^{\$} x_t + B_{2n}^{\$} z_t. \tag{3.36}$$

Expressions for the coefficients $A_n^{\$}, B_{1n}^{\$}$, and $B_{2n}^{\$}$ are given in Campbell and Viceira (2001b).

Since nominal bond prices are driven by shocks to both real interest rates and inflation, they have a two-factor structure rather than the single-factor structure of indexed bond prices. Inflation affects the excess return on an n-period nominal bond over the one-period nominal interest rate, so risk premia in the nominal term structure include compensation for inflation risk. Like all other risk premia in the model, however, the risk premia on nominal bonds are constant over time; thus, the expectations hypothesis of the term structure holds for nominal as well as for real bonds.

Pricing equities

Even though our focus in this chapter is on long-term bonds, a full evaluation of bond demand requires that we include equities in our model as an attractive alternative long-term investment.

We do this as simply as possible, assuming that the unexpected log return on equities is affected by shocks to both the expected and unexpected log SDF:

$$r_{e,t+1} - E_t r_{e,t+1} = \beta_{ex}\varepsilon_{x,t+1} + \beta_{em}\varepsilon_{m,t+1}. \tag{3.37}$$

Campbell (1999) shows that this decomposition of the unexpected log equity return into a linear combination of the shocks to the expected and unexpected log SDF is consistent with a representative-agent model where expected aggregate consumption growth follows an AR(1). From the fundamental pricing equation $1 = E_t(M_{t+1}R_{t+1})$ and the lognormal structure of the model, it is easy to show that the risk premium on equities, over a one-period riskless return $r_{1,t+1}$, is given by

$$E_t(r_{e,t+1} - r_{1,t+1}) + \frac{\sigma_{et}^2}{2} = \beta_{mx}\beta_{ex}\sigma_x^2 + \beta_{em}\sigma_m^2. \tag{3.38}$$

Like all other covariances in the model, this is constant over time, so the equity premium is a constant.

Once nominal bonds and equities are included in the model, the algebraic portfolio solutions become sufficiently complicated that it is no longer helpful to write them out explicitly. Instead, we estimate the model on historical data and present numerical solutions.

3.2.2. The term structure of interest rates in the USA

Data and estimation method

We estimate the two-factor term structure model using data on US nominal interest rates, equities, and inflation. We use nominal zero-coupon yields at maturities three months, one year, three years, and ten years from McCulloch and Kwon (1993), updated through 1999(II) (the second quarter of 1999) by Kamakura Risk Information Services. We take data on equities from the Indices files on the CRSP tapes, using the value-weighted return, including dividends, on the NYSE, AMEX, and NASDAQ markets. For inflation, we use a consumer price index that retrospectively incorporates the rental-equivalence methodology, thereby avoiding any direct effect of nominal interest rates on measured inflation. Although the raw data are available monthly, we construct a quarterly dataset in order to reduce the influence of high-frequency noise in inflation and short-term movements in interest rates. We begin our sample in 1952, just after the Fed–Treasury Accord that dramatically altered the time-series behavior of nominal interest rates. Our sample ends in 1999(II) and thus adds almost three years to the sample studied by Campbell and Viceira (2001a).

To avoid the implication of the model that bond returns are driven by only two common factors, so that all bond returns can be perfectly explained by any two bond returns, we assume that bond yields are measured with error. The errors in yields are normally distributed, serially uncorrelated, and uncorrelated across bonds. Then the term structure model becomes a classic state–space model in which unobserved state variables x_t and z_t follow a linear process with normal innovations and we observe linear combinations of them with normal errors. The model can be estimated by maximum likelihood using a Kalman filter to construct the likelihood function (Hamilton 1994).

In Table 3.1 we report parameter estimates for the periods 1952–99 and 1983–99. Interest rates were unusually high and volatile in the 1979–82 period, during which the Federal Reserve Board under Paul Volcker was attempting to re-establish the credibility of anti-inflationary monetary policy and was experimenting with monetarist operating procedures. Many authors have argued that real interest rates and inflation have behaved differently in the monetary policy regime established since 1982 by Federal Reserve Chairmen Volcker and Alan Greenspan (see e.g. Clarida, Gali, and Gertler 2000). Accordingly, we report separate estimates for the period starting in 1983(I) in addition to the full sample period.

The parameter values in the table are restricted maximum likelihood estimates of the model. Unrestricted maximum likelihood estimates fit the data well in the 1952–99 sample period, but they deliver implausibly low means for short-term nominal and real interest rates in the 1983–99 sample period. (The model does not necessarily fit the sample means because the same parameters are used to fit both time-series and cross-sectional behavior; thus, the model can trade off better fit elsewhere for worse fit of mean short-term interest rates.) Accordingly, we require that the model exactly fit the sample means of nominal

Table 3.1. Term Structure Model Estimation

Parameter	1952(I)–1999(II)		1983(I)–1999(II)	
	Estimate	S.E.	Estimate	S.E.
μ_x	0.0584	0.0287	0.0503	0.0711
μ_z	0.0091		0.0081	
ϕ_x	0.8690	0.0055	0.9909	0.0035
ϕ_z	0.9992	0.0012	0.8674	0.0199
β_{mx}	−67.8663	41.5504	−25.1276	96.4208
β_{zx}	0.0779	0.0516	−0.4035	0.1746
β_{zm}	−0.0011	0.0005	0.0001	0.0010
$\beta_{\pi x}$	0.5163	0.2957	0.0435	0.8487
$\beta_{\pi m}$	−0.0084	0.0030	−0.0024	0.0038
$\beta_{\pi z}$	1.4518	0.2790	−1.7691	1.1744
β_{ex}	−3.6366	3.4219	−9.8359	5.5368
β_{em}	0.2873	0.0846	0.2533	0.1503
σ_x	0.0024	0.0001	0.0024	0.0005
σ_m	0.2849	0.0888	0.2866	0.1773
σ_z	0.0013	0.0001	0.0015	0.0002
σ_π	0.0070	0.0004	0.0073	0.0016
Log-likelihood	26.4355		26.8966	
No. of observations	190		66	
$E[r_{1,t+1}]$	1.70%		3.00%	
$E[r_{1,t+1}^\$]$	5.70%		6.29%	
$\sigma(r_{1,t+1})$	0.98%		3.52%	
$\sigma(r_{1,t+1}^\$)$	6.76%		3.41%	
$E[\pi_{t+1}]$	3.66%		3.23%	
$\sigma_t(\pi_{t+1})$	1.54%		1.55%	

interest rates and inflation. These restrictions hardly reduce the likelihood at all in 1952–99, and even in 1983–99 they cannot be rejected at conventional significance levels.

Parameter estimates

The first two columns of Table 3.1 report parameters and asymptotic standard errors for the period 1952–99.[2] All parameters are in natural units, so they are on a quarterly basis. We

---

[2] No standard error is reported for the parameter μ_z because the restrictions we have imposed on the model determine this parameter exactly.

estimate a moderately persistent process for the real interest rate; the persistence coefficient ϕ_x is 0.87, implying a half-life for shocks to real interest rates of about five quarters. The expected inflation process is much more persistent, with a coefficient ϕ_z of 0.9992 that implies a half-life for expected inflation shocks of over two centuries! Of course, the model also allows for transitory noise in realized inflation.

The final six rows of the table report the implications of the estimated parameters for the unconditional means and standard deviations of real and nominal short-term interest rates, the unconditional mean of inflation, and the conditional standard deviation of inflation, measured in percentages per year. The implied mean log yield on an indexed three-month bill is 1.70% for the 1952–99 sample period. Taken together with the mean log yield on a nominal three-month bill of 5.70% and the mean log inflation rate of 3.66% (both restricted to equal the sample means over this period), and adjusting for Jensen's inequality using one-half the conditional variance of log inflation, the implied inflation risk premium in a three-month nominal Treasury bill is 34 basis points. This fairly substantial risk premium is explained by the positive coefficient $\beta_{\pi x}$ and the negative coefficient $\beta_{\pi m}$ in Table 3.1.

Risk premia on long-term indexed bonds, relative to a three-month indexed bill, are determined by the parameter β_{mx}. This is negative, implying positive risk premia on long-term indexed bonds and an upward-sloping term structure of real interest rates. However, it is not statistically significant. Risk premia on nominal bonds, relative to indexed bonds, are determined by the inflation-risk parameters β_{zx} and β_{zm}. The former is positive but statistically insignificant, while the latter is negative and significant. Both point estimates imply positive inflation risk premia on nominal bonds relative to indexed bonds.

The parameters in Table 3.1 can also be used to calculate the volatility of the log SDF. From (3.22)–(3.24), the variance of m_{t+1} is $\sigma_x^2/(1 - \phi_x^2) + \beta_{mx}^2\sigma_x^2 + \sigma_m^2$. The estimates in Table 3.1 imply a large quarterly standard deviation of 0.33, consistent with the literature on volatility bounds for the SDF (Hansen and Jagannathan 1991; Cochrane and Hansen 1992). When financial markets are complete, the discounted marginal utility growth of each investor must be equal to the SDF. Therefore the consumption and portfolio solutions we report later in the chapter for the complete markets case imply highly volatile marginal utilities, resulting from either volatile consumption or high risk aversion. This is a manifestation of the equity premium puzzle of Mehra and Prescott (1985) in our microeconomic model with exogenous asset returns and endogenous consumption.

Implications for the term structure

Table 3.2 explores the term structure implications of our estimates in greater detail. The table compares implied and sample moments of term structure variables, measured in percentage points per year. Panel (A) reports sample moments for returns and yields on nominal bonds, together with the moments implied by our estimated model; panel (B) shows comparable implied moments for indexed bonds; and panel (C) reports sample and implied moments for equities. Row (1) of the table gives Jensen's-inequality-corrected average excess returns on n-period nominal bonds over one-period nominal bonds, while row (2) gives the standard deviations of these excess returns. Row (3) reports annualized Sharpe ratios for nominal bonds, the ratio of row (1) to row (2). Row (4) reports mean nominal yield spreads, and row (5) reports the standard deviations of nominal yield spreads. Rows (6)–(10) repeat these moments for indexed bonds. Note that the reported risk premia and Sharpe ratios for nominal and indexed bonds are not directly comparable, because they are measured relative to different short-term assets, nominal and indexed respectively.

The first two columns of the table report results for the 1952–99 sample. A comparison of the model implications in rows (1) and (6) shows that ten-year nominal bonds have a risk premium over three-month nominal bills of 1.71% per year, while ten-year indexed bonds have a risk premium over three-month indexed bills of 1.21% per year. These numbers, together with the 34-basis-point risk premium on three-month nominal bills over three-month indexed bills, imply a ten-year inflation risk premium (the risk premium on ten-year nominal bonds over ten-year indexed bonds) of 84 basis points. This number is slightly lower than the rough estimate in Campbell and Shiller (1996).

Rows (2) and (7) show that nominal bonds are much more volatile than indexed bonds; the difference in volatility increases with maturity, so that ten-year nominal bonds have a standard

Table 3.2. Sample and Implied Moments of the Term Structure

Moment	1952(I)–1999(II)		1983(I)–1999(II)	
	1 yr	10 yr	1 yr	10 yr
(A) Nominal term structure				
(1) Nominal bond premium				
Sample	0.40	1.24	0.67	5.82
Implied	0.49	1.71	0.11	1.70
(2) Nominal bond s.d.				
Sample	1.57	11.22	1.06	11.96
Implied	1.60	11.45	1.20	14.36
(3) Sharpe ratio = (1)/(2)				
Sample	0.26	0.11	0.64	0.49
Implied	0.30	0.15	0.09	0.12
(4) Mean yield spread				
Sample	0.43	1.16	0.47	1.84
Implied	0.26	0.99	0.05	0.49
(5) S.d. yield spread				
Sample	0.22	0.60	0.18	0.57
Implied	0.18	0.80	0.13	0.70
(B) Real term structure				
(6) Real bond premium				
Implied	0.42	1.21	0.17	1.86
(7) Real bond s.d.				
Implied	1.27	3.69	1.41	15.62
(8) Sharpe ratio = (6)/(7)				
Implied	0.33	0.33	0.12	0.12
(9) Mean yield spread				
Implied	0.22	0.94	0.08	0.54
(10) S.d. yield spread				
Implied	0.18	0.79	0.05	0.56
(C) Equities				
(11) Equity premium				
Sample		7.67		10.61
Implied		9.91		8.88
(12) Equity s.d.				
Sample		16.03		15.15
Implied		16.47		15.25
(13) Sharpe ratio = (11)/(12)				
Sample		0.48		0.70
Implied		0.60		0.58

deviation three times greater than ten-year indexed bonds. This difference in volatility makes the Sharpe ratio for indexed bonds in row (8) considerably higher than the Sharpe ratio for nominal bonds in row (3). Since indexed bond returns are generated by a single-factor model, the Sharpe ratio for indexed bonds is independent of maturity at 0.33. The Sharpe ratio for nominal bonds declines with maturity; short-term nominal bonds have a ratio close to that for indexed bonds, but the Sharpe ratio for ten-year nominal bonds is only 0.15. These numbers imply that in our portfolio analysis investors with low risk aversion will have a strong myopic demand for indexed bonds.

Table 3.2 can also be used to evaluate the empirical fit of the model. A comparison of the model's implied moments with the sample moments for nominal bonds shows that the model fits the volatility of excess nominal bond returns extremely well. The model somewhat overstates the average excess nominal bond return and the nominal Sharpe ratio, but this can be attributed in part to the upward drift in interest rates over the 1952–99 sample period. To the extent that investors did not anticipate this upward drift, it reduced the realized returns on nominal bonds; this causes sample means to be lower than true population means.[3]

Another way to judge the fit of the model is to ask how much of the variability of bond yields, or bond returns, is accounted for by the structural parameters as opposed to the white-noise measurement errors we have allowed in each bond yield. The estimated variances of measurement errors (not reported in Table 3.1) are zero for one-year and ten-year bonds and are extremely small for three-month bills and three-year bonds. Measurement errors are estimated to account for less than 0.5% of the variance of three-month and three-year bond yields and less than 5% of the variance of three-year bond returns. This reflects the fact that bond yields are highly persistent at all maturities, so the model fits them primarily with persistent structural processes rather than white-noise measurement errors.

---

[3] To save space, standard errors are not reported in the table. The general pattern is one of small standard errors for implied volatilities, and much larger standard errors for implied mean excess returns. This reflects the well-known result that it is much harder to obtain precise estimates of first moments than of second moments.

We can use the model to describe the history of the nominal US term structure and its components. We do this in Figure 3.1, which shows three-month nominal bill yields, real yields and expected inflation in the top panel, and the equivalent ten-year series in the bottom panel. The model attributes the low-frequency variation of nominal interest rates, particularly the runup in nominal rates from the 1960s through the early 1980s, and the slow decline thereafter to changing expected inflation. Much of the higher-frequency variation in interest rates is attributed to the real interest rate, particularly after the end of the 1960s.[4] Because real interest rate variation is less persistent than expected-inflation variation, the latter is the main determinant of the ten-year nominal yield. However, the ten-year real yield does show some residual variation. Overall, the model appears to provide a good description of the nominal US term structure, considering its parsimony and the fact that we have forced it to fit both time-series and cross-sectional features of the data.

Rows (11), (12), and (13) of Table 3.2 report summary statistics for equities: the annualized Jensen's-inequality-corrected average excess returns on equities relative to nominal bills, the standard deviation of these excess returns, and their Sharpe ratio. The model fits the standard deviation of equities extremely well, but overpredicts the equity premium and the Sharpe ratio for equities. The implied Sharpe ratio of 0.60 implies that investors with low risk aversion will have an extremely large myopic demand for equities; this is again a manifestation of the equity premium puzzle.

The right-hand sides of Tables 3.1 and 3.2 repeat these estimates for the Volcker–Greenspan period 1983–99. Many of the parameter estimates are quite similar; however, we find that in this period real interest rates are much more persistent, with $\phi_x = 0.991$ and an implied half-life for real interest rate shocks of about 19 years. The expected inflation process now mean-reverts much more rapidly, with $\phi_z = 0.867$ implying a half-life for

---

[4] Fama (1975) famously argued that the real interest rate is constant and that all variation in nominal interest rates is due to expected inflation. This was a reasonable view of his data, which ended in 1971, but certainly does not describe more recent experience. Perhaps Fama fell foul of 'Murphy's Law of Empirical Economics', that any strong characteristic of historical data will alter immediately after it has been identified by empirical researchers!

(a)

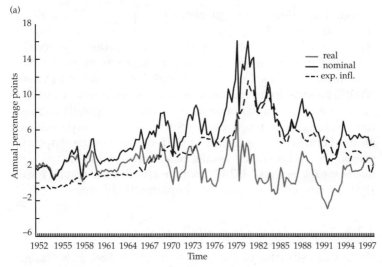

(b)

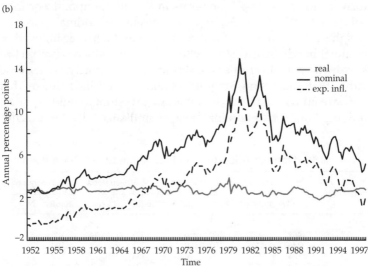

Figure 3.1. Fitted real and nominal yields and inflation, 1952–1999.
(a) Three-month yields on real/nominal bonds and expected inflation,
(b) Ten-year yields on real/nominal bonds and expected inflation.

expected-inflation shocks of about five quarters. These results are consistent with the patterns illustrated in Figure 3.1, and with the notion that since the early 1980s the Federal Reserve has controlled inflation more aggressively, at the cost of greater long-term variation in the real interest rate (Clarida, Gali, and Gertler 2000). The increase in real interest rate persistence raises the risk premia on indexed and nominal bonds, but it also greatly increases the volatility of indexed bond returns, so the Sharpe ratio for indexed bonds is lower at 0.12. In the remainder of the chapter we present portfolio choice results based on our full-sample estimates for the period 1952–99, but we also discuss results for the 1983–99 period, where they are importantly different.

3.2.3. Implications for portfolio choice

Given our estimates of the term structure model, it is straight-forward to calculate all the terms in the intertemporal portfolio solution (3.21). Table 3.3 reports percentage optimal portfolio weights for equities and for three-month and ten-year indexed or nominal bonds by investors who are unconstrained or subject to borrowing and short-sales constraints. For simplicity, we assume either that short- and long-term bonds are all indexed, or that they are all nominal; we do not allow investors to hold equities, indexed bonds, and nominal bonds simultaneously. We consider

Table 3.3. Optimal Allocations to Equities and Long-Term Bonds

Relative risk aversion	Unconstrained		Constrained		Unconstrained		Constrained	
	Equity	Indexed	Equity	Indexed	Equity	Nominal	Equity	Nominal
(A) 1952–99								
0.75	464	937	100	0	495	−14	100	0
1	348	726	100	0	371	−8	100	0
2	174	410	100	0	184	1	100	0
5	70	220	65	35	73	6	73	6
10	35	157	32	68	35	8	35	8
5,000	0	94	0	94	−2	10	0	10
(B) 1983–99								
0.75	526	−63	100	0	525	−66	100	0
1	395	−24	100	0	394	−25	100	0
2	197	35	86	14	197	36	87	13
5	79	70	38	62	79	73	36	64
10	39	82	22	78	40	86	19	81
5,000	0	90	0	93	1	98	1	98

investors with a unit intertemporal elasticity of substitution, and coefficients of relative risk aversion of 0.75 (more risk-tolerant than log utility), 1, 2, 5, 10, and 5,000 (effectively infinite). Panel (A) reports results for the 1952–99 sample, which we consider first.

The demand for inflation-indexed bonds
In a world with full indexation, the unconstrained demand for both long-term inflation-indexed bonds and equities is positive and often above 100%, implying that the investor optimally borrows to finance purchases of equities and indexed bonds. The portfolio share of inflation-indexed bonds exceeds that of equities, despite the higher Sharpe ratio of equities, because inflation-indexed bonds are much less risky than equities.[5] As the coefficient of relative risk aversion increases, the demands for both long-term bonds and equities fall, but the share of equities falls faster. In the limit, the infinitely risk-averse investor holds a portfolio equivalent to an inflation-indexed consol, as we have already discussed. With the parameter values estimated for the 1952–99 period, this portfolio consists of 94% ten-year zero-coupon inflation-indexed bonds, and 6% three-month inflation-indexed bills. When there are borrowing and short-sale constraints, investors with low risk aversion invest fully in equities as a way to maximize their risk and expected return without using leverage, while more risk-averse investors hold both inflation-indexed bonds and equities. Cash plays only a minor role in the portfolios of the most risk-averse investors as a means to synthesize an inflation-indexed consol.

These findings are related to the 'asset allocation puzzle' of Canner, Mankiw, and Weil (1997) discussed in Chapter 1. Investment advisors often suggest that more conservative investors should have a higher ratio of long-term bonds to stocks in their portfolios. Canner *et al.* document this feature of

---

[5] Recall that optimal myopic demand for a single risky investment, or for a risky investment that is independent of other risky investments, is proportional to mean excess return divided by variance. Equivalently, it is proportional to the Sharpe ratio divided by the standard deviation. Although equities have a higher Sharpe ratio than indexed bonds, their standard deviation is much higher so the optimal equity share is lower.

conventional investment advice and point out that it is inconsistent with the mutual fund theorem of static portfolio analysis,
according to which risk aversion should affect only the ratio
of cash to risky assets and not the relative weights on different
risky assets.

Our analysis shows that static portfolio analysis is not only
inappropriate in theory, but can be seriously misleading in
practice, when investment opportunities are time-varying and
investors have long time horizons. The portfolio allocations to
equities and inflation-indexed bonds in panel (A) of Table 3.3
are strikingly consistent with conventional investment advice.
Aggressive long-term investors should hold stocks, while conservative ones should hold long-term bonds and small amounts
of cash. The explanation is that long-term bonds, and not cash,
are the riskless asset for long-term investors.

The demand for nominal bonds
A weakness in this resolution of the asset allocation puzzle is that
it assumes that long-term bonds are inflation-indexed, or,
equivalently, that there is no inflation uncertainty. Panel (A) of
Table 3.3 shows that nominal bonds play a much smaller role in
optimal portfolios. In a world with no indexation, unconstrained
investors with low risk aversion actually hold short positions in
nominal bonds, while constrained investors hold only equities.
As risk aversion increases, investors move into cash rather than
long-term nominal bonds.

Figure 3.2 illustrates this point. The top panel of the figure plots
constrained optimal allocations to equities, a ten-year nominal
bond, and a three-month nominal bill, while the bottom
panel plots constrained myopic allocations. Thus, the difference
between the two panels illustrates the effect of strategic considerations on the portfolio demands of long-term investors. The
horizontal axis measures relative risk tolerance $(1/\gamma)$ rather than
relative risk aversion, because both optimal and myopic allocations are linear in risk tolerance when portfolio constraints are
not binding. Infinitely conservative investors with $1/\gamma = 0$ are
plotted at the right edge of the figure, so that as the eye moves
from left to right we see the effects of increasing risk aversion on
investment policy. As in Table 3.3, we set $\psi = 1$, but the choice of
ψ has very little effect on the results.

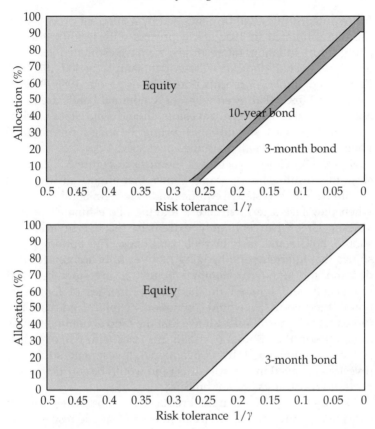

Figure 3.2. Optimal and myopic allocations to nominal bonds and equity, 1952–1999.

Risk-tolerant investors at the left of Figure 3.2 are fully invested in equities. Highly risk-averse investors hold most of their portfolios in cash, although they also hold some ten-year nominal bonds. The bottom panel shows that long-term bonds are held purely for hedging purposes. The myopic demand for long-term bonds is extremely close to zero at all levels of risk aversion.

The portfolio allocations to nominal bonds in panel (A) of Table 3.3 and Figure 3.2 do not correspond well with conventional investment advice. In order to rationalize the conventional wisdom about long-term nominal bonds, one must assume that future interest rates will be generated by a different process than the one estimated in 1952–99, a process with less uncertainty about future inflation. Interestingly, we have estimated just such a process over the Volcker–Greenspan sample period 1983–99. Panel (B) of Table 3.3 repeats panel (A) using our 1983–99 estimates, and finds that, even when only nominal bonds are available, aggressive long-term investors should hold stocks, while conservative ones should hold primarily long-term nominal bonds along with small quantities of stocks.[6]

Figure 3.3, whose structure is identical to Figure 3.2, emphasizes this result. The top panel shows that almost all investors should be fully invested in equities and long-term nominal bonds when they face a term structure like the one estimated for the Volcker–Greenspan era; only extremely risk-averse investors should hold some cash in their portfolios. The bottom panel shows that intertemporal hedging motives fully account for this demand for long-term nominal bonds. If investors behaved myopically and ignored the hedging properties of long-term bonds, their portfolios would contain only equities and cash. The top panel of Figure 3.3 also shows that the ratio of nominal bonds to equities in the optimal portfolio increases with risk aversion, just as recommended by conventional investment advice. If investors behaved myopically, this ratio would be constant when portfolio constraints are not binding.

Although our 1983–99 model replicates important features of conventional investment advice, it falls short in one respect. The optimal portfolios in Figure 3.3 contain almost no cash relative to the recommended portfolios reported by Canner, Mankiw, and Weil (1997). We do not attempt to match those portfolios more accurately, but suspect that it can be done either by using a term structure process intermediate between the two

---

[6] During the 1983–99 period the interest rate sensitivity of a ten-year inflation-indexed zero-coupon bond is considerably less than that of an inflation-indexed perpetuity. Therefore an infinitely risk-averse investor would like to hold a leveraged position in ten-year inflation-indexed zeros, which was not the case in our 1952–99 model. To maintain comparability with that model, in panel (B) of Table 3.3 and Figure 3.3 we replace the ten-year zero-coupon bond with a 20-year zero-coupon bond. This ensures that the optimal inflation-indexed portfolio for an infinitely risk-averse investor is available even when borrowing and short-sales constraints are imposed.

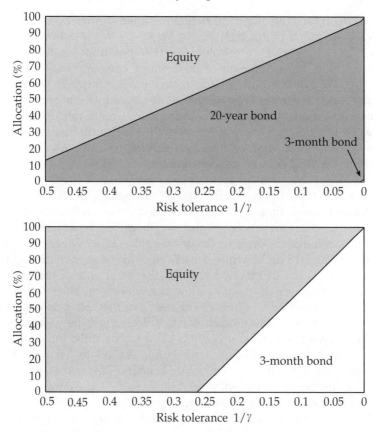

Figure 3.3. Optimal and myopic allocations to nominal bonds and equity, 1983–1999.

processes we have estimated, or by modelling liquidity motives for holding cash.

Utility benefits of indexation

We can use our solutions to consider the partial equilibrium effects on investors' utility of switching from a world where only nominal bonds are available to a world where all debt instruments are inflation-indexed or, equivalently, where inflation uncertainty has been eliminated. The analysis is partial equilibrium in that we hold constant the empirical model for interest rates even as we vary the menu of available assets. We study this question using (2.52), which gives the value function per unit wealth as a monotonic transformation of the optimal consumption–wealth ratio. We can compute an approximate value function without any need for further approximations just by substituting into this expression our approximate consumption–wealth ratio. The log value function is a linear function of the short-term interest rate, so it is time-varying, and we calculate its unconditional mean using the 1952–99 parameter estimates.

The benefits of indexation depend on whether investors are subject to portfolio constraints. If investors' portfolios are unconstrained, then both aggressive and conservative investors benefit from indexation. Aggressive investors benefit because inflation-indexed bonds have considerably higher Sharpe ratios than nominal bonds, while conservative investors benefit from the elimination of inflation risk. At the short end of the term structure, the replacement of a nominal short-term asset with an indexed short-term asset eliminates the risk of unexpected inflation; although this risk is small, it does affect the welfare of extremely conservative investors. More importantly, indexation eliminates the risk in long-term bonds caused by changes in expected future inflation. The utility benefits of indexation can be large; for an investor with $\psi = 1$ and $\gamma = 5$, for example, the benefit is equivalent to a 49% increase in wealth.

If investors' portfolios are constrained, then aggressive investors lose from indexation while conservative investors benefit. Aggressive investors prefer long-term nominal bonds as a way to take on higher risk and higher return without violating leverage constraints, but conservative investors prefer inflation-indexed bonds as a way to avoid inflation risk. In this case the utility benefits of indexation are somewhat smaller, equivalent to a 10% increase in wealth for an investor with $\psi = 1$ and $\gamma = 5$.

As one would expect, these results are sensitive to the sample period that is used to estimate the model. Results for the 1983–99 sample are qualitatively similar but imply considerably smaller benefits of bond indexation. The Volcker–Greenspan monetary regime has greatly reduced long-run uncertainty about inflation, and has correspondingly reduced the benefits of eliminating inflation risk entirely.

These findings contradict the claim of Viard (1993) that indexation has only minor effects on investors' utility. Viard models indexation as elimination of the inflation risk in a one-period asset, and studies the benefits to one-period investors. Since there is little risk in inflation over one period, Viard's result is not surprising. We get much larger benefits of indexation because we model indexation as elimination of the inflation risk in long-term assets, and study the benefits to long-term investors.[7]

Advocates of bond indexation have sometimes argued that the availability of indexed assets will stimulate saving. However, this effect depends on the elasticity of intertemporal substitution, ψ. If $\psi = 1$, then the consumption–wealth ratio is constant regardless of the available asset menu. If ψ is close to zero, as many empirical estimates suggest, then the consumption–wealth ratio approximately equals the value function. Thus, the utility gain from indexation is accompanied by an increase in consumption and a decline in saving.

These utility calculations should be treated with caution for two reasons. First, they depend on arbitrary assumptions about the menu of available assets. If we assume that investors can freely trade in nominal bonds of several maturities, then they can construct portfolios of nominal bonds that behave like inflation-indexed bonds. They can do this by shorting long-term nominal bonds, which are particularly sensitive to changes in expected inflation, and holding long positions in medium-term nominal bonds, which are comparatively sensitive to changes in real interest rates. The availability of medium-term nominal bonds reduces the utility benefits of indexation even if portfolio constraints prevent investors from shorting long-term nominal bonds.

Second, we have assumed that the process driving interest rates is invariant to the presence or absence of inflation-indexed bonds. This assumption might be defensible in a small open economy, but is unlikely to hold in the general equilibrium of a closed economy. Thus, our results are not a reliable guide to the effects of bond indexation on social welfare. They do, however, make it hard to argue the irrelevance of indexation. If bond

---

[7] Fischer (1975) also studies the benefits of indexation using a model with constant investment opportunities; thus, he too misses the effects that are captured by the intertemporal model of this chapter.

indexation does not change the stochastic process driving interest rates, it must have utility benefits for constrained conservative investors; if it does not help such investors, it must have effects on interest rates.

3.3. CONCLUSION: BONDS, JAMES, BONDS

If one uses conventional mean–variance analysis, it is hard to explain why any investors hold large positions in bonds. Mean–variance analysis treats cash as the riskless asset and bonds as merely another risky asset like stocks. Bonds are valued only for their potential contribution to the short-run excess return, relative to risk, of a diversified risky portfolio. This view tends to relegate bonds to a minor supporting role in the recommended portfolio, since excess bond returns have historically been fairly low and bond returns have been highly variable in the short run. Over the period 1952–99 reported in Table 3.2, for example, the average excess return on ten-year US Treasury zero-coupon bonds over three-month Treasury bills was only 1.2%, while the standard deviation of this return was over 11%. Accordingly, the annualized Sharpe ratio for bonds, the ratio of their average excess return to their standard deviation, was only 0.11. Over the same period the US equity market had an average excess return of 7.7% and a standard deviation of 16%, implying a Sharpe ratio of 0.48. The comparison looks more favorable for bonds in the shorter 1983–99 sample also shown in Table 3.2, but it is even less favorable for bonds if one studies the early postwar period of slowly rising inflation.

A long-horizon analysis treats bonds very differently, and assigns them a much more important role in the optimal portfolio. For long-term investors, money market investments are not riskless because they must be rolled over at uncertain future interest rates. Just as borrowers have come to appreciate that short-term debt carries a risk of having to refinance at high rates during a financial crisis, so long-term investors need to understand that short-term investments carry the risk of having to reinvest at low real rates in the future. For long-term investors, an inflation-indexed long-term bond is actually less risky than cash. Such a bond does not have a stable market value in the short term, but it delivers a predictable stream of real income and thus supports a stable standard of living in the long term.

The implications for portfolio choice depend both on the assets that are available and on investors' views about the risk of inflation. If inflation-indexed bonds are available, then long-term investors should shift out of equities and into inflation-indexed bonds as they become more conservative. Even if only nominal bonds are available, conservative long-term investors should hold large positions in long-term bonds if they believe that inflation risk is low, as we have estimated it to be in the USA in the period 1983–99. In this sense the message of this chapter might be summarized as 'Bonds, James, Bonds'.

Inflation risk is however a serious caveat. In the presence of significant inflation risk, of the sort we have estimated for the USA in the period 1952–99, nominal bonds are risky assets for long-term investors and are not good substitutes for inflation-indexed bonds. This conclusion illustrates the general point that strategic asset demands depend on many features of the environment: not just on the conditional means and variances of returns that determine myopic asset demands, but also on the processes driving relevant state variables such as inflation and real interest rates.

4

Is the Stock Market Safer for Long-Term Investors?

In Chapter 3 we studied strategic asset allocation in a model with time-varying real interest rates and inflation and with constant risk premia on all assets. We found that short-term safe assets are not riskless for long-term investors, because they must be rolled over at uncertain future rates. The riskless asset for a long-term investor is a long-term inflation-indexed bond, and nominal bonds are also close to riskless if inflation risk is low. Thus, conservative long-term investors should tilt their portfolios towards bonds, rather than towards cash as predicted by the standard short-term analysis.

The model of Chapter 3 does not imply any special role for stocks in the portfolios of long-term investors. Intertemporal hedging demand in that model is determined by covariance with future real interest rates, which is the same for stocks as for bonds of the same duration; by variance, which is higher for stocks than for bonds; and by covariances among the available assets. Thus, intertemporal hedging considerations benefit bonds rather than stocks. An aggressive long-term investor will hold stocks because of their high average returns, but this is the same consideration that influences an aggressive short-term investor.

These results contrast with the commonly held view that long-term investors can afford to increase their stockholdings because stocks are comparatively safe for such investors. Jeremy Siegel (1994, pp. 29–30) expresses this view particularly clearly in his popular book *Stocks for the Long Run*:

It is widely known that stock returns, on average, exceed bonds in the long run. But it is little known that in the long run, the risks in stocks are *less than* those found in bonds or even bills!.... Real stock returns are substantially more volatile than the returns of bonds and bills over short-term periods. But as the horizon increases, the range of stock returns narrows far more quickly than for fixed-income assets.... Stocks, in contrast to bonds or bills, have never offered investors a negative real holding period return yield over 20 years or more. Although it might appear riskier to hold stocks than bonds, precisely the opposite is true: the safest long-term investment has clearly been stocks, not bonds.

We saw in Chapter 2 that, if asset returns are independent and identically distributed (IID) over time, then there is a precise mathematical relationship between risk at a short horizon and at a long horizon. Siegel's measure of risk is the standard deviation of the annualized return, which must be inversely proportional to the square root of the horizon if returns are IID. Any evidence that risk does not scale with horizon in this way is indirect evidence for the predictability of asset returns. In order to evaluate such evidence, we need a general empirical framework that allows for predictability—not just predictability of real interest rates, as in Chapter 3, but predictability of risk premia as well.

In this chapter we use a vector autoregressive (VAR) system to capture the historical predictability of asset returns. This type of model has been used in a similar context by Kandel and Stambaugh (1987), Campbell (1991, 1996), Hodrick (1992), and Barberis (2000), among others. Section 4.1 develops the framework and solution method. Section 4.1.1 sets up the model, and Section 4.1.2 extends our approximate solution method to handle this intertemporal consumption and portfolio choice problem. Section 4.1.3 studies a special but illuminating case in which there is a constant real interest rate and the investor allocates wealth between short-term safe assets and stocks, which follow a mean-reverting process. Merton (1973), Samuelson (1991), Kim and Omberg (1996), and Campbell and Viceira (1999) have all studied versions of this special model and have used it to develop intuition about the portfolio decisions of long-term investors.

Section 4.2 is an empirical study of US bond and stock returns. Section 4.2.1 estimates a general VAR on historical US data, Section 4.2.2 derives implications for asset risks at different investment horizons, and Section 4.2.3 derives optimal portfolio weights for bills, nominal bonds, and stocks. In Section 4.2.4 we use the VAR to impute hypothetical returns on inflation-indexed bonds, redoing the portfolio analysis for the case where inflation-indexed bonds are available. Section 4.3 concludes. The empirical work in this chapter is closely based on Campbell, Chan, and Viceira (2001).

4.1. LONG-TERM PORTFOLIO CHOICE IN A VAR MODEL

4.1.1. VAR specification

We begin by establishing notation that can handle multiple risky assets and forecasting variables. We work with a risky benchmark return, $r_{0,t+1}$, and a vector of n excess returns over the benchmark return, $\mathbf{r}_{t+1} - r_{0,t+1}\iota$. We include other forecasting variables, such as the nominal interest rate or the dividend–price ratio on stocks, in a vector $\mathbf{s}_{t+1}$. We stack the benchmark return, excess risky returns, and other state variables into a single $m \times 1$ state vector $\mathbf{z}_{t+1}$:

$$\mathbf{z}_{t+1} \equiv \begin{bmatrix} r_{0,t+1} \\ \mathbf{r}_{t+1} - r_{0,t+1}\iota \\ \mathbf{s}_{t+1} \end{bmatrix}. \tag{4.1}$$

We postulate that the dynamics of $\mathbf{z}_{t+1}$ are well captured by a first-order vector autoregressive process, or VAR (1). The use of a VAR (1) is not restrictive, since any vector autoregression can be rewritten in this form through an expansion of the vector of state variables. Then we have

$$\mathbf{z}_{t+1} = \mathbf{\Phi}_0 + \mathbf{\Phi}_1\mathbf{z}_t + \mathbf{v}_{t+1}, \tag{4.2}$$

where $\mathbf{\Phi}_0$ is the $m \times 1$ vector of intercepts, $\mathbf{\Phi}_1$ is the $m \times m$ matrix of slope coefficients, and $\mathbf{v}_{t+1}$ is the $m \times 1$ vector of shocks to the state variables. We assume that $\mathbf{v}_{t+1}$ is normally distributed white noise, with mean zero and variance–covariance matrix $\mathbf{\Sigma}_v$. Thus, we allow the shocks to be cross-sectionally correlated, but assume that they are homoskedastic and independently distributed over time. The VAR framework conveniently captures the dependence of expected returns of various assets on their past histories as well as on other predictive variables. The stochastic evolution of these other state variables $\mathbf{s}_{t+1}$ is also determined by the system.

The assumption of homoskedasticity is of course restrictive. It rules out the possibility that the state variables predict changes in risk; they can affect portfolio choice only by predicting changes in expected returns. Authors such as Campbell (1987), Harvey (1989, 1991), and Glosten, Jagannathan, and Runkle (1993) have explored the ability of the state variables used here to predict risk and have found only modest effects that seem to be dominated by the effects of the state variables on expected returns. In Section 5.4, following Chacko and Viceira (1999), we show how to include changing risk in a long-term portfolio choice problem.

It is common in the continuous-time finance literature to assume that markets are complete, that is that the state variables governing investment opportunities are driven by the same stochastic processes that drive asset returns, so that innovations to investment opportunities are perfectly hedgeable using financial assets. The model (4.1) does not make this assumption. Whenever there are additional state variables s_{t+1} in the vector z_{t+1} and the variance–covariance matrix of the VAR system Σ_v has full rank, shocks to investment opportunities are imperfectly correlated with shocks to asset returns and cannot be perfectly hedged using financial assets. The ability to handle incomplete markets is an important empirical advantage of this model.

Given our homoskedastic VAR formulation, the unconditional distribution of z_t is easily derived. The state vector z_t inherits the normality of the shocks v_{t+1}. It has unconditional mean μ_z and variance–covariance matrix Σ_z that can straightforwardly be calculated from the VAR coefficients Φ_0, Φ_1, and Σ_v. We can also calculate the conditional moments of linear and quadratic combinations of the variables.

4.1.2. Solving the model

We seek a solution that satisfies the loglinear Euler equations for the Epstein–Zin model, given the approximations laid out in the previous two chapters. That is, we need to find consumption and portfolio rules that satisfy the consumption Euler equation (2.49) and the portfolio Euler equation for multiple risky assets (2.51). The consumption Euler equation can be rewritten, using our loglinear approximation to the intertemporal budget constraint, as a difference equation in $c_t - w_t$:

$$c_t - w_t = -\rho\psi \log \delta - \rho\chi_{pt} + \rho(1 - \psi)E_t(r_{p,t+1}) + \rho k$$
$$+ \rho E_t(c_{t+1} - w_{t+1}), \tag{4.3}$$

where $\chi_{pt} = (\theta/2\psi)\text{Var}_t(\Delta c_{t+1} - \psi r_{p,t+1})$. The portfolio Euler equation can be rewritten, using our approximation to the intertemporal budget constraint and the fact that $\Delta c_{t+1} = \Delta(c_{t+1} - w_{t+1}) + \Delta w_{t+1}$, as

$$E_t(\mathbf{r}_{t+1} - r_{0,t+1}\iota) + \frac{\sigma_t^2}{2} = \frac{\theta}{\psi}\sigma_{c-w,t} + \gamma\sigma_{pt} - \sigma_{0t}, \tag{4.4}$$

where σ_t^2 is a vector containing the variances of excess returns, $\sigma_{c-w,t} \equiv \text{Cov}_t(\mathbf{r}_{t+1} - r_{0,t+1}\iota, c_{t+1} - w_{t+1})$ is a vector containing the covariances of excess returns with the log consumption–wealth ratio, $\sigma_{pt} \equiv \text{Cov}_t(\mathbf{r}_{t+1} - r_{0,t+1}\iota, r_{p,t+1})$ is a vector containing the covariances of excess returns with the log portfolio return, and $\sigma_{0t} \equiv \text{Cov}_t(\mathbf{r}_{t+1} - r_{0,t+1}\iota, r_{0,t+1})$ is a vector containing the covariances of excess returns with the log return on the benchmark asset.

To solve the model, we now guess that the optimal portfolio and consumption rules take the form

$$\boldsymbol{\alpha}_t = \mathbf{a}_0 + \mathbf{A}_1\mathbf{z}_t, \tag{4.5}$$

$$c_t - w_t = b_0 + \mathbf{b}_1'\mathbf{z}_t + \mathbf{z}_t'\mathbf{B}_2\mathbf{z}_t. \tag{4.6}$$

That is, the optimal portfolio rule is linear in the VAR state vector but the optimal consumption rule is quadratic. $\mathbf{a}_0$ is an n-vector, $\mathbf{A}_1$ is an $n \times m$ matrix, b_0 is a scalar, $\mathbf{b}_1$ is an m-vector, and $\mathbf{B}_2$ is an $m \times m$ matrix.[1]

The motivation for this guess is that (4.5) is the simplest portfolio rule that allows the investor to shift his portfolio in response to changing risk premia. All the variables in the state vector $\mathbf{z}_t$ can potentially affect risk premia, and thus the portfolio vector $\boldsymbol{\alpha}_t$

---

[1] This matrix has $m(m+1)/2$ identified elements corresponding to the $m(m+1)/2$ separate cross-products of the elements of z_t. Arbitrary restrictions can be imposed on the remaining elements of $\mathbf{B}_2$.

must be free to respond to them; we assume that it does so linearly. Given a linear portfolio rule, the expected portfolio return implied by (2.23) is quadratic in the state variables. State variables affect the expected portfolio return both directly, by shifting the expected returns on existing asset holdings, and indirectly, by shifting the asset allocations. Since each of these effects is linear, their interaction is quadratic, and this makes the expected portfolio return quadratic. But then the consumption Euler equation (4.3) implies that the log consumption–wealth ratio must be at least quadratic in the state variables. The consumption Euler equation also has a conditional variance term, but this too turns out to be quadratic in the state variables, given our homoskedastic VAR specification. Kim and Omberg (1996) derived a similar linear–quadratic solution for a finite-horizon continuous-time model in which the investor has power utility defined over terminal wealth.

To verify our guess and solve for the parameters of the solution, we write the conditional moments that appear in (4.4) as functions of the VAR coefficients and the unknown parameters of (4.5) and (4.6). We then solve for the parameters that satisfy (4.4). This gives us the parameters in (4.5) as functions of the VAR coefficients and the still unknown parameters of (4.6). Next we substitute into (4.3), both sides of which are quadratic in the VAR state variables, given our conjectured quadratic form for the optimal consumption–wealth ratio. Finally, we solve this system of quadratic equations for the parameters of (4.6).

Given the loglinearization parameter ρ, this solution is analytical. Campbell and Viceira (1999) write it out explicitly for the special case in which there is a constant riskless interest rate, a single risky asset, and a single forecasting variable for the excess risky return which itself follows an AR (1) process. We explain this case in Section 4.1.3. Campbell, Chan, and Viceira (2001) extend the approach to the general VAR case, for which it is more convenient to solve the linear–quadratic equations numerically.

The solution presented here is exact in continuous time when asset prices follow continuous diffusion processes, if the consumption–wealth ratio is constant. The consumption–wealth ratio is constant if the elasticity of intertemporal substitution

$\psi = 1$, but in all other cases the solution is only an approximation. Campbell and Koo (1997) and Campbell *et al.* (2001b) evaluate the accuracy of the approximate solution, respectively, in models with exogenous portfolio returns and in models with exogenous returns on underlying assets, and find that it is acceptably accurate for elasticities of intertemporal substitution up to about 3. In particular, this implies that low elasticities of intertemporal substitution of the sort estimated by macroeconomists should be consistent with the use of the approximate solution.

The case $\psi = 1$ is also important because only in this case do we know that the value of ρ equals δ. In all other cases we must solve for ρ along with the other parameters of the model. We can do this numerically by initializing $\rho = \delta$, solving for the other parameters of the model, calculating the implied mean log consumption–wealth ratio from (4.6), recalculating ρ, and repeating until convergence. Alternatively, we can fix ρ and solve out for the implied value of δ that is consistent with it. This process generally works well except in cases where the infinite-horizon optimization problem is ill-defined (e.g. because average rates of return are too high relative to the investor's rate of time preference, so that a finite-horizon investor's utility diverges as the investment horizon increases).

An important property of the model is that, given the log-linearization parameter ρ, the optimal portfolio rule does not depend on the intertemporal elasticity of substitution ψ. ψ affects portfolio choice only to the extent that it enters into the determination of ρ. Empirically, this indirect effect through ρ seems to be minor.

4.1.3. A special case: one risky asset and a constant real interest rate

Campbell and Viceira (1999) study a special case in which there is a short-term riskless asset with a constant real log return r_f. Because this riskless real return is constant, it is a safe investment for both short-term investors and long-term investors. Thus, the issue emphasized in Chapter 3, that the identity of the riskless asset may be different for investors with different horizons, does not arise here. Campbell and Viceira also assume that there is a single risky asset ('stocks') with log return r_{t+1} given by

$$r_{t+1} - E_t r_{t+1} = u_{t+1}, \tag{4.7}$$

where u_{t+1} is the innovation to the risky asset return, normally distributed with mean zero and variance σ_u^2. The expected excess log return on the risky asset, adjusted for one-half its variance in the familiar manner, equals a state variable.[2]

$$E_t r_{t+1} - r_f + \frac{\sigma_u^2}{2} = x_t. \tag{4.8}$$

The state variable x_t follows an AR(1) process with mean μ and persistence ϕ. The innovation to x_{t+1} is written η_{t+1}, assumed to be normally distributed with mean zero and variance σ_η^2:

$$x_{t+1} = \mu + \phi(x_t - \mu) + \eta_{t+1}. \tag{4.9}$$

Modelling mean reversion
The innovations u_{t+1} and η_{t+1} can be correlated, with covariance $\sigma_{\eta u}$. In fact, this covariance is what generates intertemporal hedging demand for the risky asset by long-term investors. The state variable x_t summarizes investment opportunities at time t. Thus, the conditional covariance between the risky asset return and the state variable measures the ability of the risky asset to hedge time variation in investment opportunities. This covariance is given by

$$\text{Cov}_t(r_{t+1}, x_{t+1}) = \text{Cov}_t(r_{t+1}, r_{t+2}) = \sigma_{\eta u}. \tag{4.10}$$

The model can be solved for arbitrary $\sigma_{\eta u}$, but we focus attention on the case where $\sigma_{\eta u} < 0$. This case captures the notion that stocks are 'mean-reverting': an unexpectedly high return today reduces expected returns in the future, and thus high short-term returns tend to be offset by lower returns over the long term. This

---

[2] This is a slight change from the parameterization of Campbell and Viceira (1999), which omitted the term $\sigma_u^2/2$ on the left-hand side of (4.8). Accordingly, some equations here are slightly altered from the corresponding equations in their paper.

offset reduces the conditional variance of long-term stock returns, since

$$
\begin{aligned}
\text{Var}_t(r_{t+1} + r_{t+2}) &= 2\text{Var}_t(r_{t+1}) + 2\text{Cov}_t(r_{t+1}, r_{t+2}) \\
&= 2\text{Var}_t(r_{t+1}) + 2\sigma_{\eta u} < 2\text{Var}_t(r_{t+1}). \quad (4.11)
\end{aligned}
$$

That is, the conditional variance of stock returns does not grow in proportion with the investment horizon, but grows more slowly. If we calculate a conditional variance ratio,

$$
VR_t(K) \equiv \frac{\text{Var}_t(r_{t+1} + r_{t+2} + \cdots + r_{t+K})}{K \, \text{Var}_t(r_{t+1})}, \quad (4.12)
$$

the ratio will be less than one at all horizons K. Stocks will appear relatively safer to long-term investors.

The discussion above concentrates on conditional variances, since these are what matter to investors. The empirical literature on mean-reversion, initiated by Poterba and Summers (1988) and Fama and French (1988b), typically emphasizes unconditional variances instead. These can behave quite differently from conditional variances, since

$$
\text{Cov}(r_{t+1}, x_{t+1}) = \text{Cov}(x_t + u_{t+1}, x_{t+1}) = \phi\sigma_x^2 + \sigma_{\eta u}. \quad (4.13)
$$

Comparing the unconditional covariance in (4.13) with the conditional covariance in (4.10), we see that they differ by the autocovariance of the state variable, $\phi\sigma_x^2$. Persistence in the process for x_{t+1} can make the unconditional covariance zero, even if the conditional covariance is negative. Campbell (1991) and Campbell, Lo, and MacKinlay (1997, chapter 7) emphasize this point. More generally, the unconditional variance ratio,

$$
VR(K) \equiv \frac{\text{Var}(r_{t+1} + r_{t+2} + \cdots + r_{t+K})}{K \, \text{Var}(r_{t+1})} = \frac{VR_t(K)}{1 - R^2(K)}, \quad (4.14)
$$

where $R^2(K)$ is the explanatory power of a regression of the K-period stock return onto the state variable x_t. Thus, the unconditional variance ratio is always greater than the conditional variance ratio; empirical results using the former understate the risk reduction that is relevant for long-term investors. The difference between the two variance ratios can be substantial, since authors such as Fama and French (1988a) and Campbell and Shiller (1988) have found long-horizon R^2 statistics as large as 40%. We explore this issue empirically in Section 4.2.2.

Solving the model
The model is a special case of the general VAR system. Thus, the solution takes the form

$$\alpha_t = a_0 + a_1 x_t, \tag{4.15}$$

$$c_t - w_t = b_0 + b_1 x_t + b_2 x_t^2. \tag{4.16}$$

The quadratic expression for the consumption–wealth ratio implies that the value function in (2.52) takes the exponential-quadratic form

$$V_t = \exp\left(\frac{b_0 - \psi \log(1 - \delta)}{1 - \psi} + \frac{b_1}{1 - \psi} x_t + \frac{b_2}{1 - \psi} x_t^2\right). \tag{4.17}$$

Kim and Omberg (1996) derive a similar exponential–quadratic solution in a related continuous-time model, where a single state variable follows a continuous-time AR(1) (Ornstein–Uhlenbeck) process and the investor has power utility defined over terminal wealth. Samuelson (1991) derives similar results in a three-period version of this model.

Given the form of the value function, it should not be surprising that the ratios $b_1/(1 - \psi)$ and $b_2/(1 - \psi)$ play a key role in the solution. These ratios capture the linear and quadratic effects of the state variable x_t on utility; they have the same sign as the effects of x_t on consumption only when income effects dominate substitution effects, that is, when $\psi < 1$. Campbell and Viceira (1999) show that the parameters of the portfolio rule are related to $b_1/(1 - \psi)$ and $b_2/(1 - \psi)$ as follows:

$$a_0 = \left(1 - \frac{1}{\gamma}\right)\left[\left(\frac{b_1}{1 - \psi}\right) + 2\mu(1 - \phi)\left(\frac{b_2}{1 - \psi}\right)\right]\left(-\frac{\sigma_{\eta u}}{\sigma_u^2}\right), \tag{4.18}$$

$$a_1 = \frac{1}{\gamma\sigma_u^2} + \left(1 - \frac{1}{\gamma}\right)\left[2\phi\left(\frac{b_2}{1 - \psi}\right)\right]\left(-\frac{\sigma_{\eta u}}{\sigma_u^2}\right).\tag{4.19}$$

For a myopic investor, we would have $a_0 = 0$ and $a_1 = 1/\gamma\sigma_u^2$, so intertemporal hedging demand accounts for the entire right-hand side of (4.18) and the second term on the right-hand side of (4.19).

Campbell and Viceira (1999) show that $b_2/(1 - \psi) > 0$ and does not depend on the average excess stock return μ, while $b_1/(1 - \psi) = 0$ when $\mu = 0$ and should be expected to have the same sign as μ. The empirically relevant case is that where μ, $b_1/(1 - \psi)$, and $b_2/(1 - \psi)$ are all positive, while $\sigma_{\eta u}$ is negative so $-\sigma_{\eta u}/\sigma_u^2$ is also positive. In this case the intercept of the portfolio rule, a_0, is positive for conservative investors with $\gamma > 1$, which implies that such investors will hold stocks even when the expected excess return is zero. This is a striking result, since it contradicts the well-known principle of short-term portfolio choice that a risk-averse investor will never wish to take on risk without receiving a reward for it.

The explanation for this result is as follows. With $\sigma_{\eta u} < 0$, stocks tend to have high returns when their expected future returns fall. With $\mu > 0$, the investor is normally long in stocks, so a decline in expected future stock returns is normally a deterioration in the investment opportunity set. A conservative investor with $\gamma > 1$ wants to hedge the risk of deteriorating investment opportunities by holding assets that deliver increased wealth when investment opportunities are poor. Stocks are just such an asset, so the investor has positive intertemporal hedging demand for stock even when the current risk premium on stocks is zero.

Although the investor is normally long in stocks, if the expected excess return becomes significantly negative, a decline in expected future stock returns can represent an improvement in the investment opportunity set because it creates a profitable opportunity to short stocks. At this point in the state space the sign of intertemporal hedging demand for stocks reverses. Intertemporal hedging demand thus moves in the same direction as the state variable x_t, which explains why the slope of intertemporal hedging demand—the second term on the right-hand side of (4.19)—is positive. The positive slope of intertemporal hedging demand allows it to reverse sign for sufficiently negative

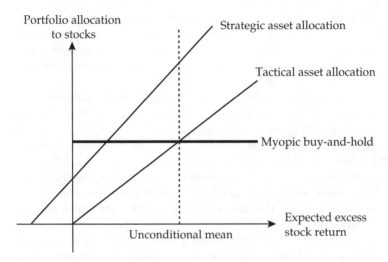

Figure 4.1. Alternative portfolio rules.

x_t.[3] Perhaps surprisingly, the positive slope of intertemporal hedging demand implies that long-term investors are more aggressive market timers than myopic investors, although the difference in slope is quite modest for empirically reasonable parameter values.

This solution is illustrated in Figure 4.1, which shows three alternative portfolio rules for a conservative investor with $\gamma > 1$ facing the benchmark case of mean-reverting stock returns. The horizontal line is a myopic buy-and-hold strategy which assumes a constant expected excess stock return equal to the true unconditional mean μ. The line marked 'Tactical asset allocation' is the optimal strategy for a single-period investor who observes the conditional expected stock return x_t. It passes through the origin, because a single-period investor should hold no risky stocks if the expected excess stock return is zero. It crosses the myopic buy-and-hold line at the point where the excess stock return equals its unconditional mean. The line marked 'Strategic asset allocation' is the optimal strategy for a long-term investor. This line is slightly steeper than the tactical asset allocation line, and is shifted upwards so that it has a positive intercept.

---

[3] Kim and Omberg (1996) give a clear account of this effect (figure 4, pp. 153–4).

The discussion so far assumes that the average level of excess stock returns, μ, is positive. Positive average excess stock returns lead the investor normally to maintain a long position in stocks for which a decrease in the expected stock return represents a deterioration in investment opportunities.

If μ were negative, however, the investor would normally have a short position in stocks for which a decrease in the expected stock return represents an improvement in investment opportunities. In this case the normal sign of intertemporal hedging demand would be negative for an investor with $\gamma > 1$. The slope of intertemporal hedging demand is unaffected by the coefficient μ, however, so in this case a sign reversal of the normal intertemporal hedging demand would occur for sufficiently positive x_t. The case $\mu = 0$ is intermediate; in this case we have a symmetric model in which the investor gains equally from increases and decreases in x_t away from its mean, and intertemporal hedging demand has a positive slope but no intercept.

The model implies that intertemporal hedging demand is not monotonic in risk aversion. At $\gamma = 1$ intertemporal hedging demand is zero, so initially it increases with risk aversion in the benchmark case. Eventually, however, intertemporal hedging demand decreases with risk aversion since a sufficiently conservative investor will hold only the safe asset; such an investor will not wish to exploit stock market opportunities and will not have any motive to hedge variation in those opportunities. One can show that, as the investor becomes infinitely risk-averse, the coefficients $b_1/(1 - \psi), b_2/(1 - \psi), a_0$, and a_1 all approach zero.

Campbell and Viceira (1999) examine the empirical implications of this model in some detail, using the log dividend–price ratio as an empirical proxy for the state variable x_t. Unfortunately, there is an error in the empirical estimates reported in that paper; the estimates understate the predictability of postwar quarterly stock returns and the absolute value of the correlation between innovations in stock returns and dividend yields, and thus understate the magnitude of hedging demands. This error is explained in Campbell and Viceira (2000), which reports corrected results.

It is interesting to relate the model of this section to the advice of Siegel (1994) that long-term investors should aggressively buy and hold equities. Siegel bases his advice on the reduced risk of stock returns at long horizons. We have seen that such reduced risk can arise only from mean reversion in stock returns, a fact recognized by Siegel (1994, p. 33) when he writes:

Stocks have what economists call mean-reverting returns, meaning that over long periods of time, high returns seem to be followed by periods of low returns and vice versa. On the other hand, over time, real returns on fixed-income assets become relatively less certain. For horizons of 20 years or more, bonds are riskier than stocks.

The difficulty with Siegel's investment advice is that mean-reversion is equivalent to predictable variation in stock returns, and such predictable variation is inconsistent with the optimality of a buy-and-hold strategy. The optimal strategy is instead a strategic market-timing strategy of the sort illustrated in Figure 4.1. Campbell and Viceira (1999, 2000) show that there are large utility losses from ignoring the market-timing aspect of the optimal investment strategy. Siegel's investment advice is clearly suboptimal unless an investor is constrained from taking on leverage, in which case the constrained optimal strategy might involve a 100% equity allocation over much of the state space. Even in this case, however, sufficiently positive past returns would drive down the expected future return to the point where the long-term investor should cut back his equity allocation.

4.2. STOCK AND BOND MARKET RISK IN HISTORICAL US DATA

4.2.1. *Data and VAR estimation*

In the previous section we developed a general theoretical framework for strategic asset allocation and explored a special case with a constant real interest rate and a mean-reverting stock return. Although that case is illuminating, it is too special to provide a solid foundation for investment advice. In this section we return to the general framework and use it to investigate how investors who differ in their consumption preferences and risk aversion should allocate their portfolios among three assets: stocks, nominal bonds, and nominal Treasury bills. Following Campbell, Chan, and Viceira (2001), we describe investment opportunities using a VAR system that includes short-term ex post real interest rates, excess stock returns, excess bond returns, and variables that have been identified as return predictors by empirical research: the short-term nominal interest rate, the dividend–price ratio, and the yield spread between long-term bonds and Treasury bills.

The short-term nominal interest rate has been used to predict stock and bond returns by authors such as Fama and Schwert (1977a), Campbell (1987), and Glosten, Jagannathan, and Runkle (1993). An alternative approach, suggested by Campbell (1991) and Hodrick (1992), is to stochastically detrend the short-term rate by subtracting a backwards moving average (usually measured over one year). For two reasons, we do not adopt this alternative here. First, we emphasize a long-term annual dataset in which we cannot measure a one-year moving average of short rates. Second, we want our model to capture inflation dynamics. If we include both the ex post real interest rate and the nominal interest rate in the VAR system, we can easily calculate inflation by subtracting one from the other. This allows us to separate nominal from real variables, so that we can extend our model to include a hypothetical inflation-indexed bond in the menu of assets. We consider this extension in Section 4.2.4.

We compute optimal portfolio rules for different values of γ, assuming $\psi = 1$ and $\delta = \rho = 0.92$ in annual terms. Portfolio allocations are similar for the power utility case $\psi = 1/\gamma$, which we omit to save space.

Data description

Our calibration exercise is based on annual and quarterly data for the US stock market. We emphasize results from the annual dataset, which covers over a century from 1890 to 1998. Its source is the data used in Grossman and Shiller (1981), updated for the recent period following the procedures of Campbell (1999).[4] This dataset contains data on prices and dividends on S&P 500 stocks as well as data on inflation and short-term interest rates. The equity price index is the end-December S&P 500 Index, and the price index is the Producer Price Index. The short rate is the return on six-month commercial paper bought in January and rolled over July. We use this dataset to construct time series of

---

[4] See the Data Appendix to Campbell (1999), available on the author's website: http://kuznets.fas.harvard.edu/~campbell/papers.html.

short-term nominal and ex post real interest rates, excess returns on equities, and dividend yields. Finally, we obtain data on long-term nominal bonds from the long-yield series in Shiller (1989), which we have updated using the Moody's AAA corporate bond yield average. We construct the long bond return from this series using the loglinear approximation technique described in chapter 10 of Campbell, Lo and MacKinlay (1997):

$$r_{n,t+1} \approx D_{nt}y_{nt} - (D_{nt} - 1)y_{n-1,t+1},$$

where n is bond maturity, the bond yield is written Y_{nt}, the log bond yield $y_{nt} = \log(1 + Y_{nt})$, and D_{nt} is bond duration. We calculate duration at time t as

$$D_{nt} \approx \frac{1 - (1 + Y_{nt})^{-n}}{1 - (1 + Y_{nt})^{-1}},$$

and we set n to 20 years. We also approximate $y_{n-1,t+1}$ by $y_{n,t+1}$.

For comparison, we also study a quarterly dataset that begins in 1952(I), shortly after the Fed–Treasury Accord that fundamentally changed the stochastic process for nominal interest rates, and ends in 1999(IV). We obtain our quarterly data from the Center for Research in Security Prices (CRSP). We construct the ex post real Treasury bill rate as the difference of the log return (or yield) on a 90-day bill and log inflation, and the excess log stock return as the difference between the log return on a stock index and the log return on the 90-day bill. We use the value-weighted return, including dividends, on the NYSE, NASDAQ, and AMEX markets. We construct the excess log bond return in a similar way, using the five-year bond return from the US Treasury and Inflation Series (CTI) file in CRSP.

The nominal yield on Treasury bills is the log yield on a 90-day bill. To calculate the dividend–price ratio, we first construct the dividend payout series using the value-weighted return including dividends, and the price index series associated with the value-weighted return excluding dividends. Following the standard convention in the literature, we take the dividend series to be the sum of dividend payments over the past year. The dividend–price ratio is then the log dividend less the log price index. The yield spread is the difference between the five-year zero-coupon bond yield from the CRSP Fama–Bliss data file (the longest yield available in the file) and the bill rate.

VAR estimation

Table 4.1 gives the first and second sample moments of the data. Except for the dividend–price ratio, the sample statistics are in annualized percentage units. Mean excess log returns are adjusted by one-half their variance to account for Jensen's inequality. For the postwar quarterly dataset, Treasury bills offer a low average real return (a mere 1.5% per year) along with low variability. Stocks have an excess return of 7.6% per year compared with 1.1% for the five-year bond. Although volatility is much higher for stocks than for bonds (16.2% vs 5.6%), the Sharpe ratio is two and a half times as high for stocks as for bonds. The average Treasury bill rate and yield spread are 5.5% and 0.95%, respectively.

Covering a century of data, the annual dataset gives a different description of the relative performance of each asset. The real return on short-term nominal debt is quite volatile, owing to greater volatility in both real interest rates and inflation before World War II. Stocks offer a slightly lower excess return, and yet a higher standard deviation, than the postwar quarterly data. The Depression period is largely responsible for this result. The

Table 4.1. Sample Statistics for Asset Returns

Sample moment	1952(I)–1999(IV)	1890–1998
(1) Mean real interest rate	1.52	2.11
(2) S.d. real interest rate	1.35	8.77
(3) Equity premium	7.59	6.74
(4) Equity s.d.	16.21	18.11
(5) Equity $SR = (3)/(4)$	0.47	0.37
(6) Nominal bond premium	1.05	0.66
(7) Nominal bond s.d.	5.62	6.51
(8) Nominal bond $SR = (6)/(7)$	0.19	0.10
(9) Mean nominal interest rate	5.48	4.36
(10) S.d. nominal interest rate	1.42	2.58
(11) Mean log dividend–price ratio	−3.42	−3.10
(12) S.d. log dividend–price ratio	0.31	0.30
(13) Mean yield spread	0.95	0.90
(14) S.d. yield spread	0.51	1.44

Table 4.2. VAR Estimation Results: Annual Sample (1890–1998)

Dependent variable	rtb_t (t)	xr_t (t)	xb_t (t)	$y_t^\$$ (t)	$(d-p)_t$ (t)	spr_t (t)	R^2 (p)
VAR coefficients							
rtb_{t+1}	0.306 (2.456)	−0.054 (−1.363)	0.119 (0.873)	0.677 (2.279)	−0.006 (−0.208)	−0.808 (−1.288)	0.238 (0.000)
xr_{t+1}	0.111 (0.420)	0.080 (0.646)	−0.082 (−0.275)	−0.020 (−0.029)	0.135 (2.388)	1.365 (1.012)	0.052 (0.378)
xb_{t+1}	0.201 (3.077)	0.106 (2.984)	−0.197 (−1.505)	−0.115 (−0.328)	0.012 (0.606)	2.623 (5.276)	0.391 (0.000)
$y_{t+1}^\$$	−0.042 (−1.916)	−0.012 (−1.806)	0.036 (1.310)	0.920 (12.285)	−0.005 (−1.144)	−0.019 (−0.155)	0.775 (0.000)
$(d-p)_{t+1}$	−0.562 (−2.253)	−0.129 (−1.194)	0.348 (1.074)	−0.652 (−1.028)	0.837 (13.297)	−1.739 (−1.248)	0.713 (0.000)
spr_{t+1}	0.020 (1.108)	0.002 (0.441)	−0.013 (−0.649)	0.087 (1.660)	0.004 (1.201)	0.823 (8.924)	0.540 (0.000)

	rtb	xr	xb	$y^\$$	$(d-p)$	spr
Standard deviations and correlations of residuals						
rtb	7.652	−0.188	−0.014	0.124	0.126	−0.168
xr	—	17.632	−0.025	−0.144	−0.733	0.199
xb	—	—	5.081	0.646	−0.048	0.259
$y^\$$	—	—	—	1.225	0.188	−0.895
$(d-p)$	—	—	—	—	16.233	−0.185
spr	—	—	—	—	—	0.979

long-term bond also performs rather poorly, giving a Sharpe ratio of only 0.10 versus a Sharpe ratio of 0.37 for stocks. The bill rate has a lower mean in the annual dataset, and both bill rates and yield spreads have higher standard deviations.

Table 4.2 reports the estimation results for the VAR system in the annual dataset. The top section of the table reports coefficient estimates (with t-statistics in parentheses) and the R^2 statistic (with the p-value of the F test of joint significance in parentheses) for each equation in the system.[5] The bottom section of the table shows the covariance structure of the innovations in the VAR

---

[5] We estimate the VAR imposing the restriction that the unconditional means of the variables implied by the VAR coefficient estimates equal their full-sample arithmetic counterparts. Standard, unconstrained least squares fits exactly the mean of the variables in the VAR excluding the first observation. We use constrained least squares to ensure that we fit the full-sample means.

system. The entries above the main diagonal are correlation statistics, and the entries on the main diagonal are standard deviations multiplied by 100. To save space, we do not present a separate table for quarterly data; quarterly results can be found in Campbell, Chan, and Viceira (2001) and are summarized briefly here.

The first row of the table shows the annual forecasting equation for the real bill rate rtb. The lagged real bill rate and the lagged nominal bill rate $y^\$$ are statistically significant in predicting the real interest rate one year ahead. The second row shows the equation for the excess stock return xr. Predicting excess stock returns is difficult: this equation has the lowest R^2 in the system at 5%. The log dividend–price ratio $(d - p)$, with a positive coefficient, is the only variable with a t-statistic above 2. The third row shows the equation for the excess bond return xb. Lagged excess stock returns, real Treasury bill rates, and yield spreads all help predict future excess bond returns. The R^2 of the equation is surprisingly high at 39%. In part, this may reflect approximation error in our procedure for constructing annual bond returns; the possibility of such error should be kept in mind when interpreting our results. The last three rows report the estimation results for the remaining state variables, each of which is fairly well described by a persistent univariate AR(1) process.

Forecasting results for postwar quarterly data are generally quite similar, but there are some interesting differences. In the real bill rate equation the yield spread enters with a positive sign; in the excess stock return equation the nominal short rate enters with a negative sign; excess bond returns are much less forecastable than in the annual data, but lagged excess stock returns and yield spreads are significant predictors; and the log dividend–price ratio is highly persistent, with a coefficient on its own first lag of 0.965, reflecting the long decline in this ratio during the 1980s and 1990s.

The bottom section of the table describes the covariance structure of the innovations in the VAR system. Unexpected log excess stock returns are highly negatively correlated with shocks to the log dividend–price ratio. This result is consistent with previous empirical results in Campbell (1991), Campbell and Viceira (1999), Stambaugh (1999), and others. Unexpected log excess bond returns are negatively correlated with shocks to the nominal bill rate, but are weakly positively correlated with the yield spread. The same patterns appear in the postwar quarterly data.

The signs of these correlations help to explain the contrasting results of recent studies that apply Monte Carlo analysis to judge the statistical evidence for predictability in stock and bond returns. Stock market studies typically find that asymptotic tests overstate the evidence for predictability of stock returns (Hodrick 1992, Goetzmann and Jorion 1993, Nelson and Kim 1993). Bond-market studies, on the other hand, find that asymptotic procedures are actually conservative and understate the evidence for predictability of bond returns (Bekaert, Hodrick, and Marshall 1997a). The reason for the discrepancy is that asymptotic results in the stock market are based on positive regression coefficients of stock returns on the dividend–price ratio, while asymptotic results in the bond market are based on positive regression coefficients of bond returns on the yield spread. Stambaugh (1999) shows that the small-sample bias in such regressions has the opposite sign to the sign of the correlation between innovations in returns and innovations in the predictive variable. In the stock market the log dividend–price ratio is negatively correlated with returns, leading to a positive small-sample bias which helps to explain some apparent predictability; in the bond market, on the other hand, the yield spread is positively correlated with returns, leading to a negative small-sample bias which cannot explain the positive regression coefficient found in the data.

The signs of these correlations also have important effects on the volatility of bond and stock returns over long holding periods. We now explore these effects in some detail as they are highly relevant for long-term investors.

4.2.2. Return volatility at short and long horizons

Our estimated VAR system implies that there are important horizon effects on the relative volatilities of different investment strategies. In Figure 4.2 we plot the annualized standard deviations of real returns on stocks and bills implied by our annual VAR for investment horizons up to 100 years (panel (a)) and implied by our quarterly VAR for investment horizons up to 100 quarters or 25 years (panel (b)).[6] These standard deviations are

---

[6] Note that we are not looking directly at the long-horizon properties of returns, but at the long-horizon properties of returns imputed from our first-order VAR. Thus, provided that our VAR captures adequately the dynamics of the data, we can consistently estimate the moments of returns over any desired horizon.

conditional; that is, they take out movements that are predictable in advance and thus represent variation in investment opportunities rather than risk. In order to annualize, we divide the conditional standard deviation of the cumulative return over the investment horizon by the square root of the horizon; this means that if returns were unpredictable the standard deviations would be independent of the horizon and we would see flat lines in the figure. The slopes of the lines in Figure 4.2 reflect the predictability of returns in our VAR system.

We also plot conditional standard deviations for two alternative investment strategies using nominal bonds. The 'long bond rolled' strategy keeps the maturity of the long bond constant at 20 years (or five years in the quarterly dataset), buying a 20-year bond each year and selling it the next year in order to invest in a new 20-year bond. This is the strategy implicitly assumed in virtually all time series of long-term bond returns. The 'bond held to maturity' strategy assumes that an investor with horizon K buys a nominal bond with K years to maturity and holds it until maturity. The standard deviation of the real return on this strategy is just the standard deviation of cumulative inflation from time t to time $t + K$, since a nominal bond held to maturity is riskless in nominal terms.

Figure 4.2(a) shows results for the long-term annual dataset. We see that stocks are mean-reverting—their long-horizon returns are less volatile than their short-horizon returns—while bills are mean-averting—their long-horizon returns are actually more volatile than their short-horizon returns. The mean-reversion of stock returns cuts their standard deviation from 18% at a one-year horizon to 14% at a 25-year horizon. The mean-aversion of bill returns is caused by persistent variation in the real interest rate, which amplifies the volatility of returns when Treasury bills are reinvested over long horizons. These effects are strong enough to make bills actually riskier than stocks at sufficiently long investment horizons, a point emphasized by Siegel (1994). Nominal bond returns also show some mean-aversion, but the safest investment strategy for a long investment horizon is to buy a long-term nominal bond and hold it to maturity. The risk of this strategy is the risk of cumulative inflation over the investment horizon, and for a long enough horizon this risk is smaller than stock market risk or real interest rate risk.

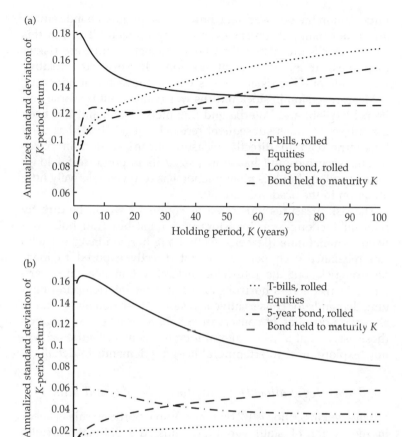

Figure 4.2. Variability of multi-period asset returns. (a) Annual data, 1890–1998, (b) Quarterly data, 1952(I)–1999(IV).

In the quarterly postwar dataset, illustrated in Figure 4.2(b), we again see mean-reversion in stock returns, which cuts the annualized standard deviation of return from 16% to 8% as one moves from a one-quarter horizon to a 25-year horizon. In this dataset there is much less mean-aversion in bill returns because the real interest rate is more stable. Inflation risk is still extremely important in the postwar data, however, so nominal bond returns are riskier than bill returns even at long horizons. Thus, in this dataset stocks are riskier than bonds, which in turn are riskier than bills, at all investment horizons; however, the relative magnitude of these risks changes with the investment horizon.

Mean-reversion in stock returns was pointed out by Fama and French (1988b) and Poterba and Summers (1988), and has been the subject of much subsequent research. Siegel (1994) has used long-term data to directly measure mean-aversion in fixed-income securities and has emphasized its importance for long-term investors, but this phenomenon has received relatively little attention in the academic literature.

The risk measures illustrated in Figure 4.2 would be directly relevant for long-term investors who must buy and hold to a fixed terminal date (Barberis 2000). Long-horizon investors who can rebalance each period are not directly exposed to long-horizon risk, but the return predictability that generates variations in risk across horizons also generates intertemporal hedging demands for conservative investors. These demands tend to shift the portfolios of conservative long-term investors towards those assets that appear safer at long horizons in Figure 4.2. We now explore these intertemporal hedging demands in detail.

4.2.3. Strategic allocations to stocks, bonds, and bills

We showed in Section 4.1.2 that the optimal portfolio rule is linear in the vector of state variables. Thus, the optimal portfolio allocations to stocks, bonds, and bills change over time. We now characterize the portfolio rule by examining its mean and volatility.

Figure 4.3 plots mean allocations to stocks and bonds as solid lines, together with their myopic components as dotted lines, using the estimated annual VAR from Table 4.2. In this figure the horizontal axis shows risk tolerance $1/\gamma$ rather than risk aversion γ, both in order to display the behavior of highly conservative investors more compactly, and because myopic portfolio demands are linear in risk tolerance. As in Figures 3.2 and 3.3, infinitely conservative investors with $1/\gamma = 0$ are plotted at the right edge of the figure, so that as the eye moves from left to right we see the effects of increasing risk aversion on asset allocation. We assume that the elasticity of intertemporal substitution $\psi = 1$.

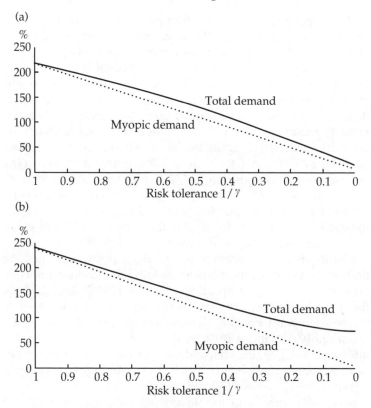

Figure 4.3. Optimal allocations to stocks and
nominal bonds in annual VAR. (a) Allocation to stocks,
(b) Allocation to nominal bonds.

Conservative investors, with risk aversion $\gamma > 1$, have a positive intertemporal hedging demand for stocks. This demand
shows up in the gap between the two lines in Figure 4.3(a). The
intertemporal hedging demand is a hump-shaped function of
risk tolerance $1/\gamma$, because investors with unit risk aversion have
no intertemporal hedging demand while extremely conservative
investors seek to hold a risk-minimizing portfolio which contains
almost no equities and thus are almost indifferent to shifts in
expected stock returns. The myopic portfolio demand for stocks
is, as always, a linear function of $1/\gamma$. The intertemporal hedging
demand for equities is smaller than the myopic demand, but it is

far from negligible; at $\gamma = 5$, for example, the mean myopic weight on equities is 50% while the intertemporal hedging demand contributes 17% for a total mean equity demand of 67%.

Conservative investors also have a large positive intertemporal hedging demand for nominal bonds. This should not be surprising, given the variation in the real interest rate in the annual dataset, a risk that can be hedged using long-term bonds as we emphasized in Chapter 3. At $\gamma = 5$, the mean myopic weight on nominal bonds is 51% while the intertemporal hedging demand contributes 40% for a total mean bond demand of 91%. (The optimal mean cash position is −58% to finance bond and stock positions that exceed 100% of the portfolio.) As risk aversion increases above 5, the intertemporal hedging demand for bonds increases and accounts for almost the entire portfolio of extremely conservative long-term investors.

Results are very different in the quarterly postwar dataset. We find strong positive intertemporal hedging demand for stocks, of the sort reported by Campbell and Viceira (1999, 2000).[7] At $\gamma = 5$, for example, the mean myopic weight on equities is 101% while the intertemporal hedging demand contributes 60% for a total mean equity demand of 161%. At the same time, we find negative intertemporal hedging demand for bonds; at $\gamma = 5$ the mean myopic weight on bonds is 28% but the intertemporal hedging demand is −123% for a total mean demand of −94%.

Several differences in the underlying data account for these different portfolio choices. First, in the postwar period stocks have a higher Sharpe ratio; this increases the myopic demand for stocks and the importance of hedging variations in expected stock returns. Since stocks are estimated to be mean-reverting, stocks themselves can be used to hedge these variations. Second, there is less variability in the real interest rate in the postwar period. This reduces the importance of long-term bonds as

---

[7] Campbell and Viceira (1999) made an error in estimating their model, understating the predictability of postwar quarterly stock returns and the absolute value of the correlation between innovations to stock returns and dividend yields. This error is explained in Campbell and Viceira (2000), which reports complete corrected results. Here we are using updated data that include the late 1990s. Although the predictability of stock returns is lower in recent years, which tends to diminish the intertemporal hedging demand for stock, the estimated persistence of the dividend–price ratio is higher, which tends to increase intertemporal hedging demand.

a hedge against shocks to real interest rates. Third, persistent variation in inflation in the postwar period makes nominal bonds risky assets for conservative long-term investors, a factor we emphasized in Chapter 3. Fourth, bond and stock returns are positively correlated, so a positive intertemporal hedging demand for equities tends to produce a negative intertemporal hedging demand for bonds as investors hedge their aggressive equity positions with short positions in bonds.

We can also use our model to decompose the variability of asset demands. We can write the optimal portfolio rule as

$$\alpha_{it} = \alpha_{it}^m + \alpha_{it}^h, \tag{4.20}$$

where i denotes stocks or bonds, m denotes myopic demand, and h denotes intertemporal hedging demand. Thus,

$$\text{Var}(\alpha_{it}) = \text{Var}(\alpha_{it}^m) + \text{Var}(\alpha_{it}^h) + 2\text{Cov}(\alpha_{it}^m, \alpha_{it}^h). \tag{4.21}$$

We have calculated this variance decomposition for the case $\gamma = 5$ and $\psi = 1$. The variance of the myopic demand explains almost all the variance in asset demands in the annual dataset; in the quarterly dataset it explains just over 50% of the variance in stock demand and about 60% in bond demand, while the variance of the intertemporal hedging demand explains 15% and 22% respectively, and the remainder is attributed to covariance of the two components. Thus, the intertemporal hedging component of demand is comparatively stable over time.

Kim and Omberg (1996) and Campbell and Viceira (1999) give an intuitive explanation for this result, showing that intertemporal hedging demand can change sign only in extreme circumstances where investors have replaced their normal long positions with short positions in risky assets. To a first approximation, intertemporal hedging shifts the intercept of risky asset demand rather than the slope with respect to state variables; put another way, long-term investors should 'time the markets' just as aggressively as short-term investors. We illustrated this in Figure 4.1 for a model with a single state variable.

Which state variables matter?
The analysis so far has focused on the shape of asset demands and their intertemporal hedging components. It is equally important

to understand the effects of various state variables on the level and variability of asset demands. To analyze these effects, we estimate a series of restricted VAR specifications. The first VAR system only has a constant term in each regression, corresponding to the case in which risk premia are constant and realized returns on all assets, including the short-term real interest rate, are IID. The second system includes an intercept term, the ex post real bill rate, and log excess returns on stocks and bonds. We then add sequentially the nominal bill rate, the dividend yield, and the yield spread. Thus, we estimate five VAR systems in total.

There are important changes in the magnitude of intertemporal hedging demands as we consider new state variables in the investor information set. In the case of stocks, intertemporal hedging demand is fairly small when only lagged interest rates and excess returns are included in the VAR. It shoots up dramatically when the dividend–price ratio is introduced into the VAR as a regressor. The inclusion of the yield spread has little further effect on the intertemporal hedging demand for stocks.

The correlation structure of the VAR residuals shown in Table 4.2 helps to explain these results. There is a strong negative correlation between unexpected excess returns on stocks and shocks to the dividend–price ratio, while the magnitude of all other correlations is much smaller. These correlations are not sensitive to the inclusion or exclusion of state variables in the VAR. The presence of the dividend–price ratio in the investor information set increases the intertemporal hedging demand for stocks because negative shocks to the dividend–price ratio, which drive down expected returns on stocks, tend to coincide with positive realized excess returns on stocks. This negative correlation is even stronger in the quarterly dataset, which explains the large intertemporal hedging demands in this dataset.

The intertemporal hedging demand for bonds is more complex. In the annual model it becomes positive as soon as the VAR includes any variables that predict the real interest rate, such as the lagged real interest rate or the nominal interest rate. Addition of further variables tends to increase the hedging demand for bonds. In the quarterly model the intertemporal hedging demand becomes negative once the VAR includes nominal and real interest rates and thus captures the dynamics of real returns and inflation.

We can also analyze the importance of each state variable for the variability of asset demands. In the case $\gamma = 5$ and $\psi = 1$, the dividend–price ratio explains over 80% of the variance of total demand for stocks in both the annual and the quarterly models. The short rate is also a major source of variability of stock demand in the quarterly sample. The dividend–price ratio plays a much less important role in explaining the variability of bond demand, which is driven primarily by the yield spread and the short-term nominal interest rate.

4.2.4. Strategic asset allocation with inflation-indexed bonds

Our VAR analysis has generalized the model of Chapter 3 to allow for arbitrary patterns of predictability in real interest rates and excess returns. We have found that mean-reversion in the stock market creates positive intertemporal hedging demand for equities by conservative investors, consistent with the view that stocks are in some sense 'safer assets' for long-term investors. The sign of the intertemporal hedging demand for long-term bonds is also positive in our long-term annual model, but it is negative in our quarterly model.

Inflation risk is more important relative to real interest rate risk in the postwar period, and it is natural to suppose that this accounts for the negative intertemporal hedging demand for bonds in our postwar model. To check the validity of this explanation, Campbell, Chan, and Viceira (CCV) (2001) extend the model to include an inflation-indexed consol in the menu of available assets. This requires them to construct hypothetical real bond returns because inflation-indexed bonds have only recently been issued by the US Treasury and thus data on these bonds are very limited. The VAR framework is well suited for this purpose, provided that we make the assumption that expected real returns on real bonds of all maturities and the expected return on short-term nominal bills differ only by a constant. This amounts to assuming that the inflation risk premium on nominal bills is constant. We now briefly describe the construction procedure, which is adapted from the work of Campbell and Shiller (1996).

CCV (2001) first use the estimates of the coefficient matrices in the VAR to construct returns on hypothetical real consols. The procedure assumes a zero inflation risk premium. As noted in Campbell and Shiller (1996), if the inflation risk premium is not zero but constant, the procedure will miss the average level of the yield curve but will still capture the dynamics of the curve. This is important, because intertemporal hedging demand depends sensitively on the dynamics of asset returns. With the correct dynamics in hand, CCV adjust the mean return to several alternative levels.[8] Finally, CCV include the imputed excess return on real consols in a new VAR system that includes both nominal bonds and real consols.

The results of this exercise are as follows. In a model without predictability of real interest rates or excess returns, extremely conservative investors hold the short-term minimum-variance portfolio. In the annual data this portfolio places roughly equal weights on the short-term bill and the real consol; in the quarterly data it is dominated by the short-term bill. Portfolio choices are very different in the estimated VAR model with predictable interest rates and excess returns. In that model the intertemporal hedging demand for the real consol is increasing in risk aversion; it drives total demand for the real perpetuity to 100% of the portfolio as the investor becomes infinitely conservative. By contrast, the total portfolio demand for stocks, the nominal bill, and the nominal bond are decreasing in γ, approaching 0% as the investor becomes infinitely conservative. Thus, inflation-indexed bonds drive out cash from the portfolios of conservative investors. This is a generalization of the result of Chapter 3 to a world in which both interest rates and expected excess returns are time-varying. Thus, the negative intertemporal hedging demand for nominal bonds in postwar quarterly data is the result of inflation risk; inflation-indexed bonds, or nominal bonds in a low-inflation environment, remain attractive investments for conservative long-term investors, as shown in Chapter 3.

---

[8] Intertemporal hedging demands are similar if one sets the Sharpe ratio of the real consol bond equal to zero or to the Sharpe ratio of stocks or bonds.

4.3. CONCLUSION

In this chapter we have explored optimal investment strategies when both riskless interest rates and risk premia change over time. In this situation a long-term investor with constant risk aversion should both exploit and hedge against variations in investment opportunities. As in Chapter 3, a conservative long-term investor should hedge real interest rate risk by holding long-term inflation-indexed bonds, or nominal bonds if inflation risk is low. In addition, the investor should respond to mean-reverting stock returns by increasing the average allocation to equities.

The strategic equity allocation responds slightly more strongly than the myopic allocation to changes in the equity premium, so it involves an element of market timing. Since the state variables that predict excess returns are generally slow-moving, however, the variation in asset allocation should also be gradual. In practice, individuals might implement the strategy by periodic revisions in asset allocation within retirement savings accounts, while institutions might implement it by periodically resetting their strategic policy portfolios. This sort of market timing has little to do with the volatile high-frequency trading that might be recommended by 'tactical asset allocation' programs.

It is interesting to relate these results to recent discussions of stock market risk. Equities have traditionally been regarded as risky assets. They may be attractive because of their high average returns, but these returns represent compensation for risk; thus, equities should be treated with caution by all but the most aggressive investors. In recent years, however, several authors have argued that equities are actually relatively safe assets for investors who are able to hold for the long term. We have already quoted Jeremy Siegel (1994) on this point; a more extreme version of this revisionist view is promoted by James Glassman and Kevin Hassett (1999), who argue in their book *Dow 36,000* that stocks are just as safe as bonds or Treasury bills.

The revisionist view that stocks are safe assets is based on evidence that excess stock returns are less volatile when they are measured over long holding periods. Mathematically, such a reduction in stock market risk at long horizons can only be due to mean-reversion in excess stock returns, which is equivalent to time variation in the equity premium. Yet revisionist investment advice typically ignores the implications of a time-varying equity premium. Siegel (1994) recommends an aggressive buy-and-hold strategy, like the horizontal line in Figure 4.1 but shifted upwards to reflect the reduced risk of stocks for long-term investors. The optimal policy is instead the sloped line marked 'Strategic asset allocation' in Figure 4.1.

The difference between the optimal strategy and the strategy recommended by Siegel is particularly dramatic at times such as the turn of the millennium, when recent stock returns have been spectacular. At such a time, the optimal equity allocation may be no higher—it may even be lower—than the allocation implied by a traditional short-term portfolio analysis. To put it another way, investors who are attracted to the stock market by the prospect of high returns combined with low long-term risk are trying to have their cake and eat it too. If expected stock returns are constant over time, then one can hope to earn high stock returns in the future similar to the high returns of the past; but in this case stocks are much riskier than bonds in the long term, just as they are in the short term. If instead stocks mean-revert, then they are relatively safe assets for long-term investors; but in this case future returns are likely to be meagre, as mean-reversion unwinds the spectacular stock market runup of the past decade.

It is important to keep in mind two limitations of our analysis in this chapter. First, we ignore portfolio constraints that might prevent investors from short-selling or from borrowing to invest in risky assets. The Siegel strategy of buying and holding stocks might be much closer to optimal for an aggressive investor who cannot borrow to leverage a stock market position, and who therefore normally holds the maximum 100% weight in equities.[9]

Second, we have studied a partial equilibrium model. We have solved the microeconomic problem of an investor facing exogenous asset returns, but we do not show how these asset returns could be consistent with general equilibrium. The difficulty is particularly severe in this chapter, since we find that all investors

---

[9] Campbell *et al.* (2001b) present a numerical analysis of the model of Section 4.1.3. They verify the accuracy of the loglinear approximate solution, except at the extremes of the state space, and also explore the effects of portfolio constraints. They find that the constrained solution resembles a smoothed version of the unconstrained solution with the constraints imposed.

should change their portfolio allocations in the same direction as state variables change, regardless of their preferences. That is, all investors should buy and sell assets at the same time. This cannot be consistent with a general equilibrium model that makes realistic assumptions about asset supplies.

One possible resolution of this difficulty is that the representative investor has different preferences from those assumed here, perhaps the habit formation preferences of Campbell and Cochrane (1999), which can generate shifts in risk aversion and hence can change risk premia with a constant riskless interest rate. Under this interpretation, the results of this chapter should be used only by investors with constant risk aversion, who cannot be typical of the market as a whole.

5

Strategic Asset Allocation in Continuous Time

In the first part of this book we have developed a discrete-time model that can be used to analyze optimal long-term portfolio choice when the conditions for myopic portfolio choice fail. In particular, we have asked how long-term investors should react to time variation in interest rates and risk premia. This chapter extends the previous analysis in several ways.

First, we show how to approach similar problems in a continuous-time framework. The use of continuous-time mathematics to analyze dynamic portfolio choice has a long tradition that goes back at least to the seminal work by Robert Merton (1969, 1971, 1973). Duffie (1996), Karatzas and Shreve (1998), and Merton (1990) provide general treatments of portfolio choice in continuous time. We show that, when exact analytical solutions are not available, we can still obtain approximate analytical solutions of the same nature as the ones we have presented in previous chapters. Furthermore, when investors have recursive utility, we can obtain exact analytical solutions for investors with unit elasticity of intertemporal substitution.

Second, we explore the investment implications of time-varying risk. A continuous-time framework is convenient for this purpose because continuous-time models of stochastic volatility are parsimonious and readily restrict volatility to be positive. Our analysis of this problem closely follows Chacko and Viceira (1999). We continue to assume that investors have financial wealth but no labor income.

Third, we briefly discuss the implications of parameter uncertainty for portfolio choice. The models elsewhere in this book assume that investors know with certainty the stochastic process determining asset returns. In other words, investors are assumed to be completely confident about the means, variances, and predictability of returns. This assumption is clearly unrealistic, but it is hard to relax it while retaining a tractable model. The continuous-time framework helps here too, as is shown in recent papers by Brennan (1998) and Brennan and Xia (2001).

This chapter is written at a higher technical level than other chapters in the book. Readers who are unfamiliar with continuous-time mathematics—in particular, Itô's lemma—should consult a primer such as Neftci (1996) or could skip this chapter altogether.

The organization of the chapter is as follows. Section 5.1 develops the dynamic programming approach to optimal consumption and portfolio choice in continuous time, as introduced originally by Merton. Section 5.1.1 explains the Bellman optimality principle in continuous time, Section 5.1.2 introduces an example that is a continuous-time equivalent of the real term structure model in Chapter 3, and Section 5.1.3 derives a continuous-time loglinear approximate solution to the model, a continuous-time equivalent of the solution derived in Chapter 3.

Section 5.2 explains the martingale solution method, the leading continuous-time alternative to the dynamic programming approach. Section 5.2.1 explains the role of the stochastic discount factor (SDF) in continuous-time models, Section 5.2.2 shows how the properties of the SDF help one to solve dynamic portfolio choice problems, and Section 5.2.3 revisits the term structure example of Section 5.1.2.

For simplicity, both Sections 5.1 and 5.2 work with time-separable power utility. Section 5.3 presents recursive utility, the continuous-time equivalent of the Epstein–Zin preferences introduced in Chapter 2.

Sections 5.4 and 5.5 present new applications. Section 5.4 uses the methods of this chapter to solve a long-term portfolio choice problem with time-varying stock market volatility, while Section 5.5 discusses the portfolio choice problem of an investor who is learning about the moments of asset returns.

5.1. THE DYNAMIC PROGRAMMING APPROACH

5.1.1. The Bellman optimality principle

We start by deriving the Bellman equation for optimality in a simple setting. The Bellman optimality principle is a useful tool for solving dynamic portfolio problems because it allows the transformation of a dynamic optimization problem into a differential equation, for which several solution methods are available.

For notational convenience, we assume there are only two assets available to the investor, a risky asset with instantaneous total return dP_t/P_t,[1] and an instantaneously riskless asset with return dB_t/B_t. There is also a single state variable S_t driving the dynamics of the investment opportunity set. It is conceptually straightforward to extend the analysis to multiple assets and state variables.

We assume that both returns and the state variable follow diffusion processes:

$$\frac{dP_t}{P_t} = \mu_P(S,t)\,dt + \sigma_P(S,t)\,dZ_{Pt}, \tag{5.1}$$

$$\frac{dB_t}{B_t} = r(S,t)\,dt, \tag{5.2}$$

$$dS_t = \mu_s(S,t)\,dt + \sigma_s(S,t)\,dZ_{st}, \tag{5.3}$$

where dZ_{Pt} and dZ_{st} are Wiener processes with $dZ_{Pt}dZ_{st} = \rho_{PS}(S,t)dt$. Note that the drifts, volatilities, and correlations of the asset prices and the state variable may be functions of the state variable and time. In the following equations, however, we often omit this dependence, writing for example μ_P instead of $\mu_P(S,t)$; this simpler notation is less careful but more readable.

Given time-separable preferences defined over consumption, and given initial wealth $W_0 > 0$, we can formulate the optimal portfolio and consumption problem for a long-term investor as

$$\max_{C,\alpha} E_0 \left[\int_0^\infty U(C,t)\,dt \right], \tag{5.4}$$

subject to the continuous-time intertemporal budget constraint,

$$dW_t = [(\alpha_t(\mu_P - r) + r)W_t - C_t]\,dt + \alpha_t W_t \sigma_P\,dZ_{Pt}, \tag{5.5}$$

---

[1] If the risky asset does not pay dividends, P_t is simply the price of the asset. If it does pay dividends, P_t represents an index whose instantaneous rate of change dP_t/P_t equals the instantaneous total return on the asset.

and the constraints $W_t > 0$ and $C_t > 0$. Here α denotes the fraction of wealth invested in the risky asset, and C denotes consumption.

Let $J(W, S, t)$ denote the maximized utility function, or value function, of this problem. The Bellman principle implies:

$$0 = \max_{c, \alpha} \left\{ U(C, t) + \frac{1}{dt} E_t[dJ(W, S, t)] \right\}. \tag{5.6}$$

At the optimum, the investor has traded off the value of present and future consumption perfectly. Consumption today is achieved at the expense of current resources that otherwise could increase consumption in the future. The investor chooses a level of current consumption whose utility value exactly offsets the expected utility cost of lost future consumption.[2]

Under suitable regularity conditions, Itô's lemma implies that

$$dJ(W, S, t) = J_w \, dW + J_s \, dS + \left(\frac{\partial J}{\partial t} \right) dt$$

$$+ \frac{1}{2} J_{ww} (dW)^2 + J_{ws} \, dW \, dS + \frac{1}{2} J_{ss} (dS)^2. \tag{5.7}$$

Here we use subscripts to denote partial derivatives, except that we write out the partial time derivative of J explicitly as $\partial J / \partial t$ to avoid any possibility of confusion with the value of the function J at time t. Using the stochastic differential equations for dS and dW given in (5.3) and (5.5) and the rules of stochastic calculus, we can easily compute an expression for the expected instantaneous change in the value function. Substitution of the expression for $E_t[dJ(W, S, t)]/dt$ into (5.6) gives an equation that depends on C, α, and the value function:

$$0 = \max_{c, \alpha} \left\{ U(C, t) + J_w[(\alpha(\mu_p - r) + r)W - C] + J_s \mu_s \right.$$

$$\left. + \frac{\partial J}{\partial t} + \frac{1}{2} J_{ww} \alpha^2 W^2 \sigma_p^2 + J_{ws} \alpha W \sigma_p \sigma_s \rho_{ps} + \frac{1}{2} J_{ss} \sigma_s^2 \right\}. \tag{5.8}$$

---

[2] Merton (1971, 1973) first stated this result. Later work summarized in Karatzas and Shreve (1998) completed Merton's analysis.

Merton (1969) notes that this equation must satisfy the boundary condition

$$\lim_{t \to \infty} E_0[J(W, S, t)] = 0. \tag{5.9}$$

This is a condition for the convergence of the integral in (5.4). It is a transversality condition ensuring that the value function is bounded in the limit, i.e. that there is no investment strategy that allows the investor to achieve infinite utility.

We can compute the first-order conditions of the problem by taking derivatives of (5.8) with respect to C and α. We obtain a pair of expressions for consumption and portfolio choice as a function of wealth:

$$U_C = J_W, \tag{5.10}$$

$$\alpha = \frac{1}{-J_{WW} W / J_W} \left(\frac{\mu_P - r}{\sigma_P^2} \right) - \frac{J_{WS}}{J_{WW} W} \left(\frac{\sigma_S}{\sigma_P} \rho_{PS} \right). \tag{5.11}$$

Here consumption and the derivatives of the value function all depend on the variables W, S, and t, while the riskless rate and the moments of the risky asset return all depend on S and t. For simplicity these dependences are omitted from the notation, but they should not be forgotten.

Equation (5.10) determines the optimal consumption policy. It is known as the 'envelope condition', because it implies that at the optimum an extra unit of current consumption is as valuable to the investor as an extra unit of wealth to finance future consumption.

Equation (5.11) determines the optimal portfolio allocation to the risky asset. It is the continuous-time counterpart of (3.14). The first term of this equation is the familiar myopic portfolio rule: the optimal allocation to the risky asset is proportional to the asset's risk premium, and inversely proportional to its volatility and the relative risk aversion of the investor's value function. The second term is the intertemporal hedging component. It is non-zero as long as investment opportunities are time-varying ($\sigma_S > 0$), are correlated with instantaneous realized returns on the risky asset ($\rho_{PS} \neq 0$), and affect the marginal utility of wealth ($J_{WS} \neq 0$).

Equations (5.10) and (5.11) are not a complete solution to the model because they depend on the value function, which is still unknown. However, substitution of these expressions for optimal consumption and portfolio choice back into the Bellman equation (5.8) delivers a second-order partial differential equation (PDE) for the value function $J(W, S, t)$. Once we have solved this equation for the value function, we can obtain the optimal policies by substituting the value function into the first-order conditions for consumption and portfolio choice and inverting (5.10) to get $C = U_C^{-1}(J_W)$.

Unfortunately, it is not generally straightforward to find an analytical solution for the PDE that gives the value function. This type of equation is solved analytically using the method of undetermined coefficients. That is, one makes a guess about the functional form of the solution and shows that it verifies the partial differential equation (PDE) for some values of the parameters defining the functional guess. However, finding such a function is not always easy. In some cases, it is possible to transform the PDE into an ordinary differential equation (ODE), and there are handbooks such as Polyanin and Zaitsev (1995) that help identify ODEs with known exact solutions. But if no exact solution is known, it is necessary to resort to numerical algorithms such as those explained in Judd (1998) or Rogers and Talay (1997).

The special cases with known analytical solutions can be listed quite briefly.[3] Merton (1969, 1971, 1973) showed that (5.6) has an exact analytical solution if investors' utility of consumption is logarithmic, or if utility is power and investment opportunities are constant. In both cases, as we noted in Chapter 2, the inter-temporal asset allocation problem is essentially equivalent to a one-period problem, and optimal portfolio choice is myopic.

More recently, Kim and Omberg (1996) have considered a model with a constant riskless interest rate and a single risky asset whose expected return follows an Ornstein–Uhlenbeck (continuous-time AR(1)) process. This model is the continuous-time equivalent of the discrete-time model discussed in Section 4.1.3. Kim and Omberg have found exact solutions for investors

---

[3] We confine attention here to solutions for models with constant relative risk aversion. Solutions are also available for models with constant absolute risk aversion (Svensson and Werner 1993), but, as we explained in Chapter 2, we regard these models as less relevant. We revisit this issue in Chapter 6.

who maximize power utility defined over terminal wealth at some fixed horizon.

Wachter (2002) has solved this model when investors maximize power utility defined over consumption each period, provided that the process for the expected return on the risky asset is instantaneously perfectly correlated with the realized return—that is, provided that markets are complete. In this case the solution involves an integral that must be evaluated numerically, but is otherwise analytical.

Even when markets are not complete and investors value consumption rather than terminal wealth, this model can be solved analytically if investors have recursive utility with a unit elasticity of intertemporal substitution. Campbell and Viceira (1999) state this result in discrete time with an approximation to the intertemporal budget constraint that becomes exact in continuous time, while Chacko and Viceira (2000) state the result in continuous time.

Analytical solutions are also available in continuous-time affine term structure models related to the discrete-time term structure models of Chapter 3. The same three sets of assumptions—power utility of terminal wealth, power utility of consumption with complete markets, recursive utility with unit elasticity of substitution—deliver closed-form solutions in this context, as shown by Wachter (2000), Brennan and Xia (2001), and the results presented later in this chapter.

Analytical solutions can also be found in a model with stochastic volatility. Chacko and Viceira (1999) solve a model with a constant riskless interest rate and a constant risk premium, but a mean-reverting square-root process for the precision—the inverse of volatility—of the risky asset return. We present this model in Section 5.4.

All these papers consider particular cases of a general model in which the vector of state variables S has a drift that is a linear function of S and a variance–covariance matrix that is a quadratic function of S; the riskless interest rate $r(S, t)$ is a linear or quadratic function of S; and the market price of risk $(\mu_P(S, t) - r(S, t))/\sigma_P(S, t)$ is a linear or a square-root function of S. In two recent methodological papers, Schroder and Skiadas (1999) and Liu (2001) explore this general framework more systematically. Their main result is that there is no analytical solution to the general model, but that analytical solutions do exist under various sets of parameter restrictions. The required restrictions vary depending on three considerations: first, whether markets are complete or incomplete; second, whether utility is defined over terminal wealth or intermediate consumption; and third, whether investors have power utility or recursive utility. Schroder and Skiadas (1999) assume complete markets and utility defined over consumption, while Liu (2001) assumes either power utility defined over wealth or complete markets and power utility defined over consumption.

While the theoretical literature has made considerable progress in recent years, the cases with known exact analytical solutions are still relatively few, and the solutions often have complicated forms that are hard to interpret; for example, they may involve integrals that must be evaluated numerically. Thus it is often useful to apply an approximate analytical solution method of the sort we introduced in previous chapters for discrete-time problems. We illustrate this approach in the next section by studying an example, the continuous-time counterpart of the model with time-varying real interest rates introduced in Chapter 3.

5.1.2. An example with time-varying interest rates

The derivation of the Bellman equation shown in the previous section is general, except for the limited number of assets and state variables. To apply this solution method to a particular problem, we need to be more specific about the direct utility function $U(\cdot)$ and the investment opportunity set. In this section we solve a simple example, where investors have time-separable power utility over consumption with constant relative risk aversion γ, $U(C_t) = C_t^{1-\gamma}/(1-\gamma)$, and where time variation in investment opportunities is created by a time-varying real interest rate, so that $S_t = r_t$. To keep our notation as simple as possible, we also assume that the investor can choose only between an instantaneous short-term real bond paying $r_t\,dt$ and a long-term real bond.

We assume that the real interest rate follows an Ornstein–Uhlenbeck or continuous-time AR(1) process as in Vasicek (1977):

$$dr_t = \kappa(\theta - r_t)dt + \sigma\,dZ_{rt}, \tag{5.12}$$

where $\kappa \in (0,1)$ and $\theta > 0$. Let $P(r_t, T - t)$ denote the price of a real zero-coupon bond with $T - t$ periods to maturity. Vasicek (1977) shows that no arbitrage, together with a constant price of interest-rate risk, implies the following dynamics for bond returns:

$$\frac{dP(r_t, T - t)}{P(r_t, T - t)} = [r_t + \lambda b(T - t)]\, dt - b(T - t)\sigma\, dZ_{rt}, \qquad (5.13)$$

where λ determines the risk premium on the bond and $b(T - t) \equiv \kappa^{-1}\{1 - \exp[-\kappa(T - t)]\} = -P_r/P$. Thus, real bonds in this model have a constant expected excess return equal to $\lambda b(T - t)$ and a constant instantaneous return volatility equal to $b(T - t)\sigma$. There is only one source of uncertainty in this model, and bond returns are perfectly negatively correlated with the short-term real interest rate. This is the continuous-time counterpart of the real-interest-rate model in Chapter 3.

The investor's dynamic portfolio and consumption problem can now be written as

$$\max_{C,\alpha} E_0\left[\int_0^\infty e^{-\beta t} \frac{C_t^{1-\gamma}}{1 - \gamma}\, dt\right] \qquad (5.14)$$

subject to

$$dW_t = [(\alpha_t \lambda b(T - t) + r_t)W_t - C_t]\, dt - \alpha_t W_t b(T - t)\sigma\, dZ_{rt}. \qquad (5.15)$$

To find the optimal consumption and portfolio policies for this model, we follow the steps described in Section 5.1.1. The Bellman equation for this problem is

$$0 = \max_{\alpha,C}\left\{ e^{-\beta t} \frac{C^{1-\gamma}}{1 - \gamma} + J_w(\alpha \lambda b W + rW - C) + J_r \kappa(\theta - r) + \frac{\partial J}{\partial t} \right.$$

$$\left. + \frac{1}{2}J_{ww}\alpha^2 W^2 b^2 \sigma^2 - J_{wr}\alpha W b \sigma^2 + \frac{1}{2}J_{rr}\sigma^2 \right\}, \qquad (5.16)$$

where for brevity we have set $b(T - t) \equiv b$ and have suppressed time subscripts.

From this Bellman equation, the first-order conditions for optimal consumption and portfolio choice are

$$C = (e^{\beta t}J_w)^{-(1/\gamma)}, \tag{5.17}$$

$$\alpha = \left(\frac{1}{-J_{ww}W/J_w}\right)\frac{\lambda}{b\sigma_r^2} + \left(\frac{J_{wr}}{J_{ww}W}\right)\frac{1}{b}. \tag{5.18}$$

Substitution of these conditions into (5.16) gives a second-order PDE for the value function $J(W, r, t)$. To solve this equation, we guess that the value function takes the form

$$J(W, r, t) = e^{-\beta t}H(r_t)^{\gamma}\frac{W_t^{1-\gamma}}{1-\gamma}, \tag{5.19}$$

where $H(r_t)$ is a function only of the instantaneous interest rate. In other words, we guess that wealth has a multiplicative effect on the value function and is scaled in the natural way for power utility with relative risk aversion γ. This guess implies, after some simplifications, a second-order ODE for the function $H(r_t)$:

$$0 = \frac{\gamma}{1-\gamma}\left(\frac{1}{H}\right) + \left(\frac{\lambda^2}{2\gamma\sigma^2} - \frac{\beta}{1-\gamma} + r\right)$$
$$+ \left(\frac{\gamma\kappa}{1-\gamma}(\theta - r) - \lambda\right)\left(\frac{H_r}{H}\right) + \frac{\gamma\sigma^2}{2(1-\gamma)}\left(\frac{H_{rr}}{H}\right). \tag{5.20}$$

Equation (5.20) is a non-homogeneous ODE, whose associated homogeneous equation belongs to the degenerate hypergeometric equation class. This equation has an exact solution given in Polyanin and Zaitsev (1995). Unfortunately, this solution is a complicated expression involving gamma functions which is extremely hard to interpret.

5.1.3. An approximate analytical solution

We now show that it is possible to find an approximate analytical solution to the problem. The solution is based on a loglinear expansion of the consumption–wealth ratio around its unconditional mean. This is exactly the same type of approximation that we used in Chapters 3 and 4, but instead of using it to linearize the intertemporal budget constraint, we use it here to solve the Bellman equation.

To understand this approach, note that the envelope condition (5.17) and the form of the value function (5.19) imply

$$\frac{C_t}{W_t} = \exp(c_t - w_t) = \frac{1}{H(r_t)}, \tag{5.21}$$

where $c_t - w_t = \log(C_t/W_t)$. Therefore, we can approximate $1/H(r_t)$ as

$$\frac{1}{H(r_t)} \approx h_0 + h_1(c_t - w_t) = h_0 - h_1 \log(H(r_t)), \tag{5.22}$$

where $h_0 = \exp(\overline{c - w})[1 - (\overline{c - w})], h_1 = \exp(\overline{c - w})$, and $(\overline{c - w}) = E(c_t - w_t)$. Substituting (5.22) for $1/H(r_t)$ in the first term of (5.20), it is easy to see that the resulting ODE has a solution of the form $H(r_t) = \exp(C_0 + C_1 r_t)$. This implies that the log consumption–wealth ratio is linear in the riskless real interest rate: $c_t - w_t = -C_1 r_t - C_0$.

The first term in the ODE (5.20) is the term that makes the equation hard to solve. We replace this term with a loglinear approximation, thereby transforming (5.20) into another ODE with a known analytical solution. If the loglinear approximation is accurate, the exact analytical solution to the approximate ODE will also verify the original ODE subject to some approximation error and can be regarded as an approximate analytical solution to the original ODE. We will also show that there is no approximation error in the known special cases where the investor has log utility or faces constant investment opportunities.

The approximate ODE leads to two algebraic equations for C_1 and C_0, given in Campbell and Viceira (2001b). The first equation is linear in the coefficient C_1 with solution

$$C_1 = -\left(1 - \frac{1}{\gamma}\right)\frac{1}{h_1 + \kappa}. \tag{5.23}$$

The second equation involves both coefficients, but it is linear in C_0 given C_1. Its solution is a function of all the parameters in the model.

The approximate solution implies the value function

$$J(W, r, t) = \exp(-\beta t + \gamma C_0 + \gamma C_1 r_t) \frac{W_t^{1-\gamma}}{1-\gamma}, \tag{5.24}$$

and the optimal policies

$$c_t - w_t = -C_0 + \left(1 - \frac{1}{\gamma}\right) \frac{1}{h_1 + \kappa} r_t, \tag{5.25}$$

$$\alpha = \frac{1}{\gamma} \frac{\lambda}{b(T-t)\sigma^2} + \left(1 - \frac{1}{\gamma}\right) \frac{1}{b(T-t)(h_1 + \kappa)}. \tag{5.26}$$

This is the continuous-time equivalent of the discrete-time approximate solution given in Chapter 3. The optimal portfolio policy is a weighted average of two terms, with weights given by the investor's coefficient of relative risk tolerance and one minus this coefficient. Both terms are constant over time, so the portfolio weights are constant over time. It is straightforward to show that the solution is exact in the log-utility case where $\gamma = 1$. In this case, $C_t/W_t = \beta$ and $\alpha = \lambda/b(T-t)\sigma^2$. This is the exact solution implied by the Bellman equation (5.20) with $\gamma = 1$.

5.1.4. *An alternative approximate analytical solution*

The approximate analytical solutions presented so far are based on an expansion of the optimal log consumption–wealth ratio around its unconditional mean, $E(c_t - w_t)$. The optimal rules (5.25)–(5.26) depend on this mean through the loglinearization coefficient $h_1 \equiv \exp(E[c_t - w_t])$. Except in those special cases where h_1 is a known constant, we need to solve numerically for h_1 to compute values for the optimal policies. As we have discussed in Chapters 3 and 4, we can find h_1 using a simple recursive procedure. We can also derive a number of properties of the solution without solving explicitly for h_1, using the fact that it lies between zero and one. For example, $h_1 > 0$ implies that the intertemporal hedging demand for bonds in (5.26) is always positive when $\gamma > 1$.

The approximate loglinear solution will be accurate provided that the log consumption–wealth ratio is not too variable around its unconditional mean. It is exact in those special cases in which the optimal consumption–wealth ratio is constant. With time-varying investment opportunities and power utility, the only special case with a constant consumption–wealth ratio is the uninteresting case where $\gamma = 1$ and portfolio choice is myopic, but in Section 5.4 we introduce continuous-time recursive utility and show that the consumption–wealth ratio is constant if the elasticity of intertemporal substitution equals one.

Kogan and Uppal (2000) have suggested an alternative approximate analytical solution around the exact solution that obtains when $\gamma = 1$. Their approach works by substituting the guess for the value function (5.19) into the first-order conditions (5.17) and (5.18) and expanding the resulting expressions around $\gamma = 1$. Their solution can be understood as a particular case of our loglinear solution procedure that sets $\mathrm{E}(c_t - w_t) = \log \beta$, the exact value of this expectation when $\gamma = 1$. To see this in our example, note that substitution of guess (5.19) into the first-order condition for consumption (5.17) leads to (5.21). Expanding this equation around $\gamma = 1$, we obtain:

$$
\begin{aligned}
\frac{C_t}{W_t} &= \exp(-h(r_t)) \\
&\approx \exp(-\bar{h}) - \exp(-\bar{h})(h(r_t) - \bar{h})|_{\bar{h} = -\log \beta} \\
&= \beta(1 - \log \beta) + \beta(-h(r_t)),
\end{aligned} \tag{5.27}
$$

where $h(r_t) = \log H(r_t)$ and $\bar{h} = -\log \beta$ is the known, exact value of the function $h(r_t)$ when $\gamma = 1$.

Direct comparison of (5.22) and (5.27), using the fact that $-h(r_t) = c_t - w_t$, shows that the alternative approximate solution is a particular case of the loglinear solution based on (5.22), with $h_1 = \beta$. It is also straightforward to check that substitution of (5.27) into the Bellman equation (5.20) leads to an optimal portfolio rule that is identical to (5.26), with $h_1 = \beta$.

The approximate analytical solution around $\gamma = 1$ is fully analytical in the sense that it simply sets h_1 equal to the discount factor β, so that no numerical procedure is necessary to find h_1. Kogan and Uppal (2000) note that this solution will be accurate for values of γ close to one. Our interpretation of the solution as a particular case of the loglinear solution suggests that it will also be accurate for values of γ further away from one, provided the mean log optimal consumption–wealth ratio is not far from log β. Unfortunately, the consumption–wealth ratio is highly sensitive to the parameters of utility, as shown by Campbell and Viceira (1999, 2001a) for the empirical models presented in Chapters 3 and 4. This suggests that simply setting the loglinearization parameter h_1 to β will often deliver less accurate solutions than using a numerical recursion to find h_1. Campbell (1993) offers some evidence that supports this conjecture in a model where there is only one asset, and the individual's only choice is consumption. He solves for optimal consumption using numerical methods, the loglinear approximation method, and the approximation that sets $h_1 = \beta$, and finds that the approximation error produced by setting $h_1 = \beta$ can be many times larger than the error produced by the loglinear method, even for values of γ as close to log utility as 0.5 or 2.

5.2. THE MARTINGALE APPROACH

Cox and Huang (1989), Cox and Leland (1982), Karatzas, Lehoczky, and Shreve (1987), and Pliska (1986) have suggested an alternative approach to intertemporal consumption and portfolio choice that takes advantage of the properties of the SDF under complete markets. Their approach works by transforming the dynamic problem into a static problem whose unknown is optimally invested wealth rather than the value function. This transformation delivers a differential equation for optimally invested wealth that is sometimes easier to solve than the Bellman equation for the value function. In this section we offer a 'hands-on' explanation of this approach. We start by describing the properties of the SDF in continuous time.

5.2.1. The SDF in continuous time

The SDF in continuous time is defined as the process M_t such that, for any security with price V_t and instantaneous payoff X_s at some future date $s \geq t$, we have

$$V_t = E_t\left(\frac{M_s}{M_t} X_s\right). \tag{5.28}$$

The SDF is also known as the pricing kernel or state–price density. An important property of the SDF is that it is unique if markets are complete and there are no opportunities for arbitrage in the economy.

If we are considering a security that does not pay dividends, we have $X_s = V_s$, and (5.28) becomes

$$M_t V_t = E_t(M_s V_s),\qquad(5.29)$$

which in turn implies that $M_t V_t$ follows a martingale:

$$E_t(d(M_t V_t)) = 0.\qquad(5.30)$$

If the security pays an instantaneous dividend of $D_t\,dt$ each period, we have $X_s = V_s + D_s\,dt$, and (5.28) becomes

$$E_t(d(M_t V_t) + M_t D_t\,dt) = 0.\qquad(5.31)$$

We can still use (5.30) to analyze a security that pays dividends, provided that we interpret V_t as an index whose instantaneous rate of change equals the total return on the security.

Given a process for the SDF, we can price any security in the market. Harrison and Kreps (1979) show that we can also work the other way around and find the SDF that is consistent with a set of observed equilibrium prices in the economy. For example, suppose that the only securities in the market are security P_t, whose total return follows the process (5.1), and an instantaneously riskless asset given in (5.2). Further, assume that markets are complete, i.e. that the vector of traded security prices perfectly spans the vector of state variables.

In our example, the complete-markets assumption means that innovations to the state variable and innovations to the risky asset return must be perfectly correlated so that there is only one source of uncertainty in the model (i.e. $dZ_{Pt} = dZ_{st}$). In this case, the SDF follows a diffusion process with only one diffusion term:

$$\frac{dM_t}{M_t} = \mu_M(S,t)\,dt + \sigma_M(S,t)\,dZ_{Pt}.\qquad(5.32)$$

We can use the martingale property (5.30) to solve for μ_M and σ_M as functions of the drift and diffusion coefficients of security prices. Equation (5.30) implies that $E_t(d(M_tP_t)) = 0$ and $E_t(d(M_tB_t)) = 0$. That is, the drift terms of $d(M_tP_t)$ and $d(M_tB_t)$ must be equal to zero. From Itô's lemma, we have

$$d(M_tP_t) = M_tP_t\left(\frac{dP_t}{P_t} + \frac{dM_t}{M_t} + \sigma_P\sigma_M\, dt\right)$$
$$= M_tP_t[(\mu_P + \mu_M + \sigma_P\sigma_M)\, dt + (\sigma_P + \sigma_M)\, dZ_{Pt}].$$
$$(5.33)$$

Thus the martingale property $E_t(d(M_tP_t)) = 0$ holds if and only if

$$\mu_P + \mu_M + \sigma_P\sigma_M = 0. \tag{5.34}$$

Similarly, for the instantaneously riskless bond we have

$$d(M_tB_t) = M_tB_t(dB_t + dM_t)$$
$$= M_tB_t[(r + \mu_M)\, dt + \sigma_M\, dZ_{Pt}], \tag{5.35}$$

and the martingale property requires

$$r + \mu_M = 0. \tag{5.36}$$

Equations (5.34) and (5.36) define a system of two linear equations with two unknowns, whose unique solution is

$$\mu_M(S, t) = -r(S, t), \tag{5.37}$$

$$\sigma_M(S, t) = -\frac{\mu_P(S, t) - r(S, t)}{\sigma_P(S, t)}. \tag{5.38}$$

That is, the instantaneous expected return on the SDF is the negative of the instantaneous interest rate, and the diffusion term is the negative of the price of risk (or the Sharpe ratio of the risky asset). Note that if markets are not complete the innovations to the SDF will depend on both dZ_{Pt} and dZ_{st}, and it will not be possible to uniquely identify the drift and diffusion terms of the process for the SDF.

It is straightforward to extend this approach to any number of securities. In this case, $d\mathbf{P}_t/\mathbf{P}_t$ becomes a vector, and σ_{Pt} a vector such that $\sigma_{Pt}\sigma'_{Pt} = \Sigma_{Pt}$, where Σ_{Pt} is the instantaneous variance–covariance matrix of returns.

5.2.2. Using the SDF to solve portfolio and consumption problems

Transforming the dynamic problem into a static problem

The martingale approach uses the properties of the SDF under complete markets to solve portfolio and consumption problems. In (5.4) and (5.5) we defined the optimal portfolio and consumption problem for a long-term investor as

$$\max_{C,\alpha} E_0 \left[\int_0^\infty U(C,t)\, dt \right],$$

subject to

$$dW_t = \left[(\alpha_t (\mu_P - r) + r) W_t - C_t \right] dt + \alpha_t W_t \sigma_P \, dZ_{Pt},$$

and positive initial wealth $W_0 > 0$. Note that by simply reordering terms we can rewrite the intertemporal budget constraint (5.5) as

$$\frac{dW_t + C_t\, dt}{W_t} = \left[\alpha_t \mu_P + (1 - \alpha_t) r \right] dt + \alpha_t \sigma_P \, dZ_{Pt}. \tag{5.39}$$

This expression interprets the dynamic budget constraint as the total return on an asset whose price is W_t and that has an instantaneous dividend each period equal to optimal consumption C_t. Under this interpretation, optimally invested wealth W_t must verify

$$W_t = E_t \left(\int_t^\infty C_s \frac{M_s}{M_t} \, ds \right). \tag{5.40}$$

That is, optimally invested wealth is the expected present value of optimal future consumption discounted using the SDF. Optimally invested wealth at any time must be able to finance expected consumption under the optimal consumption plan determined at t.

With this reinterpretation of the budget constraint, we can transform the dynamic optimization problem (5.4)–(5.5) into the following problem:

$$\max_C E_0 \left[\int_0^\infty U(C,t) \, dt \right] \tag{5.41}$$

subject to

$$W_0 = E_0 \left(\int_0^\infty C_t \frac{M_t}{M_0} \, dt \right), \tag{5.42}$$

where we omit α from the argument of the max operator because we assume that W_0 and C_t in (5.42) denote optimally invested wealth and optimal consumption, respectively. Cox and Huang (1989) show that this problem has the same solution as the original problem. At the same time, (5.41)–(5.42) is a static problem that we can solve using the standard Lagrangian method.

The first-order conditions for the static problem (5.41)–(5.42) are

$$U_c(C_t) = \ell M_t \Longrightarrow C_t = U_c^{-1}(\ell M_t), \tag{5.43}$$

where ℓ denotes the Lagrange multiplier, and (5.42); that is, the budget constraint must hold along the optimal path. Note that ℓ does not have a time subscript; it is a constant determined at time 0. Substituting (5.43) into (5.42), we have

$$W_0 = E_0 \left(\int_0^\infty U_c^{-1}(\ell M_t) \frac{M_t}{M_0} \, dt \right). \tag{5.44}$$

We can simplify this expression by defining a new variable,

$$X_t = (\ell M_t)^{-1}. \tag{5.45}$$

This definition implies that $M_t/M_0 = X_0/X_t$. It also implies the following dynamics for X_t:

$$\begin{aligned}
\frac{dX_t}{X_t} &= -\frac{dM_t}{M_t} + \frac{(dM_t)^2}{M_t^2} \\
&= (-\mu_M(S,t) + \sigma_M^2(S,t)) \, dt - \sigma_M(S,t) \, dZ_{Pt},
\end{aligned} \tag{5.46}$$

where the first line follows from Itô's lemma, and the second line follows from (5.32). Cox and Huang (1989) give an interesting interpretation of the variable X_t, noting that it is the value of the 'growth-optimal portfolio' when all dividends are reinvested. We showed in Section 2.1.3 that this is the portfolio that maximizes the log return on wealth, and it is the optimal portfolio for an investor with log utility of consumption or terminal wealth.

Substituting back into (5.44) and noting that (5.44) must hold at all times, we obtain the following equality for optimally invested wealth:

$$
\begin{aligned}
W_t &= \mathrm{E}_t \left(\int_t^\infty U_C^{-1}(X_s^{-1}) \frac{X_t}{X_s} \, ds \right) \\
&= X_t \mathrm{E}_t \left(\int_t^\infty U_C^{-1}(X_s^{-1}) X_s^{-1} \, ds \right).
\end{aligned}
\tag{5.47}
$$

Given the Markovian structure of the dynamics for X_t and S_t (see (5.3) and (5.46)), this expectation will be some function F of the current value of X. If the process for X_t depends on the state variable, it will be also a function of the current value of S:

$$
W_t = F(X, S, t). \tag{5.48}
$$

This observation has important implications for the role of time-varying expected returns, variances, and covariances on portfolio choice. Note that the process for X depends only on the instantaneous interest rate, $-\mu_M = r$, and on the price of risk, $-\sigma_M = (\mu_P - r)/\sigma_P$, but it does not depend on the expected return on the risky asset μ_P or its instantaneous standard deviation σ_P in isolation. Thus, if both the instantaneous interest rate and the price of risk are constant, optimally invested wealth will not depend on S, even if μ_P and σ_P are functions of S individually. Optimal portfolio choice and consumption will also be independent of the process for the state variable because they depend on the state variable only indirectly through optimally invested wealth.

Nielsen and Vassalou (2000), working with utility defined over terminal wealth, show that this result holds more generally, regardless of the dimensions of the state vector and the vector of risky assets, and regardless of whether or not markets are complete. They note that the interest rate is the intercept of the instantaneous capital market line, and the price of risk (or the Sharpe ratio) is the slope. Their result implies that the only time variation that matters for portfolio choice is time variation in the slope and intercept of the instantaneous capital market line.

Solving for optimally invested wealth

We can use the martingale property (5.31) to solve for the function $F(X, S, t)$. The martingale property implies

$$E_t(d(M_t W_t) + M_t C_t \, dt) = E_t(d(M_t F_t) + M_t U_C^{-1}(X_t^{-1}) \, dt) = 0, \tag{5.49}$$

where the second term on the right-hand side comes from the fact that optimally invested wealth pays an instantaneous 'dividend' equal to $C_t \, dt$. We now show that the expectation (5.49) implies a second-order PDE for optimally invested wealth.

To compute the expectation (5.49), we need first to compute $d(M_t F_t)$. By Itô's lemma, we have that

$$d(M_t F_t) = F_t \, dM_t + M_t \, dF_t + dM_t \, dF_t. \tag{5.50}$$

We have already derived the dynamics for dM_t in (5.32). We can obtain the dynamics for dF by using Itô's lemma once again:

$$\begin{aligned} dF = {}& F_X \, dX + F_s \, dS + \frac{\partial F}{\partial t} \, dt \\ & + \frac{1}{2} F_{XX} (dX)^2 + \frac{1}{2} F_{ss} (dS)^2 + F_{XS} \, dX \, dS, \end{aligned} \tag{5.51}$$

where sub-indices denote partial derivatives—for example, $F_s = \partial F / \partial S$—with the exception that we write $\partial F / \partial t$ rather than F_t to avoid any confusion with the value of the function F at time t.

Direct substitution of (5.50) and (5.51) in (5.49) implies that the argument of the expectation follows an Itô process. Thus, the expectation in (5.49) is zero only if the drift of this process is zero. Setting the drift to zero, we obtain a second-order PDE for optimally invested wealth:

$$\begin{aligned} & U_C^{-1}(X^{-1}) + (r + \sigma_M^2) X F_X + \mu_s F_s + \frac{\partial F}{\partial t} - rF \\ & + \frac{1}{2} \sigma_M^2 X^2 F_{XX} + \frac{1}{2} \sigma_{s}^2 F_{ss} - \sigma_M \sigma_s X F_{XS} \\ & = \sigma_M^2 F_X X - \sigma_M \sigma_s F_s, \end{aligned} \tag{5.52}$$

with boundary condition

$$\lim_{t \to \infty} E_0(F(X, S, t)) = 0. \tag{5.53}$$

Solving for optimal consumption and portfolio choice
Once we have solved for optimally invested wealth $W_t \equiv F(X, S, t)$, we can easily solve for consumption and portfolio choice. To solve for consumption, we use the first-order condition (5.43):

$$C_t = U_c^{-1}\left(\frac{1}{X_t}\right) = U_c^{-1}\left(\frac{1}{F^{-1}(W, S, t)}\right), \tag{5.54}$$

where we have assumed that $F(X, S, t)$ is invertible, so $W_t \equiv F(X, S, t) \Longrightarrow X_t = F^{-1}(W, S, t)$.

To solve for optimal portfolio choice, we simply equate the diffusion terms of the intertemporal budget constraint (5.5) and the equation describing the dynamics of optimally invested wealth (5.51), since both must be the same along the optimal path:

$$
\begin{aligned}
\alpha F \sigma_P \, dZ_{Pt} &= -F_X X \sigma_M \, dZ_{Pt} + F_s \sigma_s \, dZ_{st} \\
&= \left(\frac{\mu_P - r}{\sigma_P}\right) F_X X \, dZ_{Pt} + F_s \sigma_s \, dZ_{st}.
\end{aligned}
\tag{5.55}
$$

This equation highlights the importance of the complete-markets assumption in the martingale approach. The left-hand side of this equation depends only on dZ_{Pt}, but the right-hand side depends on both dZ_{Pt} and dZ_{st}. To identify α, we need either that $F_s = 0$, or the complete-markets assumption that dZ_{Pt} and dZ_{st} are perfectly correlated so that $dZ_{st} = dZ_{Pt}$. Since F_s need not be zero in general, solving for α requires the assumption that markets are complete. Under this assumption, the optimal portfolio rule is

$$\alpha = \frac{F_X X}{F}\left(\frac{\mu_P(S, t) - r(S, t)}{\sigma_P^2(S, t)}\right) + \frac{F_s}{F}\left(\frac{\sigma_s(S, t)}{\sigma_P(S, t)}\right). \tag{5.56}$$

By analogy with (5.11) with $\rho_{s,P}(S, t) = 1$, we can identify the first component of (5.56) as the myopic component of the optimal portfolio rule, and the second component as the hedging component. As Cox and Huang (1989) note, (5.11) and (5.56) also allow us to relate the dynamic programming approach and the martingale approach. Direct comparison of these equations shows that the value function and optimally invested wealth verify the following identities:

$$F_X X = -\frac{J_w}{J_{ww}}, \qquad F_s = -\frac{J_{ws}}{J_{ww}}. \tag{5.57}$$

5.2.3. *Our example revisited*

We can easily apply these results to the example of optimal portfolio choice with time-varying interest rates and power utility given in Section 5.1.2. First, note that the dynamics for the instantaneous interest rate and the return on a long-term bond imply the following process for the stochastic discount factor:

$$\frac{dM_t}{M_t} = -r_t \, dt + \frac{\lambda}{\sigma} \, dZ_{rt}. \tag{5.58}$$

This process implies that $dX_t/X_t = (r + \lambda^2/\sigma^2)dt - (\lambda/\sigma)dZ_r$, and $dX_t \, dS_t \equiv dX_t \, dr_t = -\lambda dt$. With power utility defined over consumption, $U(C_t) = e^{-\beta t}C_t^{1-\gamma}/(1-\gamma)$. Thus,

$$C_t = e^{-\beta t/\gamma}X_l^{1/\gamma} = U_c^{-1}(X_t^{-1}). \tag{5.59}$$

Substituting these results into (5.52), we obtain

$$0 = e^{-\beta t/\gamma}X^{1/\gamma} - rF + rXF_x + [\kappa(\theta - r) + \lambda]F_r + \frac{\partial F}{\partial t}$$
$$+ \frac{1}{2}\frac{\lambda^2}{\sigma^2}X^2 F_{xx} + \frac{1}{2}\sigma^2 F_{rr} - \lambda X F_{xr}, \tag{5.60}$$

subject to the boundary condition $\lim_{t\to\infty} E_0(F(X,r,t)) = 0$.

Wachter (2000) shows that this equation has a solution of the form

$$F(X,r,t) = e^{-\beta t/\gamma}X^{1/\gamma}\int_0^\infty \Psi(r_t,s)ds, \tag{5.61}$$

where

$$\Psi(r_t,s) = \exp\left(\frac{(1-\gamma)b(s)}{\gamma}r_t + A(s) - \frac{\beta}{\gamma}s\right), \tag{5.62}$$

and $A(s)$ is a function of s. Wachter notes that the limit of the function $\Psi(r_t,s)$ as $\gamma \to \infty$ is the price of a zero-coupon bond with maturity s that pays one unit of consumption at maturity: $\lim_{\gamma \to \infty} \Psi(r_t, s) = P(r, s) = \exp(-b(s)r_t + A(s))$. This has important implications for the interpretation of the optimal consumption and portfolio rules.

The optimal rules can be found by direct substitution of $F(X, r, t)$ into (5.54) and (5.56). The optimal consumption rule is

$$\frac{C_t}{W_t} = \frac{U_C^{-1}(X_t^{-1})}{F(X, r, t)} = \left(\int_0^\infty \Psi(r_t, s)\, ds \right)^{-1}. \tag{5.63}$$

Since $\lim_{\gamma \to \infty} \Psi(r_t, s)$ is the price of a zero-coupon bond with maturity s, the limit as $\gamma \to \infty$ of the integral expression in (5.63) must be the price of a real consol bond that pays one unit of consumption each period for ever. Optimally invested wealth for an infinitely risk-averse investor is equal to the value of a real consol bond that pays C units of consumption each period.

For an investor who is not infinitely risk-averse, a similar interpretation is still possible. Wachter (2000) shows that $\Psi(r_t, s)$ is the current value of optimally chosen consumption s periods ahead per dollar of optimally chosen consumption today. Therefore, the integral expression in (5.63) is the value of the entire optimal consumption stream, as a ratio to current consumption.

The optimal portfolio allocation to long-term bonds is

$$\alpha = \frac{XF_X}{F} \frac{\lambda}{\sigma_r^2 b(T-t)} - \frac{F_r}{F} \frac{1}{b(T-t)}$$

$$= \frac{1}{\gamma} \frac{\lambda}{b(T-t)\sigma_r^2} + \left(1 - \frac{1}{\gamma} \right) \frac{1}{b(T-t)} \frac{\int_0^\infty \Psi(r_t, s)\, b(s)\, ds}{\int_0^\infty \Psi(r_t, s)\, ds}, \tag{5.64}$$

where the first term of α is the myopic demand for long-term bonds and the second term is the intertemporal hedging component. The ratio of integrals in the intertemporal hedging component is a weighted average of interest sensitivities for bonds of different maturities, where the weight on maturity s is the function $\Psi(r_t, s)$. This is the interest sensitivity of the optimal consumption stream, or, in the language of fixed-income security analysis, it is the duration of optimal consumption. The position in long-term bonds is chosen so that the portfolio has the appropriate interest sensitivity to support the optimal consumption plan. Wachter

(2000) shows that, as $\gamma \to \infty$, α converges to a position in the available zero-coupon bond that, in combination with the instantaneously riskless asset, replicates the payments on a real consol bond.

Although this martingale analysis delivers many insights, it does not lead to a closed-form solution of the problem. Equation (5.61) writes the solution of the PDE (5.60) in integral form, and numerical integration would be required to evaluate this function. Once again, however, approximation methods can be used to get a closed-form solution; not surprisingly, the approximate solution is identical to the solution we obtained using dynamic programming. To see this, note that the first term of (5.60) is simply the consumption–wealth ratio. Thus, we can approximate this ratio using the same loglinear approximation as in Section 5.1.3. First, we substitute $h_0 + h_1(c_t - f_t)$ for the first term in the equation. Next, we guess that

$$F(X, r, t) = e^{-\beta t/\gamma} X_t^{1/\gamma} \exp(C_0 + C_1 r_t), \tag{5.65}$$

and we use this guess to compute all the expressions in the PDE (5.60) involving F or its derivatives. We also note that this guess implies $c_t - f_t = -C_0 - C_1 r_t$. Substitution of the guess into the approximated PDE leads to the same approximate analytical solution for the optimal portfolio policy and the optimal consumption–wealth ratio that we obtained before in (5.25) and (5.26).

Equation (5.64) offers a new way to understand the nature of the loglinear approximate solution. The optimal portfolio is constructed to have an interest sensitivity or duration identical to that of the optimal consumption stream. The approximate solution replaces the time-varying duration in (5.64) with a constant duration based on the mean optimal log consumption–wealth ratio. Thus, it is analogous to the approximate analysis of bond returns presented by Shiller, Campbell, and Schoenholtz (1983) and reviewed in Campbell, Lo, and MacKinlay (1997, chapter 10).

5.3. RECURSIVE UTILITY IN CONTINUOUS TIME

In Chapter 2 we introduced recursive Epstein–Zin preferences as a way to generalize the standard, time-separable power utility model to separate relative risk aversion from the elasticity of intertemporal substitution of consumption. Svensson (1989), Duffie and Epstein (1992a,b), and Fisher and Gilles (1998) derive a continuous-time analogue of the Epstein–Zin utility function. We adopt the Duffie–Epstein (1992b) parameterization of recursive utility:

$$J_t = E_t \left(\int_t^\infty f(C_s, J_s)\, ds \right), \tag{5.66}$$

where f(C, J) is a normalized aggregator of current consumption and continuation utility that takes the form

$$f(C, J) = \frac{\beta}{1 - (1/\psi)} (1 - \gamma)J \left[\left(\frac{C}{((1 - \gamma)J)^{1/(1-\gamma)}} \right)^{1-1/\psi} - 1 \right]. \tag{5.67}$$

Here $\beta > 0$ is the rate of time preference, $\gamma > 0$ is the coefficient of relative risk aversion, and $\psi > 0$ is the elasticity of intertemporal substitution. Power utility obtains from (5.67) by setting $\psi = 1/\gamma$.

The normalized aggregator f(C, J) takes the following form when $\psi \to 1$:

$$f(C, J) = \beta(1 - \gamma)J \left[\log C - \frac{1}{1 - \gamma} \log((1 - \gamma)J) \right]. \tag{5.68}$$

Duffie and Epstein (1992a,b) show that the Bellman principle of optimality applies to recursive utility. From a computational perspective, the only difference from the standard additive utility case is that we need to substitute the normalized aggregator f(C, J) for the instantaneous utility function U(C) in the Bellman equation (5.6).

5.3.1. Our example revisited once more: an exact solution with unit elasticity of intertemporal substitution

This section derives a solution to the model with stochastic interest rates under recursive utility. This is the continuous-time counterpart of the model with inflation-indexed bonds that we solved in Section 3.2. We argued in Chapters 3 and 4 that our discrete-time approximate analytical solution is exact in continuous time with diffusions for asset prices, provided that the elasticity of intertemporal substitution is one. We now prove this claim.

The Bellman equation for the recursive utility model with $\psi = 1$ is identical to (5.16), except that we substitute (5.68) for the instantaneous power utility of consumption $e^{-\beta t} C^{1-\gamma}/(1 - \gamma)$. The first-order condition for consumption (the envelope condition) becomes

$$C = \beta(1 - \gamma)\frac{J}{J_w}, \tag{5.69}$$

and the first-order condition for α is identical to (5.18). We now guess that the solution to the Bellman equation has the form

$$J(W, r_t) = I(r_t)\frac{W^{1-\gamma}}{1 - \gamma}. \tag{5.70}$$

Substitution of this guess and the first-order conditions into the Bellman equation lead to the following ODE:

$$0 = -\frac{\beta}{1 - \gamma}\log I + \left(\beta \log \beta - \beta + \frac{\lambda^2}{2\gamma\sigma^2} + r\right) + \frac{\sigma^2}{2\gamma}\left(\frac{I_r}{I}\right)^2$$
$$+ \left(\frac{\kappa}{1 - \gamma}(\theta - r) - \frac{\lambda}{\gamma}\right)\frac{I_r}{I} + \frac{\sigma^2}{2(1 - \gamma)}\frac{I_{rr}}{I}. \tag{5.71}$$

This equation has an exact solution of the form

$$I(r_t) = \exp(C_0 + C_1 r_t), \tag{5.72}$$

where $C_1 = (1 - \gamma)/(\beta + \kappa)$, and C_0 is given in Campbell and Viceira (2001b). This solution implies a constant consumption–wealth ratio equal to β, and a constant optimal portfolio rule given by (5.26) with $h_1 = \beta$.

When the elasticity of intertemporal substitution is not equal to one, we can still obtain an approximate analytical solution along the lines of the solution we presented in Section 5.1. The Bellman equation is once again identical to (5.16), except that we substitute

(5.67) for the instantaneous power utility of consumption. The first-order condition for consumption is now

$$C = \frac{[(1-\gamma)J]^{((1-\gamma\psi)/(1-\gamma))}\beta^{\psi}}{J_W^{-\psi}},\tag{5.73}$$

and the first-order condition for portfolio choice is again identical to (5.18). We guess a solution of the form

$$J(W,r,t) = H(r_t)^{-((1-\gamma)/(1-\psi))}\frac{W_t^{1-\gamma}}{1-\gamma},\tag{5.74}$$

which leads to the following non-homogeneous ODE:

$$0 = \frac{\gamma}{1-\gamma}\beta^{\psi}\left(\frac{1}{H}\right) + \left(-\frac{(1-\psi)\lambda^2}{2(1-\gamma)\sigma^2} - \frac{\gamma\psi\beta}{1-\gamma} - \frac{(1-\psi)\gamma}{1-\gamma}r\right)$$
$$+ \left(\frac{\gamma\kappa}{1-\gamma}(\theta-r)-\lambda\right)\left(\frac{H_r}{H}\right) - \left(\frac{1}{1-\psi}+\frac{\gamma}{1-\gamma}\right)\frac{\sigma^2}{2}\left(\frac{H_r}{H}\right)^2$$
$$+ \frac{\gamma\sigma^2}{2(1-\gamma)}\left(\frac{H_{rr}}{H}\right).\tag{5.75}$$

Equation (5.75) reduces to (5.20) when $\psi = 1/\gamma$, i.e. when recursive utility reduces to time-additive power utility. We can find an approximate analytical solution to this equation using the same approach as in Section 5.1. Once again, the envelope condition (5.73) implies that the first term of the equation, $\beta^{\psi}(1/H)$, is the optimal consumption–wealth ratio. Using the log-linear approximation $\beta^{\psi}(1/H) \approx h_0 + h_1(c_t - w_t) = h_0 + \psi \log(\beta) - h_1 \log(H(r_t))$, the resulting ODE has a solution of the form $H(r_t) = \exp(C_0 + C_1 r_t)$, with $C_1 = -(1-\psi)/(h_1+\kappa)$. The optimal log consumption–wealth ratio is given by

$$c_t - w_t = \psi \log \beta - C_0 + \frac{1-\psi}{h_1+\kappa}r_t,\tag{5.76}$$

and the optimal portfolio rule is identical to the optimal rule under power utility (see (5.26)). Thus, the optimal portfolio rule depends on the investor's willingness to substitute consumption intertemporally only indirectly, through the parameter h_1 that determines the mean log consumption–wealth ratio.

5.4. SHOULD LONG-TERM INVESTORS HEDGE VOLATILITY RISK?

The continuous-time approach that we have just presented is especially helpful in showing how long-term investors should react to time-varying risk. Motivated by empirical evidence, Chapter 3 and 4 examined the relevance of time variation in interest rates and expected excess bond and stock returns for long-term portfolio choice. There is equally strong empirical evidence that the volatility of stock returns is time-varying. Partial surveys of the enormous literature on time-varying volatility are given by Bollerslev, Chou, and Kroner (1992), Hentschel (1995), Ghysels, Harvey, and Renault (1996), and Campbell, Lo, and MacKinlay (1997, chapter 12).

Chacko and Viceira (1999) explore the implications of changing volatility for long-term portfolio choice. They assume that the only source of time variation in investment opportunities is time variation in instantaneous precision, the inverse of the instantaneous variance of stock returns. Writing q_t for instantaneous precision, (5.1)–(5.3) become

$$\frac{dP_t}{P_t} = \mu_p \, dt + \sqrt{\frac{1}{q_t}} \, dZ_{Pt}, \tag{5.77}$$

$$\frac{dB_t}{B_t} = r \, dt, \tag{5.78}$$

$$dq_t = \kappa_q(\theta_q - q_t)dt + \sigma_q \, dZ_{qt}, \tag{5.79}$$

and $dZ_{Pt} \, dZ_{qt} = \rho_{Pq} \, dt$. We use subscripts on parameters to make it clear that κ_q, θ_q, and σ_q are parameters of the process for precision q. Precision follows a mean-reverting process correlated with stock returns, with long-term mean equal to θ_q and reversion parameter $\kappa_q > 0$. In order to satisfy standard integrability conditions, Chacko and Viceira assume that $2\kappa_q\theta_q > \sigma_q^2$.

This model of changing risk implies that the ratio of the mean expected excess stock return to the variance of stock returns, which determines the myopic portfolio, is linear in the state variable (precision). However, the Sharpe ratio is not a linear function of the state variable, but a square-root function. Thus, this model is not mathematically equivalent to the model we discussed in Chapter 4 with a linear, mean-reverting process for the expected excess return; that model implies both a linear Sharpe ratio and a linear ratio of mean excess return to variance.

The stochastic process for precision implies a mean-reverting process for instantaneous volatility $v_t = 1/q_t$. The process for v_t can be found by applying Itô's lemma to (5.79):

$$\frac{dv_t}{v_t} = \kappa_v(\theta_v - v_t)dt - \sigma_q\sqrt{v_t}\,dZ_{qt},\tag{5.80}$$

where $\theta_v = 1/(\theta_q - \sigma_q^2/\kappa_q)$ and $\kappa_v = \kappa_q/\theta_v$. Equation (5.80) implies that proportional changes in volatility are correlated with stock returns, with instantaneous correlation

$$\text{Corr}_t\left(\frac{dv_t}{v_t}, \frac{dP_t}{P_t}\right) = -\rho_{Pq}.\tag{5.81}$$

Equation (5.80) can capture the main stylized facts about stock return volatility, in particular its mean-reversion and negative correlation with stock returns. Moreover, proportional changes in volatility are more pronounced in times of high volatility than in times of low volatility. Table 5.1, taken from Chacko and

Table 5.1. Stochastic Volatility Model Estimation

	1926(1)–1997(12)	1871–1997
$\mu_P - r$	0.080	0.084
	(0.024)	(0.037)
κ_q	0.341	0.043
	(0.311)	(0.045)
θ_q	27.709	24.772
	(1.815)	(12.695)
σ_q	0.651	1.179
	(0.486)	(0.707)
ρ_{Pq}	0.536	0.371
	(0.238)	(0.377)

Viceira (1999), shows estimates of (5.77)–(5.80) for US monthly stock returns from January 1926 through December 1997, and annual stock returns for 1871–1997.[4] Standard errors appear in parentheses, and parameter estimates are annualized to facilitate their interpretation.

The estimates in Table 5.1 imply a mean excess stock return of about 8% per year, and an unconditional standard deviation of stock returns of around 20% per year. The instantaneous correlation between shocks to volatility and stock returns ($-\rho_{Pq}$) is negative and relatively large in absolute value—almost -0.54 in the monthly sample and -0.37 in the annual sample. The estimate of the mean-version parameter κ_q implies a half-life for precision of about two years in the monthly sample, and about 16 years in the annual sample. French, Schwert, and Stambaugh (1987) and Campbell and Hentschel (1992) have also found a relatively slow decay rate for volatility shocks in low-frequency data. This slow reversion to the mean in low-frequency data contrasts with the fast decay rate detected in high-frequency data by Andersen, Benzoni, and Lund (1998) and Chacko and Viceira (1998).[5]

We assume that investors' preferences are described by the Duffie–Epstein recursive utility function (5.67)–(5.68), and the intertemporal budget constraint is given by

$$dW_t = [\alpha_t(\mu - r)W_t + rW_t - C_t]\,dt + \alpha_t W_t \sqrt{\frac{1}{q_t}}\,dZ_{Pt}. \qquad (5.82)$$

Chacko and Viceira (1999) present an exact solution for the case with unit elasticity of intertemporal substitution, and an

---

[4] These estimates are obtained using the Spectral Generalized Method of Moments of Chacko and Viceira (1998) and Singleton (2001). This estimation method is essentially a generalized method of moments based on the characteristic function of the stock return process. The source of the monthly data is CRSP, while the source of the annual data is Shiller (1989) and subsequent updates.

[5] Chacko and Viceira (1998) estimate the half-life for precision to be about three months in weekly data for the period 1962–98. These results suggest the presence of both high-frequency and low-frequency components in stock market volatility. They show that a model of multiple additive components in stock return volatility, each one operating at a different frequency, can account for this pattern in the estimates of κ_q when stock returns are sampled at different frequencies.

approximate solution for all other cases. They show that, consistent with the results of Chapter 3 and 4, empirically the effect of intertemporal substitution on the optimal portfolio rule is negligible. Thus, we present only their exact solution with $\psi = 1$. In this case, (5.68) and (5.82) imply the following Bellman equation:

$$0 = \max_{\pi, C} \left\{ f(C, J) + [\alpha(\mu - r)W + rW - C]J_w + \frac{1}{2}\alpha^2 W^2 J_{ww} \frac{1}{q} \right.$$
$$\left. + \kappa_q(\theta_q - q)J_q + \frac{1}{2}\sigma_q^2 J_{qq}q + \rho_{Pq}\sigma_q \alpha W J_{wq} \right\}, \tag{5.83}$$

where $f(C, J)$ is given in (5.68) and subscripts on J denote partial derivatives.

The first-order condition for consumption is identical to (5.83), and the first-order condition for portfolio choice is

$$\alpha_t = \frac{1}{-W J_{ww}/J_w}(\mu - r)q_t - \frac{J_{wq}}{W J_{ww}}\rho_{Pq}\sigma_q q_t. \tag{5.84}$$

Substitution of the first-order conditions into the Bellman equation and a guess for the value function of the form $J(W, q, t) = I(q_t)W_t^{1-\gamma}/(1 - \gamma)$ yield the following ODE:

$$0 = \left(\beta \log \beta - \beta - \frac{\beta\gamma}{1-\gamma}\log(1-\gamma) + \frac{(\mu-r)^2}{2\gamma}q + r \right)$$
$$- \frac{1}{1-\gamma}\beta \log I + \left(\frac{\rho_{Pq}\sigma_q(\mu-r)}{\gamma}q + \frac{\kappa_q}{1-\gamma}(\theta_q - q) \right)\left(\frac{I_q}{I} \right)$$
$$+ \frac{\rho_{Pq}^2\sigma_q^2}{2\gamma}q\left(\frac{I_q}{I} \right)^2 + \frac{\sigma_q^2}{2(1-\gamma)}q\left(\frac{I_{qq}}{I} \right). \tag{5.85}$$

Equation (5.85) has an exact solution of the form $I = \exp(C_0 + C_1 q_t)$ that leads to two algebraic equations for C_0 and C_1 given in Campbell and Viceira (2001b). This solution implies the following optimal portfolio rule:

$$\alpha_t = \frac{1}{\gamma}(\mu - r)q_t + \left(1 - \frac{1}{\gamma} \right)\rho_{Pq}\sigma_q \tilde{C}_1 q_t, \tag{5.86}$$

where $\tilde{C}_1 = C_1/(1 - \gamma) > 0$.

The optimal demand for stocks has two components. As always, the first component is myopic demand, which depends only on the risk premium, risk aversion, and precision or volatility. The second component is intertemporal hedging demand. The sign of this demand depends on the sign of the correlation between unexpected returns and changes in volatility $(-\rho_{Pq})$ and the sign of $(1 - 1/\gamma)$. Table 5.1 shows that empirically the correlation ρ_{Pq} is negative, which implies that investors with $\gamma > 1$ have a negative intertemporal hedging demand for stocks.

Table 5.2 reports the optimal portfolio allocations to stocks implied by the parameter estimates given in Table 5.1. It assumes a rate of time preference (β) equal to 6% annually; when $\psi = 1$, this is also the optimal, constant consumption–wealth ratio. For each sample period the table has two columns. The first column ('Mean') reports the mean percentage allocation to stocks, and the second ('Ratio'), the percentage ratio of the hedging demand to the myopic demand, which is constant in (5.86). This ratio tells us the reduction in portfolio demand that is due to hedging considerations.

The estimated volatility process implies only a small impact of time-varying volatility on the demand for stocks. In the monthly sample intertemporal hedging demand reduces the demand for stocks by at most 3.2%, for highly risk-averse investors with $\gamma = 40$, and in the annual sample the reduction in demand is at most 12%. This impact is relatively modest when compared with the effects of time variation in interest rates or risk premia that we explored in Chapters 3 and 4.

Table 5.2. Mean Optimal Percentage Allocation to Stocks and Percentage Hedging Demand over Myopic Demand

γ	1926(1)–1997(12)		1871–1997	
	Mean	Ratio	Mean	Ratio
1.0	221.4	0.0	208.3	0.0
1.5	145.9	− 1.1	131.9	− 5.1
2.0	108.8	− 1.7	96.8	− 7.1
4.0	54.0	− 2.5	47.0	− 9.7
10	21.5	− 2.9	18.5	− 11.1
20	10.7	− 3.1	9.2	− 11.6
40	5.4	− 3.2	4.6	− 11.8

It is interesting that the annual volatility estimates imply a much larger negative intertemporal hedging demand. The parameters causing this difference must be the mean-reversion parameter κ_q and the correlation between shocks to volatility and stock returns ρ_{pq}, because these are the only parameters whose magnitude is significantly different across samples. The mean-reversion parameter affects the optimal portfolio demand for stocks through the coefficient $\tilde{C}_1$. Chacko and Viceira (1999) show that the absolute size of the hedging demand for stocks is increasing in the persistence of volatility shocks when $\gamma > 1$.

Figure 5.1 and 5.2 illustrate the effects of each parameter on the ratio of hedging demand to myopic demand. Figure 5.1 plots the ratio of hedging demand to myopic demand for values of κ_q implying a half-life of a shock between six months and 30 years,

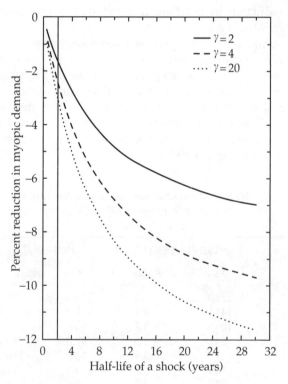

Figure 5.1. Effect of persistence on portfolio demand.

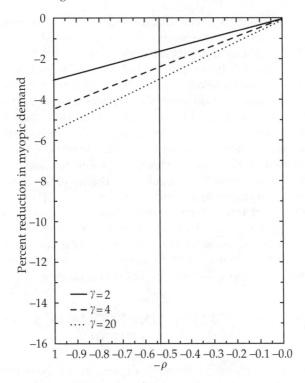

Figure 5.2. Effect of correlation on portfolio demand.

holding constant the other parameters at the values implied by the monthly dataset. Figure 5.2 repeats the experiment, this time varying the correlation coefficient and holding constant the other parameters. The vertical line in each plot intersects the horizontal axis at the parameter value implied by the monthly dataset.

These figures show that hedging demand is more sensitive to the persistence of volatility shocks than to the correlation between volatility shocks and stock returns. Figure 5.1 shows that increasing persistence produces a noticeable reduction in stock demand, even for investors with low coefficients of relative risk aversion. For example, an investor with $\gamma = 4$ would reduce his myopic demand by approximately 10% instead of 2.5% if the half-life of a shock were ten years instead of two years. By contrast, the effect of changing the correlation is much smaller. Even if the correlation between unexpected returns and shocks to volatility were -1, intertemporal hedging would not reduce myopic demand by more than 6% for an investor with $\gamma = 20$.

A limitation of the empirical analysis in this section is that we have assumed constant expected excess stock returns when studying volatility. A fully general model would allow a set of state variables to shift both the equity premium and stock market volatility jointly. As we have noted, hedging demands would then depend on the implied process for the Sharpe ratio. Authors such as Campbell (1987), Harvey (1989, 1991), Glosten, Jagannathan, and Runkle (1993), and Ait-Sahalia and Brandt (2001) have modelled time-varying returns and volatility jointly. These studies typically find that the effects of state variables on expected returns are stronger than their effects on volatility, which suggests that the negative hedging demand associated with volatility risk will be modest even in a framework that combines time-varying volatility with the time-varying returns modelled in Chapter 4.

5.5. PARAMETER UNCERTAINTY AND PORTFOLIO CHOICE

Strategic asset allocation decisions depend on all the parameters of the stochastic process generating asset returns. So far we have assumed that investors know these parameters with certainty, and we have reported illustrative results using parameters estimated from historical data. Of course, we are not certain that the estimated parameter values correctly describe the process generating the data.

If investors share our uncertainty about parameter values, this should affect their portfolio decisions. As investors observe asset returns over time, they will learn more about the true parameter values; anticipating this learning, investors may alter their portfolio decisions today. In this section we briefly consider the impact of learning on portfolio choice, using a simple example taken from Brennan (1998). We can offer only a glimpse of this topic, important early contributions to which include Williams (1977), Detemple (1986), Dothan and Feldman (1986), and Gennotte (1986).

Consider the power utility investor of Section 5.1, except that the investor has a finite horizon T. Investment opportunities are constant, and the investor knows this to be the case. Instantaneous returns on the riskless and risky assets are given by

$$\frac{dB_t}{B_t} = r\,dt$$

and

$$\frac{dP_t}{P_t} = \mu_P\,dt + \sigma_P\,dZ_{Pt}, \tag{5.87}$$

where both the instantaneous expected return μ_P and standard deviation of return σ_P are constants.

In the absence of uncertainty about these parameters, the investor would invest a fraction $\alpha = (\mu_P - r)/\gamma\sigma_P^2$ of his wealth in the risky asset. However, we assume that the investor does not observe μ_P and σ_P, and must estimate them from the data. The investor faces two problems simultaneously: an asset allocation problem, and an inference (or learning) problem. He has prior beliefs about μ_P and σ_P, and updates these beliefs over time as he observes returns.

The process for the risky asset return excludes jumps, implying that P_t follows a continuous path. Merton (1980) pointed out that an observer of a continuous price path can estimate a constant σ_P with arbitrary precision over an arbitrarily short period of calendar time, provided he has access to arbitrarily high-frequency data. Nelson and Foster (1994) extended this result to models in which σ_P is smoothly time-varying. The precision of the estimate of μ_P, by contrast, depends on the length of the sample period rather than the frequency of the data available. Thus, in our setting, where P_t follows a continuous path and the investor observes realized returns at every instant of time, we can safely assume that the investor knows the true value of σ_P but must learn about μ_P.[6]

In order to derive the effects of learning on portfolio choice, we need to be specific about the rules the investor uses to update his

---

[6] In a discrete-time setting, as in Barberis (2000), the investor must also learn about σ. If there is only a single discrete period, as in Bawa, Brown, and Klein (1979), Kandel and Stambaugh (1996), and Pastor (2000), the investor updates his priors only once, so that there is no dynamic learning. In discrete-time models parameter uncertainty increases the risk perceived by an investor over a single period. We ignore this estimation risk here. There is also uncertainty about higher moments of returns in continuous-time models that allow jumps in asset prices (Comon 2001).

prior beliefs about μ_p. It is standard to assume that the investor has a normal prior at time 0, with mean g_0 and variance v_0, and that he uses a Bayesian rule to update his prior as he observes new realizations of the return process. Liptser and Shiryaev (1978) show that under this rule the conditional distribution of μ_p is normal at every point of time, with moments that evolve according to the following differential equations:

$$dg_t = \frac{v_t}{\sigma_p^2} \left(\frac{dP_t}{P_t} - g_t \, dt \right) \tag{5.88}$$

and

$$dv_t = -\frac{v_t^2}{\sigma_p^2} \, dt, \tag{5.89}$$

where g_t and v_t are the conditional expectation and the conditional variance of μ_p given the history of P_t. Gennotte (1986) shows how these equations result from a continuous-time generalization of the formulae for the bivariate conditional mean and variance of a normal distribution.

Equations (5.88) and (5.89) have two important implications for portfolio choice. First, the conditional mean g_t evolves randomly, but the conditional variance v_t does not. v_t is a deterministic function of time, with solution

$$v_t = \frac{v_0 \sigma_p^2}{v_0 t + \sigma_p^2}, \tag{5.90}$$

whose limit as $t \to \infty$ is zero. In this model with constant underlying parameters, the investor eventually learns the true value of μ_p. This means that the effects of learning on portfolio choice are inherently transitional. Earlier in this book we made assumptions, such as infinite investment horizons, that allowed us to derive time-independent portfolio rules; we cannot do this in the present context without making the uninteresting assumption that all learning has already occurred.[7]

---

[7] Of course one can assume that μ_p itself is random, with fixed 'deep parameters' that govern its movements. In this case the investor must still learn about the current value of μ_p no matter how much return history has been observed. See Gennotte (1986).

Second, we can rewrite (5.87) and (5.88) as

$$\frac{dP_t}{P_t} = g_t \, dt + \sigma_P \, dZ_{gt} \tag{5.91}$$

and

$$dg_t = \frac{v_t}{\sigma_P^2} \, dZ_{gt}, \tag{5.92}$$

where $dZ_{gt} = (dP_t/P_t - g_t \, dt)/\sigma_P$ is a Wiener process conditional on the investor's information set, and v_t is given in (5.90). Note that dg_t and dP_t/P_t are perfectly positively correlated.

The investor must make portfolio and consumption decisions at the same time that he is learning about the unobservable parameters of the return generating process. Since he does not observe μ_P, g_t becomes a state variable for the investor's problem. That is, while the true investment opportunity set is constant, the investor sees it as time-varying, with a state variable g_t that is perfectly positively correlated with observed returns.

From the investor's perspective, the value function at time 0 can be written as

$$J(W, g, 0) \equiv \max_{C, \alpha} \mathrm{E}_0 \left[\int_0^T e^{-\beta t} \frac{C_t^{1-\gamma}}{1 - \gamma} dt \right],$$

subject to (5.91), (5.92),

$$dW_t = [(\alpha_t(g_t - r) + r)W_t - C_t]dt + \alpha_t W_t \sigma_P \, dZ_{gt},$$

and the boundary condition $J(W, g, T) = C_T^{1-\gamma}/(1 - \gamma)$. Note that we have substituted g_t for μ_P everywhere. Formally we are now in a model with time-varying expected returns.

We can solve this problem using the dynamic programming approach described in Section 5.1 or, since the state variable is perfectly correlated with the risky asset return, using the martingale approach described in Section 5.2. If we use the dynamic programming approach, we can guess that the value function takes the form

$$J(W, g, t) = H(g_t) \frac{W_t^{1-\gamma}}{1 - \gamma},$$

where the dependence of the value function on time t follows from the dependence of the conditional variance v_t on time. This implies the following first-order condition for portfolio choice:

$$\alpha_t = \frac{g_t - r}{\gamma \sigma_p^2} + \frac{1}{\gamma} \frac{H_g}{H} \frac{v_t}{\sigma_p^2}. \tag{5.93}$$

The first term of (5.93) is the familiar expression for myopic optimal portfolio choice, where g_t is the investor's expectation of the risky asset return. The second term of (5.93) is the intertemporal hedging demand caused by the unobservability of μ_p. This term is zero when $H_g = 0$, that is, when μ_p is known and the investor does not need to learn about it. Brennan (1998) notes that non-satiation in preferences implies $J_g = H_g W^{1-\gamma}/(1 - \gamma) > 0$, so that $H_g < 0$ when $\gamma > 1$. That is, intertemporal hedging demand is negative for investors who are more risk-averse than a log-utility investor.

We can understand the negative intertemporal hedging demand for a conservative investor by noting that a positive realized return leads to an upward revision of the investor's estimate of the expected return—that is, an improvement in perceived investment opportunities. From a conservative investor's perspective this makes the risky asset less attractive, because it delivers wealth in good states when he needs wealth the least. The learning effect is therefore the opposite of the mean-reversion effect discussed in Chapter 4. Learning creates a positive correlation between realized returns and revisions in expected returns, while mean-reversion creates a negative correlation.

Learning about predictability
Brennan's (1998) learning model assumes that investment opportunities are constant, and the investor has only to learn about the long-run mean return on the risky asset. In Chapter 4, however, we presented empirical evidence that there is predictable time variation in the expected excess returns of stocks and long-term bonds. We solved for optimal portfolios assuming that the investor is certain that the estimated processes for returns are the true return-generating processes.

We also noted in Chapter 4 that there is considerable uncertainty about the true predictability of stock returns. Xia (2001) extends Brennan's learning model to incorporate this form of uncertainty. Instead of assuming that the mean risky asset return μ_p is a constant, she models it as a linear function of a state variable S_t:

$$\mu_p(S,t) = \bar{\mu} + \beta(S_t - \bar{S}), \tag{5.94}$$

where $\bar{\mu}$ is known to the investor and β is unobservable. The state variable follows the Ornstein–Uhlenbeck process,

$$dS_t = \kappa(\bar{S} - S_t)\, dt + \sigma_s\, dZ_{st}.$$

Both the continuous history of S_t and the parameters $\bar{S}$, κ and σ_S are known to the investor. The Brownian motions driving the risky asset price and the state variable, dZ_{pt} and dZ_{st}, can be correlated.

When $\beta \neq 0$ the expected risky asset return is a linear function of the state variable S_t, so it follows a mean-reverting process. However, the investor does not know the value of β. In particular, the investor does not know whether this parameter is zero, in which case there is no predictable variation at all in expected returns. This model is fundamentally different from the previous model, because here the investor knows the true long-term mean stock return, but does not know the short-term dynamics of expected returns.

The additional state variable in this model implies that revisions in the investor's estimate of the unknown parameter are no longer perfectly, positively correlated with innovations in stock returns. In fact, they are positively correlated or negatively correlated depending on whether the state variable S_t is above its long-term mean $\bar{S}$ or below. If $S_t > \bar{S}$ and there is an unusually positive realized return, the investor will revise upwards his estimate of the slope coefficient β; but if $S_t < \bar{S}$, an unusually positive realized return will drive down the estimate of β.

Xia (2001) derives the optimal Bayesian learning rules for β, and provides a numerical solution to the model calibrated to monthly US data for the postwar period. We used a dataset similar to this in Chapter 4, and showed that the negative correlation between innovations in the dividend yield and unexpected stock returns leads to a positive intertemporal hedging demand for stocks by conservative investors with risk aversion greater than one. Xia finds that uncertainty about β generates an additional intertemporal hedging term in the demand for stocks whose sign is negative, thus offsetting (wholly or partially) the positive intertemporal term.

The absolute magnitude of this additional term is increasing in the dividend yield. This is because when the dividend yield is high a positive stock return increases the estimate of β, and increases both the expected excess stock return today and the long-run opportunities to profit from predictability; when the dividend yield is below its mean, however, a positive stock return reduces the estimate of β, again increasing the expected excess stock return today but reducing the long-run opportunities to profit from predictability. Thus, learning about predictability generates a larger covariance between stock returns and revisions in expected investment opportunities when the dividend yield is initially high than when it is initially low.

5.6. CONCLUSION

This chapter has examined the solutions to dynamic asset allocation problems in a continuous-time framework. We have linked the approximate solution methodology used in this book to the vast literature on continuous-time portfolio choice.

Continuous-time methods are particularly suitable for modelling time variation in volatility, so this chapter has explored the implications of volatility movements for asset demand. Empirically, increases in stock market volatility tend to persist for some time, and they are often associated with low realized excess stock returns. Short-term investors should respond by reducing the allocation to equities when volatility increases. Long-term investors should go further. The persistence of volatility shocks, and the negative correlation of these shocks with realized excess stock returns, suggest that long-term investors should hedge volatility risk by reducing their allocation to equities. However, shocks to volatility in the US stock market do not seem to be sufficiently persistent and negatively correlated with stock returns to justify a large negative intertemporal hedging portfolio demand for stocks. When compared with the size of intertemporal hedging demands induced by changes in interest rates and risk premia, the negative intertemporal hedging demand created by time-varying risk is relatively modest.

Continuous-time methods also help us understand the effects of parameter uncertainty on portfolio choice. In a continuous-time model with continuous price paths (i.e. where jumps in asset prices are ruled out), investors can be highly confident about the variance and covariances of asset returns if they observe high-frequency data. Thus, parameter uncertainty concerns the means of asset returns rather than their higher moments. If investors use realized returns to update their beliefs about mean returns, positive realized returns will increase expected future mean returns, an effect that is the opposite of the mean-reversion effect discussed in Chapter 4. This generates a negative intertemporal hedging demand that dampens the demand for stocks by conservative investors. Of course, the magnitude of this effect depends on investors' initial uncertainty. In a model with fixed underlying parameters, the learning effect is transitional and will eventually disappear as investors become more and more confident about the true data-generating process.

6

Human Wealth and Financial Wealth

In the first part of this book we have investigated asset allocation strategies under a wide variety of assumptions about available investment opportunities and the ways in which they vary over time. Throughout, we have assumed that investors' wealth consists only of readily tradable financial assets. This is a reasonable assumption for many institutional investors and retired individual investors. It is not, however, a realistic description of individual investors who are working and saving for retirement. These investors own tradable financial assets as part of their total wealth portfolio, but they also own a valuable asset that is not readily tradable. This asset is their human wealth, the expected present discounted value of their future labor earnings.[1]

From the perspective of financial economics, an individual's labor income can be seen as a dividend on the individual's implicit holding of human wealth. Human wealth is a non-tradable asset, because it is difficult or impossible to sell claims against future labor income. The reason is a standard moral hazard problem. Contracts that commit an individual to work are not legally enforceable (since they amount to a form of slavery), and thus an individual always has the legal right to stop working. Having sold a claim against future income, an individual has no incentive to continue working; recognizing this, the buyer of a claim against labor income will understand that the claim is likely to be worthless.

This chapter explores the implications for asset allocation of the non-tradability of human wealth. To motivate the analysis that follows, we begin with a simple case, taken from Bodie, Merton,

---

[1] Human wealth can also be understood more broadly to include the value of privately owned businesses. Proprietorial income from private businesses can be seen as a form of labor income, albeit one that is more risky than income from employment. This point is emphasized by Heaton and Lucas (2000) and is explored further in Chapter 7. Institutions such as universities can also have human wealth in the form of alumni donations.

and Samuelson (1992), that delivers important insights. Consider a long-horizon investor endowed with a riskless stream of labor income. The investor maximizes power utility of consumption and has two assets available for investment: a riskless asset, and risky stocks. The riskless asset has a constant log return r_f per period. Stocks have a risky log return r_{t+1} per period, with constant mean log excess return $E_t(r_{t+1} - r_f) \equiv \mu$ and variance $Var_t(r_{t+1}) \equiv \sigma^2$. We denote by W_t and H_t the investor's financial wealth and human wealth, respectively. The investor's total wealth is $W_t + H_t$.

We have already studied in Chapter 2 the optimal asset allocation for this investor when all wealth is tradable. From that analysis we know that, unconstrained, the investor would sell claims against his human wealth for H_t dollars, and invest $\hat{\alpha}(W_t + H_t)$ dollars of his total wealth in stocks, and the remaining $(1 - \hat{\alpha})(W_t + H_t)$ dollars in the riskless asset, where $\hat{\alpha} = (\mu + \sigma^2/2)/(\gamma\sigma^2)$, and γ is relative risk aversion. Given that the investor is constrained to hold H_t dollars in human wealth, how should he allocate his financial wealth W_t to stocks and the riskless asset? The answer to this question is not difficult once we realize that, because labor income is riskless in this example, human wealth H_t is the present value of all future earnings discounted at the riskless interest rate and is equivalent to an investment in the riskless asset.

Since the investor has implicit holdings of H_t in the riskless asset, he should adjust his financial portfolio so that his total dollar holdings of each asset equal the optimal unconstrained holdings. He can easily do this by investing $\hat{\alpha}(W_t + H_t)$ dollars in stocks, and $(1 - \hat{\alpha})(W_t + H_t) - H_t$ dollars in the riskless asset. The optimal share of stocks in financial wealth is then

$$\alpha = \frac{\hat{\alpha}(W_t + H_t)}{W_t} = \frac{\mu + \sigma^2/2}{\gamma\sigma^2}\left(1 + \frac{H_t}{W_t}\right). \tag{6.1}$$

Equation (6.1) implies that $\alpha \geq \hat{\alpha}$, since H_t and W_t are non-negative.[2] That is, an investor endowed with riskless, non-tradable human wealth should tilt his financial portfolio toward stocks relative to an investor who owns only tradable assets.

---

[2] The assumption that the investor cannot borrow against future labor income ensures that $W_t \geq 0$. However, the optimal dollar holdings of the riskless asset,

The share of stocks in financial wealth is increasing in the ratio of human to financial wealth (H_t/W_t). This ratio changes over the investor's life cycle. At retirement the ratio H_t/W_t is zero. Early in adult life the ratio is typically large, for two reasons: first, the investor expects to receive labor earnings for many years to come so H_t is large; second, he has had little time to accumulate financial wealth so W_t is low. Thus, (6.1) says that, when labor income is riskless, the share of financial wealth invested in stocks should change over the life cycle. A young, employed investor should invest more in stocks than a retired investor with identical risk aversion and financial wealth. This is consistent with the typical recommendations of financial advisors.

The ratio of human to financial wealth also changes with financial asset returns. If the stock market performs well, the investor's financial wealth grows relative to his human wealth. This should lead to a reduction in the share of financial wealth invested in stocks. Thus, this model predicts a 'contrarian' investment strategy that not only rebalances the portfolio regularly, but goes further to reduce the equity share after stocks have performed well.

This simple model with riskless labor income reveals the basic mechanisms that link together human wealth and the optimal allocation of financial assets. However, it ignores some important characteristics of human wealth that complicate the analysis.

First, future labor earnings are uncertain for most investors, making human wealth a risky rather than a safe non-tradable asset. The risk characteristics of human wealth should affect both the allocation of financial assets and the amount saved. In Section 6.1.1 we develop a simple two-period model to illustrate the effect of risky human wealth on asset allocation with fixed saving; in Section 6.2 we extend the model to many periods and endogenize the savings decision. Section 6.1.1 follows Viceira (1998), while Section 6.1.2 is based on Viceira (2001). Heaton and Lucas (1997) and Koo (1998, 1999) consider similar issues.

We focus on two aspects of labor income risk: the variance of labor income, and the correlation of labor income with the returns on risky financial assets. We first consider idiosyncratic labor

---

$(1 - \widehat{\alpha})(W_t + H_t) - H_t$, may be negative when H_t is very large relative to W_t. In that case the investor may want to hold a leveraged position in stocks.

income risk that is uncorrelated with risky asset returns. We show that all investors with labor income, no matter how idiosyncratically risky, should tilt their portfolios towards risky financial assets. As the variance of labor income increases, however, the tilt towards risky assets diminishes. In the limit, as labor income becomes arbitrarily risky, the allocation to risky assets approaches that of a retired investor with no labor income.

A positive correlation between labor income and risky asset returns further reduces the optimal allocation to risky assets. In the extreme case where labor income is perfectly positively correlated with the return on a risky asset, human wealth is an implicit investment in that asset; the investor should compensate by tilting the financial portfolio away from such an asset. This result is relevant for an investor whose labor income is highly correlated with the fortunes of the company he works for. Such an investor should not only avoid holding an undiversified position in his employer's stock, but should actually underweight the company stock relative to an index fund.[3]

A second important characteristic of human wealth is that investors can influence its value by varying how much they work. The ability to vary work effort allows individuals to hold riskier portfolios because they can work harder if they need extra labor income to compensate for losses in their financial portfolios. We study this effect in Section 6.1.2, using a simple two-period model to extend the influential work of Bodie, Merton, and Samuelson (1992) to cases in which labor income risk is idiosyncratic.

We do not try to model some other important characteristics of human wealth. Individuals may choose to invest in their own human wealth, increasing its value through education. They may also have some control over the risk characteristics of their human wealth through their choice of career. These are important research topics at the intersection of financial economics and labor economics that remain relatively unexplored.

This chapter addresses one other issue that is formally related to labor income. We discuss the notion that investors may have

---

[3] Similarly, a university whose alumni donations are highly correlated with returns to the aggregate stock market should hold a more conservative endowment portfolio. A university whose donations are highly correlated with a particular sector, such as technology, should underweight that sector in the endowment portfolio.

minimum required consumption levels that they wish at all costs to support. A natural way to model such a minimum or subsistence level of consumption is to define utility over the difference between consumption and the subsistence level. Rubinstein (1976a,b) explored models with fixed subsistence levels; more recently, there has been great interest in 'habit formation' models with subsistence levels that depend on the past history of consumption and thus evolve through time. A simple way to understand the effect of a subsistence level on asset allocation is to think of the subsistence level as negative labor income. Just as labor income increases the utility that is generated by a given level of financial wealth, so a subsistence level reduces that utility. We make this intuition more precise in Section 6.1.3.

The introduction of labor income significantly complicates the analysis of portfolio choice. In order to keep the analysis tractable, we simplify several other aspects of the problem. First, we are no longer able to work with Epstein–Zin utility but must use the traditional power utility model in which the elasticity of intertemporal substitution is the reciprocal of the coefficient of relative risk aversion. The reason for this is that the Epstein–Zin derivation of the Euler equations, discussed in Chapter 2, assumes that all assets are tradable; the Euler equations are unknown for the case in which some assets are non-tradable. Second, we assume that asset returns are independent and identically distributed (IID), abstracting from the time variation in investment opportunities that was the subject of Chapters 3 and 4. Finally, in this chapter we assume either a single-period investment problem or a stylized infinite-horizon problem in which there is a fixed probability of retirement each period. The investor's effective investment horizon depends on the retirement probability, but the horizon does not shrink over time as it would in a life-cycle model. In the next chapter we move to a life-cycle context and use numerical methods to solve the model.

Much of the literature on income risk makes an alternative simplification by assuming that income risk is normally distributed and that consumers have constant absolute risk aversion (CARA) utility. These two assumptions allow the derivation of exact closed-form solutions for consumption and portfolio choice (Caballero 1990, Svensson and Werner 1993, Davis and Willen 2000). However, the use of CARA utility has important disadvantages. First, it is inconsistent with the stability of risk premia and interest rates in the face of long-term consumption growth unless one arbitrarily introduces a trend in the aggregate risk-bearing capacity of the economy in the manner of Campbell and Kyle (1993).

Second, CARA utility implies that risky asset holdings are independent of wealth. If an investor receives an extra dollar of wealth, he invests the whole dollar in the riskless asset; thus, riskless labor income, or income that is uncorrelated with risky asset returns, has no effect on the risky asset demand of a CARA investor. This is the feature that makes the CARA model so simple to analyze, but it is neither intuitive nor consistent with empirical evidence on household portfolio choice. Because of these difficulties with CARA utility, we continue to assume in this chapter that relative risk aversion, rather than absolute risk aversion, is independent of wealth.

6.1. SINGLE-PERIOD MODELS WITH LABOR INCOME

6.1.1. A model with fixed labor supply

In this section we consider a simple model of portfolio choice with an investment horizon of one period. An investor, endowed with some initial fixed amount of financial wealth W_t, makes a portfolio decision at time t and consumes the liquidation value of his portfolio W_{t+1} plus the realization of a non-negative random variable L_{t+1} ('labor income') one period later.

The conditional distribution of labor income is lognormal, with $l_{t+1} \equiv \log(L_{t+1}) \sim N(l, \sigma_l^2)$. The investor cannot borrow against future labor income and use the proceeds to finance initial investment. Therefore, human wealth is a non-tradable asset. Since the investor receives labor income only at time $t + 1$, human wealth H_t is proportional to $E_t L_{t+1}$.

The investment opportunity set is the same as in our introductory example. There are two assets available for investment: a riskless asset and a risky asset. The riskless asset has a fixed simple return R_f, with $r_f \equiv \log(1 + R_f)$. The risky asset has a random simple return R_{t+1}, with constant expected log excess return $E_t[r_{t+1} - r_f] \equiv \mu$; the unexpected log return on the risky asset, denoted by u_{t+1}, is conditionally normal, with mean zero and variance σ_u^2. The return on the risky asset may be correlated with labor income, with $\text{Cov}_t(l_{t+1}, r_{t+1}) \equiv \sigma_{lu}$. Finally, we assume that the investor is risk-averse, with preferences over consumption described by a standard power utility function with constant relative risk aversion coefficient γ.

The investor's optimization problem is to choose the share of W_t invested in the risky asset (α_t) that maximizes the expected utility of his consumption at the end of the period (C_{t+1}),

$$\max_{\alpha_t} E_t \left[\delta \frac{C_{t+1}^{1-\gamma}}{1-\gamma} \right] \tag{6.2}$$

subject to the budget constraint

$$C_{t+1} = W_t(1 + R_{p,t+1}) + L_{t+1}, \tag{6.3}$$

where

$$R_{p,t+1} = \alpha_t(R_{t+1} - R_f) + R_f. \tag{6.4}$$

This is a simple problem that involves only a portfolio decision—there is no saving decision involved here. Yet no exact analytical solutions are available even in a model as simple as this. Therefore we extend the loglinear solution methods of previous chapters to find an approximate analytical solution.[4]

To compute the log return on wealth, we use the same approximation as in previous chapters (see, e.g. (2.21)):

$$r_{p,t+1} = \alpha_t(r_{t+1} - r_f) + r_f + \tfrac{1}{2}\alpha_t(1 - \alpha_t)\sigma_u^2. \tag{6.5}$$

To derive a loglinear approximation to the budget constraint, we first take logs of (6.3) after dividing both sides of the equation by L_{t+1}. Then we use a first-order Taylor expansion of the log of the right-hand side around the mean log return on wealth

---

[4] Loglinearization is possible in this model because all quantities involved are positive. W_t and L_{t+1} are both positive by assumption, and the form of the utility function implies that the investor will ensure positive C_{t+1}. As in previous chapters, we use a continuous-time approximation to the portfolio return that implies $(1 + R_{p,t+1}) > 0$.

$E[\log(1 + R_{p,t+1})] \equiv r_p$ and the mean log wealth–income ratio $E[\log(W_t/L_{t+1})] \equiv w - l$. This gives

$$c_{t+1} - l_{t+1} = \log[\exp(r_{p,t+1} + w_t - l_{t+1}) + 1]$$
$$\approx k + \rho(w_t + r_{p,t+1} - l_{t+1}), \tag{6.6}$$

where ρ and k denote loglinearization constants and lower-case letters denote variables in logs. The loglinearization constant ρ is given by

$$\rho \equiv \frac{\exp(r_p + w - l)}{1 + \exp(r_p + w - l)} < 1. \tag{6.7}$$

In this single-period problem, the budget constraint (6.6) also describes optimal consumption given the return on the optimal portfolio. Adding l_{t+1} to both sides and rearranging, we have

$$c_{t+1} \approx k + \rho(w_t + r_{p,t+1}) + (1 - \rho)l_{t+1}. \tag{6.8}$$

Log optimal consumption is (up to a constant k) a weighted average of end-of-period log financial wealth $(w_t + r_{p,t+1})$ and log labor income (l_{t+1}), with weights given by ρ and $(1 - \rho)$, respectively. The loglinearization parameter ρ has a natural interpretation as the elasticity of consumption with respect to financial wealth, while $(1 - \rho)$ is the elasticity of consumption with respect to labor income. Because $0 < \rho < 1$, the consumption function is a strictly concave function of financial wealth and labor income.[5]

The elasticity of consumption with respect to financial wealth not only determines the curvature of the consumption function, but also plays a crucial role in the determination of optimal portfolio choice. In fact, it is the link between portfolio choice and consumption. To see this, consider the first-order condition of the problem:

$$E_t[\delta C_{t+1}^{-\gamma}(1 + R_{t+1})] = E_t[\delta C_{t+1}^{-\gamma}(1 + R_f)]. \tag{6.9}$$

---

[5] Carroll and Kimball (1996) have shown that the optimal consumption function must be strictly concave with constant relative risk aversion and labor income uncertainty. See also Koo (1998, 1999).

A second-order Taylor expansion of this equation around the conditional means of c_{t+1} and r_{t+1} gives

$$
\begin{aligned}
E_t(r_{t+1} - r_f) + \tfrac{1}{2}\sigma_t^2 &= \gamma \operatorname{Cov}_t(c_{t+1}, r_{t+1}) \\
&= \gamma \operatorname{Cov}_t\big[k + \rho(w_t + r_{p,t+1}) + (1 - \rho)l_{t+1}, r_{t+1}\big] \\
&= \gamma\big[\rho\alpha_t\sigma_t^2 + (1 - \rho)\operatorname{Cov}_t(l_{t+1}, r_{t+1})\big],
\end{aligned}
\tag{6.10}
$$

where the second line substitutes the consumption function (6.8) into the first line, and the third line substitutes the log return on wealth $r_{p,t+1}$ as given by (6.5) into the second line.

Solving (6.10) for the portfolio rule, we obtain

$$
\alpha_t = \frac{1}{\rho}\left(\frac{\mu + \sigma_u^2/2}{\gamma\sigma_u^2}\right) + \left(1 - \frac{1}{\rho}\right)\left(\frac{\sigma_{lu}}{\sigma_u^2}\right),
\tag{6.11}
$$

where we have substituted in the moments of returns and labor income.

The optimal allocation to the risky asset has two components. The first describes the optimal allocation when labor income risk is idiosyncratic, that is, uncorrelated with the risky asset. This component is inversely proportional to the wealth elasticity of consumption ρ.

The second component of (6.11) is an income hedging component. The desirability of the risky asset depends not only on its expected excess return relative to its variance, but also on its ability to hedge consumption against a bad realization of labor income. If the covariance between the risky asset return and labor income is negative, then the risky asset offers a good hedge against negative income shocks, and this increases the optimal allocation. This component of risky asset demand is proportional to $(1 - 1/\rho)$.

When labor income risk is idiosyncratic ($\sigma_{lu} = 0$), the second component of (6.11) is zero and we are left with the first component, $\alpha_t = (\mu + \sigma_u^2/2)/(\rho\gamma\sigma_u^2)$. Since $0 < \rho < 1$, we have that $\alpha_t > (\mu + \sigma_u^2/2)/(\gamma\sigma_u^2)$. The right-hand side of this inequality is the optimal share of the risky asset in the portfolio of an investor without labor income, whose wealth is entirely tradable. Thus, the result we obtained in our introductory example with riskless labor income carries over to the case in which labor income is risky, provided that labor income risk is idiosyncratic. That is, the optimal risky asset allocation is larger than the optimal allocation of an investor whose wealth is entirely tradable.

Another way to understand this result is to note that (6.7) implies

$$
\begin{aligned}
\frac{1}{\rho} &= 1 + \frac{1}{\exp(w + r_p - l)} \\
&= 1 + \frac{\exp(l)}{\exp(w + r_p)} \\
&\equiv 1 + \overline{H/W}.
\end{aligned} \tag{6.12}
$$

Substitution into (6.11) shows that the optimal portfolio with idiosyncratic labor income resembles the optimal portfolio with riskless labor income given in (6.1). In fact, the expression for α_t in (6.11) with $\sigma_{lu} = 0$ approaches (6.1) as the variance of income diminishes and the time interval shrinks.[6]

The effect of increasing labor income risk
We have shown that a single-period investor with idiosyncratically risky labor income should always hold more risky assets than an investor without labor income. We now ask how an uncompensated increase in idiosyncratic labor income risk affects portfolio choice. Because human wealth is non-tradable, investors cannot diversify away their labor income risk. There is an extensive theoretical literature that explores the effects of unavoidable 'background' risk on portfolio choice. This literature derives conditions under which investors should reduce their exposure to financial risk when there is an uncompensated increase in background risk. These conditions are quite general, and should hold in most empirically relevant cases.[7]

---

[6] In that case the value of human capital is just equal to labor income, i.e. $H_t = L_{t+1}$. Thus, $\exp(l) = L_{t+1}$. If the time interval is very short, then $\exp(r_p)$ will be small, and $W_t \exp(r_p) \approx W_t$. Therefore, $1/\rho \approx 1 + H_t/W_t$. Bodie, Merton, and Samuelson (1992) work in continuous time and consider this case.

[7] See Eeckhoudt, Gollier, and Schlesinger (1996), Elmendorf and Kimball (2000), Gollier and Pratt (1996), Kimball (1993), Koo (1998, 1999), and Pratt and Zeckhauser (1987).

Our two-period model with power utility and lognormal income risk illustrates this result. We start by defining an uncompensated increase in labor income risk as a mean-preserving increase in the variance of labor income. We continue to assume that labor income is uncorrelated with the return on stocks. We want to determine the effect of increasing risk on the optimal allocation to stocks α_t.

The lognormality of labor income implies that

$$E_t(L_{t+1}) = \exp\left(l + \tfrac{1}{2}\sigma_l^2\right) \equiv L, \tag{6.13}$$

and

$$\text{Var}_t(L_{t+1}) = \exp(2l + \sigma_l^2)[\exp(\sigma_l^2) - 1] \equiv \sigma_L^2. \tag{6.14}$$

Equation (6.14) implies that an increase in the variance of log labor income σ_l^2 is equivalent to an increase in the variance of labor income σ_L^2, since σ_L^2 is a positive monotone function of σ_l^2. We will focus on σ_l^2 instead of σ_L^2 for mathematical convenience. Equation (6.13) shows that an increase in σ_l^2 implies an increase in expected labor income L, unless it is compensated by a reduction in the mean of log labor income l. Thus, a mean-preserving increase in the variance of L_t defines an implicit linear relation between l and σ_l^2:

$$l = \log L - \frac{\sigma_l^2}{2}. \tag{6.15}$$

Our objective is to determine the sign of the total derivative $d\alpha_t/d\sigma_l^2$, subject to (6.15). The solution (6.11) with idiosyncratic labor income risk can be written as

$$\alpha_t = \frac{1}{\rho(l, r_p)} \left(\frac{\mu + \sigma_u^2/2}{\gamma\sigma_u^2} \right). \tag{6.16}$$

This shows that α_t does not depend directly on σ_l^2. However, it depends on σ_l^2 through ρ, the wealth elasticity of consumption; (6.7) shows that ρ is a function of both l and r_p, and the mean-preserving constraint (6.15) defines a linear relation between l and σ_l^2. Also, r_p is a function of α_t.

Using the chain rule of differentiation we have that

$$\frac{d\alpha_t}{d\sigma_l^2} = \frac{d\alpha_t}{d\rho}\frac{d\rho}{d\sigma_l^2}$$

$$= \frac{d\alpha_t}{d\rho}\left(\frac{\partial\rho}{\partial l}\frac{dl}{d\sigma_l^2} + \frac{\partial\rho}{\partial r_p}\frac{\partial r_p}{\partial\alpha_t}\frac{d\alpha_t}{d\sigma_l^2}\right). \tag{6.17}$$

Therefore, the total derivative of α_t with respect to a mean-preserving spread in σ_l^2 equals

$$\frac{d\alpha_t}{d\sigma_l^2} = \frac{-\frac{1}{2}(d\alpha_t/d\rho)(\partial\rho/\partial l)}{1 - (d\alpha_t/d\rho)(\partial\rho/\partial r_p)(\partial r_p/\partial\alpha_t)}, \tag{6.18}$$

where we have substituted in $dl/d\sigma_l^2 = -1/2$.

A sufficient condition for $d\alpha_t/d\sigma_l^2$ in (6.18) to be negative is that $\partial r_p/\partial\alpha_t > 0.$[8] But from (6.5)

$$\frac{\partial r_p}{\partial\alpha_t} = \left(\mu + \frac{1}{2}\sigma_u^2\right)\left(1 - \frac{1}{\rho\gamma}\right), \tag{6.19}$$

so $\partial r_p/\partial\alpha_t > 0$ if $\gamma > (1/\rho) > 1$. To understand this result, note that an investor with $\gamma = 1/\rho$ holds the growth-optimal portfolio with the highest average log return. Any more conservative investor has a lower allocation to stocks than the growth-optimal portfolio, and hence his log portfolio return increases with α_t. We conclude that sufficiently conservative investors (with risk aversion greater than $1/\rho$) should reduce their portfolio exposure to risky assets when there is a mean-preserving increase in the variance of labor income.[9]

---

[8] This is easy to show using the expressions for α_t, ρ, and l in (6.16), (6.7), and (6.15). First, note that $d\alpha_t/d\rho = -\rho^{-1}\alpha_t < 0$, and $\partial\rho/\partial l = -\rho/\exp(r_p + w - l) < 0$. Therefore, the numerator of $d\alpha_t/d\sigma_l^2$ is always negative. Second, we also have $d\alpha_t/d\rho < 0$, and $\partial\rho/\partial r_p = \rho/\exp(r_p + w - l) > 0$ in the denominator. This implies that $\partial r_p/\partial\alpha_t > 0$ is sufficient for the denominator of $d\alpha_t/d\sigma_l^2$ to be positive, and the derivative itself to be negative.

[9] This result is consistent with the analysis of Eeckhoudt, Gollier, and Schlesinger (1996). Stronger results are possible if there is an upper bound on labor income or if the increase in labor income risk takes other forms. For example, if the increase in labor income risk takes the form of adding a zero-mean risk statistically independent of financial risk, Gollier and Pratt (1996) show that power utility—in fact, any utility function in the HARA class—is sufficient for $d\alpha_t/d\sigma_y^2 < 0$ to obtain. Pratt and Zeckhauser (1987) and Kimball (1993) obtain similar results when the increase in labor income risk takes the form of adding a lottery with strictly negative payoffs, or adding a lottery that increases the marginal utility of wealth, respectively.

6.1.2. *Flexible labor supply*

So far we have assumed that labor supply is fixed. The investor cannot vary work effort in response to conditions, but must accept whatever random stream of labor income is given to him.

Bodie, Merton, and Samuelson (1992) emphasize that the ability to adjust labor supply further increases an investor's willingness to take on financial risk. If an investor can respond to adverse circumstances by increasing work effort as well as by reducing consumption, the investor has two margins of adjustment rather than one and is more tolerant of financial risk.

We illustrate Bodie *et al.*'s important point using a single-period model with separable utility over consumption and leisure:

$$U(C_{t+1}, N_{t+1}) = \frac{C_{t+1}^{1-\gamma}}{1-\gamma} + \theta \frac{(1-N_{t+1})^{1-\lambda}}{1-\lambda}. \tag{6.20}$$

Here C_{t+1} is consumption and $(1 - N_{t+1}) \leq 1$ is leisure time at date $t + 1$. We have normalized the investor's time endowment per period to one, and N_{t+1} is the fraction of this time that the investor spends at work. The curvature parameter λ measures the investor's reluctance to vary labor supply in response to incentives, while the scale parameter θ measures the overall weight of leisure versus consumption in determining utility. This parameter determines the average level of labor supply.

Macroeconomists have noted that the utility specification (6.20) is consistent with balanced growth, that is, with constant labor supply in the face of steady growth in consumption, only if $\gamma = 1$ (King, Plosser, and Rebelo 1988). Balanced growth is often thought to be a desirable property of a macroeconomic model, for the same reasons that have led us to use utility functions that are consistent with constant interest rates and risk premia in the face of consumption growth. It is unappealing to impose the restriction $\gamma = 1$, for reasons we have explored earlier in the book. However, we can get around this problem by assuming technological progress in leisure as well as in production; this is equivalent to introducing a trend in the parameter θ. Campbell and Ludvigson (2001) develop this point in detail. Here we ignore long-run growth and proceed to work with (6.20) allowing a free parameter γ.[10]

We assume that labor supply is chosen at time $t+1$. The static first-order condition for labor supply is that the marginal disutility of labor equals the real wage Z_{t+1} times the marginal utility of consumption:

$$\theta(1 - N_{t+1})^{-\lambda} = Z_{t+1}C_{t+1}^{-\gamma}. \tag{6.21}$$

To make the model tractable, we must loglinearize this first-order condition. Taking logs, approximating in our standard fashion, and rearranging, we get

$$n_{t+1} = \nu(z_{t+1} - \gamma c_{t+1} - k), \tag{6.22}$$

where ν is the elasticity of labor supply with respect to the real wage and k is a constant term. The elasticity $\nu \equiv \lambda N/(1 - N)$, where $N \equiv \exp(n)$ and n is the mean level of log labor supply.

The analysis of the rest of the model is very similar to that for the fixed-labor case. Labor income equals the real wage times labor supply, $L_{t+1} = Z_{t+1}N_{t+1}$, but otherwise our previous analysis of income risk remains valid. In particular, we still have the loglinear approximation of the budget constraint (6.8),

$$c_{t+1} = k + \rho(w_t + r_{p,t+1}) + (1 - \rho)l_{t+1}.$$

We can choose the parameter θ so that average income is the same as in the fixed-labor case; thus, there need be no change in ρ.

Substituting in for log output, $l_{t+1} = z_{t+1} + n_{t+1}$, and using (6.22) to substitute out n_{t+1}, we get

$$c_{t+1} = k^* + \beta_w(w_t + r_{p,t+1}) + \beta_z z_{t+1}, \tag{6.23}$$

where k^* is a constant and the coefficients β_w and β_z are given by

$$\beta_w = \frac{\rho}{1 + (1 - \rho)\gamma\nu} \tag{6.24}$$

---

[10] An alternative approach, advocated by Basu and Kimball (2000), is to assume a utility function that is non-separable across consumption and leisure. Chan (2000) explores portfolio choice in a non-separable model.

and

$$\beta_z = \frac{(1 - \rho)(1 + \nu)}{1 + (1 - \rho)\gamma\nu}.$$ (6.25)

As ν goes to zero, the agent becomes infinitely unwilling to adjust labor supply, and we get the previous fixed-labor case where $\beta_w = \rho$ and $\beta_z = (1 - \rho)$. As ν goes to infinity, labor supply becomes infinitely elastic, and we get $\beta_w = 0$ and $\beta_z = 1/\gamma$. In all cases, $0 \le \beta_w \le \rho$ and $\beta_z \ge 0$.[11]

Because the envelope condition holds, we know that the marginal utility of a dollar at time $t + 1$ equals the marginal utility of consuming that dollar. Separability implies that marginal utility takes the same form as in the fixed labor case. Thus we still have (6.9),

$$E_t[\delta C_{t+1}^{-\gamma}(1 + R_{t+1})] = E_t[\delta C_{t+1}^{-\gamma}(1 + R_f)].$$

A second-order Taylor expansion of this equation around the conditional means of c_{t+1} and r_{t+1} gives

$$\begin{aligned}
E_t(r_{t+1} - r_f) + \tfrac{1}{2}\sigma_t^2 &= \gamma \mathrm{Cov}_t(c_{t+1}, r_{t+1}) \\
&= \gamma \mathrm{Cov}_t[k^* + \beta_w(w_t + r_{p,t+1}) + \beta_z z_{t+1}, r_{t+1}] \\
&= \gamma[\beta_w \alpha_t \sigma_t^2 + \beta_z \mathrm{Cov}_t(z_{t+1}, r_{t+1})].
\end{aligned}$$ (6.26)

This implies the following portfolio rule:

$$\alpha_t = \frac{1}{\beta_w}\left(\frac{\mu + \sigma_u^2/2}{\gamma\sigma_u^2}\right) - \frac{\beta_z}{\beta_w}\left(\frac{\sigma_{uz}}{\sigma_u^2}\right).$$ (6.27)

Comparing the first term of this equation with the equivalent term in the fixed labor supply solution (6.11), and recalling that $\beta_w \le \rho$, we see that the ability to adjust labor supply increases the portfolio share in the risky asset if wages are uncorrelated with risky asset returns. As the elasticity of labor supply increases, the portfolio share in the risky asset increases without limit since β_w approaches zero.

---

[11] The sum $\beta_w + \beta_z = 1$ only if relative risk aversion $\gamma = 1$. This is the condition for balanced growth noted earlier.

The sensitivity of the portfolio allocation to a correlation of wages with risky asset returns is also increasing in the elasticity of labor supply. In the fixed labor model with $\nu = 0$, the coefficient $-\beta_z/\beta_w = -(1 - \rho)/\rho$; this coefficient becomes increasingly negative as ν increases, approaching negative infinity as ν goes to infinity. Investors with flexible labor supply are particularly anxious to hedge wage risk, since they respond to wage fluctuations by changing their work effort, and therefore wage shocks have particularly large effects on their labor income.

6.1.3. Asset allocation with a subsistence level

Throughout this book we have assumed that investors judge their well-being by reference to the absolute level of their consumption. An alternative view is that investors regard a large part of their consumption as necessary for subsistence and derive utility only from the excess of consumption above the subsistence level. An early proponent of this view was Mark Rubinstein (1976a,b), who worked with models in which the subsistence level is constant over time. Rubinstein pointed out that long-term investors would use long-term annuities to finance their subsistence needs; thus, he was one of the first to show that long-term inflation-indexed bonds are the riskless asset for long-term investors.

Models with constant subsistence levels have the difficulty that subsistence becomes increasingly irrelevant as consumption grows over time. More recently, there has been great interest in 'habit formation' models in which the subsistence level grows along with consumption. Models of 'internal habit formation' such as Sundaresan (1989) and Constantinides (1990) have the subsistence level depend on the past history of an individual's own consumption, while models of 'external habit formation' such as Abel (1990) and Campbell and Cochrane (1999) make it depend on the past history of aggregate consumption; in the former case the subsistence level is affected by an individual's own decisions, while in the latter case it is not.[12]

Formally, a subsistence level can be treated as negative labor income. Just as labor income provides extra resources to generate

---

[12] Habit formation models have a long earlier history, including the work of Ryder and Heal (1973) and the 'relative income hypothesis' of Duesenberry (1949) which anticipates the idea of external habit formation.

utility beyond those of financial wealth, so subsistence needs drain resources and leave only part of financial wealth available to generate utility. The subsistence level is a non-tradable liability just as labor income is a non-tradable asset. Thus, it is natural for us to consider subsistence models at this point in the book.

To see the formal analogy between labor income and subsistence needs, consider a single-period model with a utility function that is power in the surplus of consumption over subsistence X:

$$U(C_{t+1}, X_{t+1}) = \frac{(C_{t+1} - X_{t+1})^{1-\gamma}}{1 - \gamma}. \tag{6.28}$$

The problem is to maximize utility subject to the usual single-period budget constraint without labor income:

$$C_{t+1} = W_{t+1} = (1 + R_{p,t+1})W_t. \tag{6.29}$$

This model can be transformed by defining surplus consumption $C^*_{t+1} = C_{t+1} - X_{t+1}$. Then the problem is to maximize power utility of surplus consumption subject to the budget constraint

$$C^*_{t+1} = (1 + R_{p,t+1})W_t - X_{t+1}. \tag{6.30}$$

This is exactly the same as the single-period problem with labor income, except that it is the negative term $-X_{t+1}$ that appears in the budget constraint rather than the positive term L_{t+1}.

The fact that the extra term in the budget constraint is negative limits the conditions under which this problem has a solution. It is essential that the investor should have assets available that guarantee that his wealth next period will at least equal X_{t+1}. In the case where X_{t+1} is a constant, this just requires that a riskless real asset be available. In that case the investor solves the problem by investing the discounted value of subsistence, $X_{t+1}/(1 + R_f)$, in the riskless asset, and investing the surplus wealth $W_t - X_{t+1}/(1 + R_f)$ using the standard formula for power utility developed in Chapter 2. Thus, if $\hat{\alpha}$ is the share of surplus wealth invested in stocks, the share of total wealth in stocks is

$$\begin{aligned}
\alpha &= \hat{\alpha} \frac{W_t - X_{t+1}/(1 + R_f)}{W_t} \\
&= \left(\frac{\mu + \sigma_u^2/2}{\gamma \sigma_u^2}\right)\left(1 - \frac{X_{t+1}/(1 + R_f)}{W_t}\right).
\end{aligned} \tag{6.31}$$

This allocation of financial wealth to stocks is always smaller than the allocation of an investor who does not have a subsistence level. Also, it increases with wealth; thus, an investor with a subsistence level buys stocks as prices rise and sells them as prices fall.

These results are the opposite of the behavior predicted for an investor with labor income, consistent with the intuition that a subsistence level is like negative labor income. There is a related literature that explores optimal investment strategies for investors who require that their wealth always exceed a certain minimum level (Cox and Leland 1982; Brennan and Schwartz 1988; Grossman and Zhou 1996). Such 'portfolio insurance' strategies share the property that the allocation to risky assets declines as prices fall.

The subsistence model can also be analyzed using the loglinear approximate approach that we developed earlier. This allows us to relax the assumption that the subsistence level is a constant known in advance. The loglinear approximation of (6.30) is

$$c^*_{t+1} = \eta(w_t + r_{p,t+1}) + (1 - \eta)x_{t+1}, \tag{6.32}$$

so log surplus consumption is a linear combination of log financial wealth and log habit. The parameter η is given by

$$\eta = \frac{\exp(w + r_p - x)}{\exp(w + r_p - x) - 1} = \frac{W}{W - X/(1 + R_p)}, \tag{6.33}$$

the ratio of total wealth to surplus wealth. Since $\eta > 1$, surplus consumption responds more than proportionally to portfolio returns.

This approximation leads to the portfolio solution

$$\alpha_t = \frac{1}{\eta}\left(\frac{\mu + \sigma_u^2/2}{\gamma\sigma_u^2}\right) + \left(1 - \frac{1}{\eta}\right)\left(\frac{\sigma_{ux}}{\sigma_u^2}\right), \tag{6.34}$$

where σ_{ux} is the covariance between the risky asset return and the subsistence level. If the subsistence level is constant, the allocation to the risky asset is smaller than in the power utility case. If the subsistence level is positively correlated with the risky asset return, however, the allocation to the risky asset may increase above the power utility level.

In applying this approach, one must be careful to specify the model so that the investor can guarantee that his subsistence needs are met. Subsistence levels can be random only if they are driven exclusively by risky returns and thus can be perfectly hedged by the investor.

These results can be extended to a multi-period setting in which subsistence levels move over time with the path of consumption. Constantinides (1990), for example, analyzes an infinite-horizon model, set in continuous time, with power utility of surplus consumption. Lax (2000) adds a finite horizon and compares discrete-time and continuous-time versions of the model. In Lax's specification, the subsistence level evolves according to

$$X_{t+1} = \phi_1 C_t + \phi_2 X_t = \phi_1 \sum_{i=0}^{t-1} \phi_2^i C_{t-i} + \phi_2^{t+1} X_0. \tag{6.35}$$

Thus, the subsistence level at time $t+1$ is known at time t once consumption C_t has been determined.

This problem can be solved only if the investor has a minimum level of wealth, equal to the present value of current and all future subsistence levels under the assumption that surplus consumption is zero today and in the future. If the investor has more wealth than this, Lax (2000) interprets the portfolio solution as follows. Having chosen current consumption, the investor calculates the present value of all future subsistence levels assuming that surplus consumption is zero in all future periods. This amount is set aside in the riskless asset, and the remainder of invested wealth is allocated using the standard formula for power utility.[13]

This solution can be used to explore horizon effects on portfolio choice. Consider two investors with the same current subsistence level and the same wealth, but different investment horizons. Given equal current consumption for both investors, the present

---

[13] Dybvig (1995) analyzes a model in which investors derive utility from total consumption, subject to the constraint that consumption can never fall, and obtains a somewhat similar solution in which consumption increases whenever wealth reaches a new maximum, and risky investment is proportional to the surplus of wealth over the amount necessary to sustain current consumption forever.

value of future subsistence levels is higher for the investor with a longer horizon; this forces the long-horizon investor to set aside more wealth in the riskless asset to meet subsistence needs, giving the long-horizon investor a more conservative portfolio as emphasized by Samuelson (1989). Lax (2000) points out that there is a second, offsetting effect. The long-horizon investor will consume a smaller fraction of wealth today, reducing the present value of his future subsistence levels and tilting his overall portfolio toward risky assets. However, this second effect diminishes as the time interval shrinks, since the current consumption flow shrinks relative to wealth or the present value of all subsistence levels; in the limit of continuous time, the second effect disappears altogether. Thus, the Samuelson (1989) effect is the robust prediction of this model.

It is tempting to use these results to explain age patterns in portfolio choice. However, there are pitfalls in doing so. First, subsistence levels themselves may vary systematically with age. This may happen endogenously through the dynamics implied by (6.35). If young investors start life with very low subsistence levels, their subsistence levels will tend to rise over time relative to wealth, tilting their portfolios even further toward safe assets. On the other hand, if investors start life with very high subsistence levels relative to wealth, their subsistence levels will tend to fall over time relative to wealth and their portfolios may tilt toward risky assets. Alternatively, there may be pure age effects on subsistence levels, analogous to the age effects on labor income documented in Chapter 7.

Second, these results depend critically on the assumption that subsistence levels are determined by the history of an investor's own consumption. An alternative view is that subsistence levels are driven by the dynamics of aggregate consumption, as investors seek to catch up with the living standards of society as a whole ('catching up with the Joneses', in Abel's (1990) terminology). On this view, the portfolio that is required to meet subsistence needs will consist partly of the riskless asset, to support subsistence needs that have already been determined by past levels of aggregate consumption, and partly of the aggregate wealth portfolio, to support subsistence needs that will arise from future realizations of aggregate consumption. Shore and White (2001) explore a model of this sort.

6.2. LABOR INCOME, PRECAUTIONARY SAVINGS, AND LONG-HORIZON PORTFOLIO CHOICE

In Section 6.1 we developed a single-period model to help us understand some of the complex effects of human wealth on financial portfolio allocation. Because of its static nature, however, this model does not allow us to analyze dynamic aspects of the problem, such as the interaction of saving and portfolio decisions or the effect of retirement horizons on portfolio choice. Following Viceira (2001), this section extends the single-period model of Section 6.1 to a multi-period setting.

We consider an investor who maximizes the expectation of power utility of consumption over an infinite horizon. The use of an infinite horizon is analytically convenient because it implies time-invariant decision rules. We can explore retirement horizon effects in this stationary model by assuming that, each period, there is a positive probability π^r that the investor retires. We define retirement as a permanent zero-labor income state. If this state occurs, labor income is set to zero for ever; otherwise, with probability $\pi^e = 1 - \pi^r$ the investor receives a realization of a labor income process L_t. One can show that the expected time till retirement is $1/\pi^r$ so this is the investor's effective retirement horizon. Similarly, we assume that after retirement the investor may die with probability π^d each period, so $1/\pi^d$ is the investor's expected lifetime after retirement. Blanchard (1985) and Gertler (1999) have used this probabilistic device to capture horizon effects on decision-making, while preserving the analytical advantages of an infinite-horizon model. In Chapter 7 we consider a more realistic but less tractable life-cycle model with a finite horizon.

To describe the investor's human wealth in this dynamic setting, we need to specify the process for labor income. We assume that labor income is subject only to permanent, multiplicative shocks, and that expected labor income growth is constant. Thus, labor income growth Δl_{t+1} is described by

$$\Delta l_{t+1} = g + \xi_{t+1}, \tag{6.36}$$

where ξ_{t+1} is a normally distributed shock with mean zero and variance σ_ξ^2.

Microeconomic studies have found that individuals' labor income is subject to both permanent and transitory shocks, and that the rate of labor income growth changes over the life cycle (MaCurdy 1982; Abowd and Card 1989; Carroll 1992). Carroll (1997) has shown that transitory income shocks have important effects on precautionary savings decisions; however, Viceira (1998) and Letendre and Smith (2001) find that they have a small impact on portfolio choice. Accordingly, we ignore transitory shocks here to keep notation as simple as possible. In the life-cycle model of Chapter 7, we allow for transitory income shocks and relax the assumption that expected labor income growth is constant.

We make the same assumptions as in Section 6.1 regarding the assets available for investment and their returns. Thus, the riskless asset has a constant log return r_f, and the risky asset has a log return r_{t+1} with constant mean log excess return μ and variance σ_u^2. The unexpected return on the risky asset can be contemporaneously correlated with shocks to log labor income growth:

$$\text{Cov}_t(r_{t+1}, \Delta l_{t+1}) = \text{Cov}_t(u_{t+1}, \xi_{t+1}) = \sigma_{u\xi}. \tag{6.37}$$

The intertemporal optimization problem
Using the assumptions above, we can write the investor's intertemporal optimization problem as

$$\max_{(C_{t+i}, \alpha_{t+i})_{i=0}^{\infty}} \text{E}_t \sum_{i=0}^{\infty} \delta^i \frac{C_{t+i}^{1-\gamma}}{1-\gamma}, \tag{6.38}$$

subject to the intertemporal budget constraint

$$W_{t+1} = (W_t + L_t - C_t)(1 + R_{p,t+1}), \tag{6.39}$$

where $(W_t + L_t - C_t)$ is savings, defined as the value of financial assets held at time t after receiving a realization of labor income and subtracting consumption for that period, and $R_{p,t+1}$ is the simple net return on the investor's portfolio, given in (6.4).

Depending on the realized state for L_t, there are two possible sets of Euler equations for this intertemporal optimization problem. For each asset i in the employed state,

$$1 = E_t\left\{\left[\pi^e\delta\left(\frac{C_{t+1}^e}{C_t^e}\right)^{-\gamma} + (1-\pi^e)(1-\pi^d)\delta\left(\frac{C_{t+1}^r}{C_t^e}\right)^{-\gamma}\right]\right.$$
$$\left. \times (1+R_{i,t+1})\right\}, \tag{6.40}$$

and in the retired state,

$$1 = E_t\left[(1-\pi^d)\delta\left(\frac{C_{t+1}^r}{C_t^r}\right)^{-\gamma}(1+R_{i,t+1})\right]. \tag{6.41}$$

The finite expected lifetime after retirement effectively reduces the investor's discount factor in the retired state. Throughout this section, a superscript e or r on a variable denotes the labor income state that determines the value of that variable.[14]

Retired investors
The Euler equation (6.40) shows that optimal consumption and portfolio policies in the employed state depend on the optimal policies in the retired state. There is no feedback, however, from the employed state to the retired state. Thus, we first solve for the optimal policies of retired investors, and then use these to derive the optimal policies of employed investors.

The retired investor's problem is relatively simple, and we have already studied it in Section 2.2.3. The retired investor has power utility, constant investment opportunities, and only financial wealth. The exact analytical solution (up to the discrete-time approximation to the log return on wealth) can be written as

$$c_t^r = b_0^r + b_1^r w_t \tag{6.42}$$

and

$$\alpha^r = \frac{\mu + \sigma_u^2/2}{\gamma b_1^r \sigma_u^2}, \tag{6.43}$$

where $b_1^r = 1$ and b_0^r is a constant given in Campbell and Viceira (2001b).

---

[14] For some variables the timing of the variable subscript and the timing of the superscript are different. For example, the return on financial wealth at time $t+1$ depends on the portfolio decisions made at time t, so $R_{p,t+1}$ depends on the realized state for labor income at t.

Equations (6.42) and (6.43) are equivalent to (2.44) and (2.25), except that we make explicit the dependence of the optimal consumption and portfolio rules on b_1^r, the wealth elasticity of consumption. The wealth elasticity of consumption gives the percentage effect on consumption of a 1% change in financial wealth. For retired investors this elasticity is exactly one, implying that the consumption–wealth ratio for these investors is independent of wealth.

The wealth elasticity of consumption also affects optimal portfolio choice. Equation (6.43) shows that α^r is inversely proportional to γb_1^r. This product measures relative risk aversion with respect to optimally invested wealth.[15] Because the wealth elasticity of consumption is one in the retirement state, retired investors' relative risk aversion with respect to wealth is equal to their relative risk aversion with respect to consumption. However, we show next that the wealth elasticity of consumption is less than one in the employment state, implying that employed investors are less risk-averse with respect to wealth than are retired investors with similar preferences over consumption.

Employed investors
There is no exact closed-form solution for the employed investor's intertemporal choice problem. However, Viceira (2001) finds an approximate analytical solution using a loglinearization procedure similar to the one in Section 6.1. The solution uses the fact that employed investors have a target wealth–income ratio; if wealth falls below the target, they increase saving and gradually restore wealth to the target level, whereas if wealth increases above the target, they reduce saving and again restore wealth to the target level. The solution fixes the wealth elasticity of consumption at the level implied by the target wealth–income ratio. This gives portfolio allocations that are constant over time and do not respond to unexpected stock returns.

---

[15] This result is easiest to show using continuous-time mathematics. It follows immediately from the first-order condition (5.10), $J_W = U_C$. This equation implies $-J_{WW}/J_W = -(U_{CC}/U_C)C_W$, or $-J_{WW}W/J_W = -(U_{CC}C/U_C)(C_W W/C) = \gamma b_1$.

The approximate consumption and portfolio rules for employed investors can be written as follows:

$$c_t^e = b_0^e + b_1^e w_t + (1 - b_1^e)l_t, \tag{6.44}$$

and

$$\alpha^e = \left(\frac{\mu + \sigma_u^2/2}{\gamma \bar{b}_1 \sigma_u^2}\right) - \left(\frac{\pi^e(1 - b_1^e)}{\bar{b}_1}\right)\left(\frac{\sigma_{\xi u}}{\sigma_u^2}\right), \tag{6.45}$$

where

$$0 < b_1^e < 1, \qquad \bar{b}_1 = \pi^e b_1^e + (1 - \pi^e)b_1^r, \tag{6.46}$$

and b_0^e is a constant given in Campbell and Viceira (2001b).

The consumption and portfolio rules for employed investors take the same form as in the single-period model of Section 6.1.1, with (6.44) and (6.45) corresponding to (6.8) and (6.11). The earlier interpretation of these rules carries over to the dynamic model. Log consumption is a weighted average (up to a constant b_0^e) of log financial wealth w_t and log labor income l_t, with weights given by the elasticities of consumption with respect to financial wealth (b_1^e) and labor income $(1 - b_1^e)$, respectively. In the dynamic model, unlike the single-period model, b_1^e is a complicated nonlinear function of the underlying parameters of preferences and income as well as the loglinearization constants of the budget constraint. But we know that $0 < b_1^e < 1$. Therefore a negative shock to the financial wealth of an employed investor does not cause an equal proportional reduction in consumption. The employed investor can use labor income to shield consumption from unexpected declines in financial wealth.

Equation (6.45) shows that α^e has the same two components as in the single-period model. The first component gives optimal portfolio choice when labor income risk is idiosyncratic. The second component shows the effect of correlation between labor income shocks and risky asset returns. We now explore these components in detail.

Idiosyncratic labor income risk
When labor income risk is idiosyncratic ($\sigma_{\xi u} = 0$), (6.45) implies that $\alpha^e = (\mu + \sigma_u^2/2)/(\gamma \bar{b}_1 \sigma_u^2)$. This is similar to the optimal

portfolio demand of retired investors, except that the relevant wealth elasticity here is $\bar{b}_1$, the average wealth elasticity of consumption across states.[16] The inequality (6.46) for b_1^e implies that $\bar{b}_1 < b_1^r$, which in turn implies that employed investors are less risk-averse with respect to wealth than are retired investors. Therefore, when labor income is idiosyncratic, the optimal allocation to stocks is unambiguously larger for employed investors than for retired investors.

Table 6.1 illustrates this result numerically. The table reports optimal allocations to stocks for employed and retired investors with relative risk aversion coefficients of 2, 3, 5, 8, 10, or 12 and a time preference rate of 4% per year. To explore the effect of retirement horizon on portfolio choice, the table reports optimal allocations for employed investors with expected retirement horizons between 35 and 5 years.

To compute these allocations, we assume a log riskless real interest rate of 2% per year, a simple equity premium of 4% per year, and an equity standard deviation (σ_u) of 15.7% per year. The assumed equity premium is well below the long-run historical average, but represents a reasonable compromise between that average and lower forward-looking estimates based on the observation that stock prices have increased in recent years relative to corporate earnings (Campbell and Shiller 2001; Jagannathan, McGrattan, and Scherbina 2001).[17] We also assume an expected growth rate of labor income of 3% per year, with a standard deviation of innovations in log labor income (σ_ξ) of 10% per year.[18]

Panel (A) in the table reports allocations when labor income risk is idiosyncratic. As expected, the portfolio share of stocks is systematically larger for employed than for retired investors. The difference increases as we consider employed investors with

---

[16] To see why α^e depends on $\bar{b}_1$ and not just on b_1^e, note that the effects on wealth of a portfolio decision made at time t are not known until $t+1$, when the return on the risky asset is realized. Since there is uncertainty about the state of labor income next period, the investor must take this into account when making his portfolio decision.

[17] Chapter 4 presented evidence that stock returns are mean-reverting, which would imply that return forecasts should be adjusted downwards in the aftermath of high past returns. In this chapter we assume a fixed rather than a time-varying expected stock return, but pick a value below the average past return.

[18] These values are consistent with the estimates of (6.36) reported in Chamberlain and Hirano (1999) and Carroll and Samwick (1997) using data on individuals.

Table 6.1. Optimal Percentage Allocation to Stocks of Employed
and Retired Investors

γ	Expected time until retirement (years)							Retired
	35	30	25	20	15	10	5	
(A) Corr$(r_{t+1}, \Delta l_{t+1}) = 0$								
2	184	170	156	143	129	114	97	80
3	112	104	97	90	82	73	63	53
5	62	59	55	51	47	42	37	32
8	37	35	33	31	28	26	23	20
10	29	27	26	24	22	20	18	16
12	24	23	21	20	18	17	15	13
(B) Corr$(r_{t+1}, \Delta l_{t+1}) = 0.35$								
2	155	146	136	126	116	105	93	80
3	89	85	80	75	70	65	59	53
5	42	41	39	38	37	35	33	32
8	18	18	18	18	19	19	20	20
10	10	11	11	12	13	14	15	16
12	5	6	7	8	9	11	12	13
Income hedging demand (% of total)								
2	−19	−18	−16	−14	−12	−9	−5	0
3	−29	−27	−24	−21	−18	−13	−7	0
5	−57	−51	−45	−38	−30	−21	−10	0
8	−126	−109	−91	−72	−54	−35	−16	0
10	−216	−176	−139	−105	−74	−45	−19	0
12	−411	−302	−218	−153	−100	−58	−23	0

longer expected retirement horizons. To understand this pattern,
it is useful to recall the example with riskless labor income that
we discussed in the introduction to this chapter. When labor
income is riskless, human wealth is equivalent to an implicit
investment in the riskless asset. This implicit investment is larger
for investors with longer horizons because they expect to work
longer before retirement. Thus, it is optimal for investors with
longer retirement horizons to tilt their portfolios further away
from the riskless asset and to hold a larger fraction of their
financial wealth in stocks.

A qualitatively similar horizon effect holds with idiosyncratically risky labor income, but the effect is smaller than in the case

with riskless labor income because idiosyncratic labor income risk shifts downwards the optimal portfolio allocation to risky assets. One way to think about this is that the riskiness of labor income makes the investor behave as if he had an implicit investment in the riskless asset with a value below the expected present value of labor income, discounted at the riskless interest rate. Koo (1998, 1999) develops this interpretation.

Correlated labor income risk
The second component of α^e, $- (\pi^e(1 - b_1^e)/\bar{b}_1)(\sigma_{\xi u}/\sigma_u^2)$, is non-zero whenever the return on the risky asset is correlated with labor income. It represents the income-hedging component of the optimal allocation to the risky asset. It is proportional to the regression coefficient of labor income shocks on risky asset returns, $(\sigma_{\xi u}/\sigma_u^2)$, weighted by the labor income elasticity of consumption $(1 - b_1^e)$.

The sign of income-hedging demand is opposite to the sign of the correlation between labor income shocks and unexpected risky asset returns. If innovations to labor income are negatively correlated with innovations to stock returns, stocks are desirable because they offer a good hedge against unfavorable innovations in labor earnings. This creates a positive hedging demand for stocks. If the correlation is positive, the opposite is true.

Panel (B) in the table illustrates the interaction between income hedging, retirement horizons, and risk aversion for employed investors. This panel assumes a correlation of 0.35 between innovations in log labor income and realized stock returns.[19] This positive correlation between labor income risk and stock market risk creates a significant negative income-hedging demand for stocks. The ratio of income-hedging demand to total demand can be large. It increases with the expected retirement horizon, and also increases with risk aversion. For high levels of risk aversion $(\gamma \geq 8)$, income-hedging demand more than offsets the standard retirement horizon effect on portfolio choice, so that the optimal portfolio share of the risky asset increases as the expected retirement horizon falls.

---

[19] This number is comparable to the correlations reported in Table 7.1 for investors without a college education. Note however that those correlations apply only to the aggregate component of labor income, not to total labor income.

Saving for retirement

Table 6.2 reports the target ratio of financial wealth to labor income for the investors in Table 6.1. This target is defined as the exponentiated long-run mean of the log financial wealth–income ratio $(\exp[\mathrm{E}(w_t - l_t)])$. The target is important because investors choose portfolios on the basis of the wealth elasticity of consumption that prevails at the target level of wealth relative to income. The table shows that wealth–income targets are generally large, especially for conservative investors. This is the result of the assumption that investors cannot freely choose how much they want to work, so that they can only hedge their labor income risk through their savings and portfolio decisions.

The target wealth–income ratio increases as we consider investors with larger γ. In the power utility model, the coefficient γ governs not only relative risk aversion and the elasticity of intertemporal subsitution, as discussed earlier in this book, but also the strength of the precautionary savings motive. Kimball (1990) showed that precautionary savings are determined by the

Table 6.2. Optimal Long-Run Holdings of Financial Wealth Relative to Income

γ	Expected time until retirement (years)						
	35	30	25	20	15	10	5
(A) $\mathrm{Corr}(r_{t+1}, \Delta l_{t+1}) = 0$							
2	8	9	9	10	11	12	13
3	10	11	12	13	14	15	16
5	14	15	16	17	18	19	21
8	18	19	19	20	22	23	25
10	20	21	21	22	23	25	27
12	22	23	23	24	25	26	28
(B) $\mathrm{Corr}(r_{t+1}, \Delta l_{t+1}) = 0.35$							
2	8	8	9	10	11	12	13
3	10	11	11	12	14	15	16
5	13	14	15	16	17	19	21
8	16	17	18	19	20	22	25
10	18	19	19	20	22	24	26
12	20	20	21	21	23	25	27

coefficient of relative prudence, defined as $-U_{CCC}C/U_{CC}$. With power utility, relative prudence is given by $(1+\gamma)$, and thus investors with high γ subject to uncertain income save more to protect consumption against states of low income.

The target wealth–income ratio also increases as we consider investors with shorter retirement horizons, but there is smaller proportional variation in the target ratio across horizons when risk aversion is high. Retirement and precautionary saving motives explain this pattern of variation across the table. Investors facing a high probability of retirement want to accumulate more assets for retirement than investors facing a low probability. On the other hand, investors with long retirement horizons have a stronger precautionary saving motive than investors with short horizons, because for them a negative shock to labor income has a larger downward effect on expected future labor income. Table 6.2 shows that the retirement savings motive dominates the precautionary savings motive across all values of γ However, the precautionary savings effect is stronger for highly prudent investors, which results in a smaller proportional difference between the target financial wealth–labor income ratios across retirement horizons for these investors.

Panel (B) in Table 6.2 shows that a positive correlation between shocks to labor income and unexpected returns slightly lowers the financial wealth–labor income target ratio. A positive correlation results in a more conservative portfolio policy, which in turn reduces the variability of the return on financial wealth, and the need for precautionary savings against negative shocks to financial wealth.

Increasing labor income risk in a long-horizon model
A limitation of our earlier analysis of increasing risk in a single-period model is that it ignores endogenous wealth accumulation. In a multi-period model, an investor can respond to an uncompensated increase in labor income risk in two ways: by saving more, and by reducing his exposure to financial risk. To the extent that the investor saves more, his financial wealth increases relative to his human wealth, increasing his sensitivity to financial risk. We can use the dynamic model of this section to explore the effects of a mean-preserving increase in the variance of labor income shocks on portfolio choice and savings.

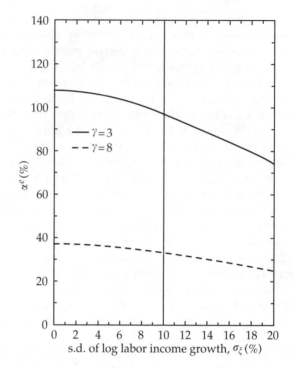

Figure 6.1. Portfolio allocation to stocks plotted against the standard deviation of log labor income growth.

Figures 6.1 and 6.2 summarize our findings. They plot α^e and the target financial wealth–labor income ratio as a function of the standard deviation of log labor income growth (σ_ξ) for $\gamma = 3$ and 8 and an expected retirement horizon of 25 years. We consider mean-preserving increases of σ_ξ in the interval [0, 0.20]. The rest of the parameter values are those assumed earlier. These figures show that an increase in labor income risk has a negative effect on the portfolio share of stocks and a positive effect on savings, consistent with the results in the dynamic models of Elmendorf and Kimball (2000) and Koo (1998, 1999).

Figure 6.1 shows that α^e declines and slowly approaches α^r, the optimal allocation to stocks of a retired investor, as the variance of labor income growth increases. This effect comes through a positive effect of σ_ξ on the wealth elasticity of consumption or, equivalently, a positive effect of σ_ξ on the relative risk aversion of

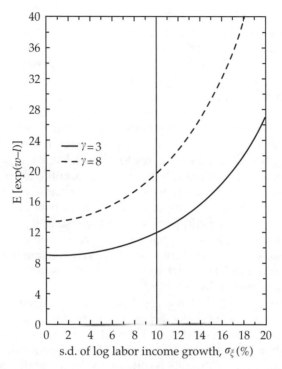

Figure 6.2. Target wealth–income ratio plotted against the standard deviation of labor income growth.

the value function. Figure 6.2 shows that labor income risk strongly stimulates asset accumulation. As the level of savings increases, labor income becomes less important relative to financial wealth as a source of consumption for the investor. Hence the employed investor becomes more like a retired investor and behaves as such when making portfolio decisions.

6.3. CONCLUSION

In this chapter we have explored some issues at the interface between financial economics and labor economics. We have used a model with constant relative risk aversion, rather than the constant absolute risk aversion that is popular in the literature on income risks (Caballero 1990; Svensson and Werner 1993; Davis and Willen 2000). Although CARA models are tractable, they achieve this tractability at a high cost in realism; in particular, they imply that the dollar amounts invested in risky assets are independent of wealth, and therefore of labor income if income risk is idiosyncratic.

In the model with constant relative risk aversion, we show that labor income affects portfolio choice by reducing the proportional sensitivity of consumption to financial asset returns, thereby reducing the investor's aversion to financial risks. In a single-period model, this effect follows directly from the fact that consumption equals financial wealth plus income; the larger the income, the smaller the proportional effect of financial wealth on consumption. In a multi-period model, consumption is chosen endogenously each period, but a similar effect will operate provided that the investor has a well-behaved consumption function. In this case the target ratio of financial wealth to income plays a key role in the analysis.

We have found that riskless labor income creates a strong portfolio tilt toward risky financial assets. Idiosyncratic labor income risk, uncorrelated with financial asset returns, can reduce this tilt but cannot reverse it. Only if labor income shocks are highly variable and strongly positively correlated with risky asset returns will an investor with labor income hold a safer portfolio than a retired investor with no labor income.

The ability to adjust labor supply also increases an investor's willingness to take financial risks. If risky investments do poorly, an investor with flexible labor supply can adjust not only by reducing consumption, but also by increasing work effort. The availability of two margins of adjustment makes the investor more tolerant of financial risk.

Finally, we have discussed optimal portfolio choice for an investor who has a minimum subsistence level of consumption. Such an investor has to commit a portion of financial wealth to meeting subsistence needs; in effect, the investor has negative labor income. Thus, all our conclusions about portfolio choice for investors with labor income apply with the opposite sign to investors with subsistence needs.

7

Investing over the Life Cycle

In describing the behavior of long-term investors, we have up to this point assumed an infinite life. We have explored horizon effects only indirectly, by varying the time discount rate. While this is a useful simplification, and may even be appropriate for institutions such as universities, it precludes any discussion of household portfolio choice over the life cycle. In this final chapter, we ask how individual investors should adjust their portfolios as they move through their life cycle from young adulthood, through middle age, and into retirement.

The complexities of the life-cycle problem prevent us from applying the loglinear approximations that we have used in previous chapters. Instead we rely heavily on numerical dynamic programming methods, using the insights from the earlier loglinear models to interpret the numerical results. The numerical methods also allow us to impose more complex borrowing and portfolio constraints than we could consider in earlier chapters. To keep the modelling problem manageable and focus on the effects of changing labor income over the life cycle, we abstract from time variation in investment opportunities.

The analysis of labor income in the previous chapter can be loosely summarized as follows. A household with labor income has an implicit holding of a non-tradable asset, human wealth, which represents a claim to the stream of future labor income. The household adjusts explicit asset holdings to compensate for the implicit holding of human wealth and to reach the desired allocation of total wealth; thus, human wealth can 'crowd out' explicit asset holdings. If labor income is literally riskless, then riskless asset holdings are strongly crowded out and the household will tilt its portfolio strongly toward risky assets. In the case where the household is constrained from borrowing to finance risky investments, the solution may be a corner at which the portfolio is 100% risky assets. If labor income is risky but uncorrelated with risky financial assets, then riskless asset holdings are still crowded out but less strongly; the portfolio tilt toward risky assets is reduced. If labor income is sufficiently positively correlated with risky financial assets, then the portfolio tilt is reversed and the household compensates for risky human wealth by increasing holdings of safe financial assets.

Under the assumption that income shocks are uncorrelated or only weakly correlated with stock returns, these results suggest that households who expect high future labor income—discounted at some appropriate rate and measured relative to financial wealth—should have the strongest desire to hold stocks. In a life-cycle model with a realistic age profile of income, the discounted value of expected future income increases relative to financial wealth in the very early part of adulthood, as peak earnings years move closer to the present and are discounted less heavily. However, the discounted value of income peaks fairly early in adult life and then declines as workers approach retirement. This suggests that fairly young (but not the very youngest) households are the most likely to be affected by borrowing constraints that limit their equity positions.

The social security system should also affect household investment policies. A stylized representation of social security is that each household is subject to a payroll tax during its working life; the proceeds of the tax are invested in riskless assets on the household's behalf, and annuitized at retirement to provide a riskless real retirement income.[1] Thus, the current social security system can be understood as a program of forced saving, invested at the riskless interest rate. This creates a non-tradable riskless asset, like human wealth, that should increase households' desire to invest in risky financial assets. Campbell *et al.* (2001a) compare optimal portfolio allocations under the current system with optimal allocations under alternative systems that invest a portion of payroll tax proceeds in risky financial assets.

In practice, many households, particularly younger and poorer ones, appear to hold no equities at all. This is inconsistent with

---

[1] This representation of social security ignores its redistributive aspects, within cohorts and across cohorts, and also ignores fluctuations in taxes and benefits over time. For more detailed discussion of these aspects of social security, see Campbell and Feldstein (2001).

simple frictionless models of optimal portfolio choice, but may be explained if there is a fixed cost of participating in equity markets. Such a fixed cost would deter young households from buying equities, but later in the life cycle these households might find it worthwhile to begin participating if their wealth levels are high enough to justify paying the cost. The existence of a fixed cost of equity investment might provide an alternative justification for social security equity investments, if the government program is able to avoid the fixed cost.

The remainder of the chapter is organized as follows. We begin in Section 7.1 by summarizing the rather fragmentary empirical evidence on how households actually do invest over the life cycle. In Section 7.2 we present a stylized model of the life-cycle portfolio choice problem. The model is originally due to Cocco, Gomes, and Maenhout (henceforth CGM 1998); the empirical results we report are taken from Campbell, Cocco, Gomes, and Maenhout (henceforth Campbell *et al.*, 2001a). Section 7.3 concludes.

7.1. WHAT DO WE KNOW ABOUT HOUSEHOLD ASSET ALLOCATION?

The empirical study of household portfolio choice faces many difficulties. Perhaps most obviously, it requires accurate data on all the components of household wealth and on demographic characteristics of households such as age, education, occupation, and income. These are formidable data requirements, since they require self-reporting by households; no single brokerage firm or pension fund gathers all these data from clients or fund participants, and government tax systems collect data on taxable income rather than wealth. Households are notoriously reluctant to share information about their wealth, and thus one should be skeptical about the accuracy of self-reported survey data in this area.

The best available US data are probably those gathered in the Federal Reserve Board's Survey of Consumer Finances (SCF) in 1983, 1989, 1992, and 1995, and in a related earlier survey, the 1962 Survey of Financial Characteristics of Consumers. Relevant data are also available in the Panel Study of Income Dynamics

(PSID).[2] A number of researchers have analyzed these data, and a few broad conclusions emerge.

First, households are extraordinarily diverse in their portfolio choices. In particular, many households hold no stocks at all. Bertaut and Haliassos (1995), for example, report that in the 1983 SCF only 20% of households held stocks or mutual funds directly; about another 15% are likely to have held stocks in defined-contribution (DC) pension plans. Mankiw and Zeldes (1991) report a similar rate of stockownership in the 1984 PSID.

Of course, many households have very little financial wealth of any kind. It may not be surprising that these households avoid the stock market, since they use financial assets as a buffer-stock against shocks to income and desired expenditures, and therefore wish to hold assets in a convenient, liquid form. Also, there may be fixed costs of stockholding (costs of establishing a brokerage account, informing oneself about the market, and so forth) which may not be worth paying for households with little financial wealth. A second conclusion of the literature is that wealthy households are more likely to hold stocks. Even among these households, however, a substantial fraction holds no stocks at all. Mankiw and Zeldes (1991), for example, report that only 48% of households with liquid assets above $100,000 held stocks in 1984.

Third, many wealthy households own private businesses. Heaton and Lucas (2000) construct a broad measure of financial wealth, including not only marketable financial assets but also proprietary businesses, pensions, trusts, and liabilities such as mortgages and consumer loans. They find that in 1989 private businesses were about half as valuable as publicly traded equities for households with financial wealth between $100,000 and $1 million; they were more valuable for households with financial wealth over $1 million. These figures conceal considerable variability across wealthy households; in 1989 fewer than half of households with financial wealth between $100,000 and $1 million owned private businesses.

---

[2] Data are also available in many other countries. A comprehensive set of international studies is collected in Guiso, Haliassos, and Jappelli (2001). Degeorge *et al.* (2000) present an interesting case study of the allocation of France Telecom shares to employees.

Private businesses are of course risky assets. Thus, the greater propensity of wealthy households to hold stocks and private businesses implies that wealthy households take more risk than poor households, a point emphasized by Carroll (2001). Heaton and Lucas (2000) report evidence that private businesses may crowd out ownership of publicly traded equities, in that wealthy households with more variable proprietary income tend to have smaller equity allocations.

Fourth, the last few decades have seen a marked increase in the propensity of households to invest in stocks. This is due largely to the growing prevalence of defined-contribution pension plans, as opposed to defined-benefit plans, and to the introduction of individual retirement accounts (IRAs) in the mid-1980s. Ameriks and Zeldes (2000) estimate that in 1962 only 24% of US households held stocks in any form (directly or through mutual funds, trusts, DC pension plans, or IRAs); by 1989 this fraction had increased to 33%, and by 1995 to 41%. No doubt it rose further during the stock market boom of the late 1990s. The fraction of US households holding stocks directly or in mutual funds was much more stable, rising only slightly, from 19% in 1962 to 23% in 1995.

Fifth, there is fragmentary evidence that households adjust their portfolios in response to tax incentives (Poterba 2001). Tax effects seem to be stronger on the timing of transactions and on the decision whether or not to hold particular assets than on the amounts that households invest in different assets.

Finally, there is troubling evidence that many households fail to diversify their risky asset holdings. For example, it is common practice to invest heavily in the stock of the company one works for (Benartzi 2001). Even households who diversify may do so naively, for example by allocating equal fractions of the portfolio to each of the options offered in a DC pension plan (Benartzi and Thaler 2001). Combined with earlier evidence on the failure to diversify internationally, surveyed by Lewis (1999), these findings make it difficult to assume that households are effectively optimizing their portfolios.

7.1.1. *The effect of age on portfolio choice*

Age effects on portfolio choice are even harder to quantify than wealth effects or time effects. Before one can even begin to study age effects, one must confront a fundamental identification problem. At any time t, a person born in year b is a_t years old, where

$$a_t = t - b. \tag{7.1}$$

Thus, it is inherently impossible to identify separate age effects, time effects, and cohort (birth-year) effects on portfolio choice. Even if one has complete panel data on portfolios of households over time, any pattern in the data can be fit equally well by age and time effects, age and cohort effects, or time and cohort effects. Ameriks and Zeldes (2000) explain this point particularly clearly.

The theory we have presented in this book suggests that there should be time effects on portfolio choice if investors perceive changes over time in the risks or expected excess returns of risky assets. Recall the classic formula (2.25) for the allocation to a single risky asset of a short-term investor:

$$\alpha_t = \frac{E_t r_{t+1} - r_{f,t+1} + \sigma_t^2/2}{\gamma \sigma_t^2}. \tag{7.2}$$

The portfolio share α_t will vary over time if the ratio of risk premium to variance changes over time. Chapter 4 showed that similar time variation is present in the optimal allocations of long-term investors.

Theory also suggests that there should be age effects on portfolio choice if older investors have shorter horizons than younger investors and investment opportunities are time-varying (Chapters 3 and 4), or if older investors have less human wealth relative to financial wealth than younger investors (Chapter 6). Thus, it seems hard to rule out either time or age effects in studying portfolio choice.

Cohort effects are more problematic. There is no reason to expect a cohort effect on portfolio choice unless different cohorts have different preferences.[3] Thus, the most natural assumption for empirical work is that cohort effects are absent; this assumption is made by Heaton and Lucas (2000) and most other studies in the area, but is questioned by Ameriks and Zeldes (2000).

---

[3] A cohort effect could also arise if different cohorts have different income histories, and thus different ratios of human to financial wealth at any given age. This is probably not a large effect in modern US conditions.

Even if one excludes cohort effects, several other empirical difficulties arise. First, there is the question of whether to measure equity relative to marketable financial assets, or relative to a broader definition of financial wealth that includes private businesses. Second, there is the question of whether to measure the share of equity in the population as a whole, the fraction of the population owning equity, or the share of equity among stockholders. These three measures may behave differently because of the heterogeneity across households that we have already discussed.

Ameriks and Zeldes (2000) estimate age effects in the 1989, 1992, and 1995 SCF surveys. They measure equity relative to marketable financial assets, including DC pension plans and IRAs. When they exclude cohort effects and allow for time effects, they estimate a hump-shaped age effect on the fraction of all household financial assets that is held in equity. The predicted equity share starts below 10% in the mid-20s, peaks at 20% in the late 40s and 50s, and declines again to 10% in the late 70s. This hump shape is largely driven by the age effect on the fraction of the population holding equities, which starts at 20% in the mid-20s, peaks at 50% around age 50, and then declines to 30% in the late 70s. There is a much smaller hump shape in the fraction of stockholders' financial assets that is held in equity.

Heaton and Lucas (2000) exclude cohort effects and confine attention to households with net worth greater than $10,000 and stockholdings greater than $500. They do not try to estimate age effects in the early part of the life cycle. Instead, they concentrate on the differences between early middle-aged households (35–49), late middle-aged households (50–64), and retired households (65 or over). When they measure the share of equity relative to marketable financial assets, they find a distinct decline in the equity share above age 65. When they broaden the measure of wealth to include private businesses, this decline in equity disappears. Stocks appear less important for middle-aged households, whose wealth is largely tied up in private businesses. As households age, they sell their private businesses and stocks play a larger role in the total portfolio.

Overall, these results suggest that there is some tendency for households to take less financial risk as they reach their retirement years. However, only a small part of the risk reduction takes the form of reduced stockholdings. Some households appear to reduce their risk by exiting the stock market altogether, and others reduce it by selling their risky private businesses. Similarly, there appears to be some tendency for young adults to increase their financial risk-taking during their 20s, but this takes the form of a decision to enter the stock market rather than a decision to increase stockholdings in a continuous fashion.

7.2. A LIFE-CYCLE MODEL OF PORTFOLIO CHOICE

7.2.1. *Model specification*

Time parameters and preferences

We now present an illustrative normative model of household portfolio choice, closely following CGM (1998) and Campbell *et al.* (2001a). We let t denote adult age. The investor is adult for a maximum of T periods, of which he works the first S periods. For simplicity, S is assumed to be exogenous and deterministic. We allow for uncertain life-span in the manner of Hubbard, Skinner, and Zeldes (1994). Let p_t denote the probability that the investor is alive at date $t+1$, conditional on his being alive at date t. Then, investor k's preferences at time t are described by the time-separable power utility function

$$\frac{C_{kt}^{1-\gamma}}{1-\gamma} + \mathrm{E}_t \sum_{i=1}^{T-t} \delta^i \left(\prod_{j=0}^{i-1} p_{t+j} \right) \frac{C_{k,t+i}^{1-\gamma}}{1-\gamma}, \tag{7.3}$$

where C_{kt} is the level of date t consumption, $\gamma > 0$ is the coefficient of relative risk aversion, and $\delta < 1$ is the discount factor. We assume that the individual derives no utility from leaving a bequest.

The labor income process

In the years before retirement, $t \leq S$, investor k's log labor income, l_{kt}, is exogenously given by

$$l_{kt} = \mathrm{f}(t, Z_{kt}) + v_{kt} + \varepsilon_{kt}, \tag{7.4}$$

where $f(t, Z_{kt})$ is a deterministic function of age and other individual characteristics Z_{kt}, ε_{kt} is an idiosyncratic temporary shock distributed as $N(0, \sigma_\varepsilon^2)$, v_{kt} is given by

$$v_{kt} = v_{k,t-1} + u_{kt}, \tag{7.5}$$

and u_{kt} is distributed as $N(0, \sigma_u^2)$ and is uncorrelated with ε_{kt}. Thus, log income is the sum of a deterministic component that can be calibrated to capture the hump shape of earnings over the life cycle and two random components, one permanent and one transitory. We assume that the temporary shock ε_{kt} is uncorrelated across households, but we decompose the permanent shock u_{kt} into an aggregate component ξ_t and an idiosyncratic component ω_{kt}, uncorrelated across households:

$$u_{kt} = \xi_t + \omega_{kt}. \tag{7.6}$$

This decomposition implies that the random component of aggregate labor income follows a random walk, an assumption made by Fama and Schwert (1977b) and Jagannathan and Wang (1996). While macroeconomists such as Campbell (1996), Campbell and Mankiw (1989), and Pischke (1995) have found empirical evidence for short-term persistence in aggregate quarterly labor income growth, the simplification to a random walk should have little effect on optimal consumption and portfolio choice over the life cycle.

Financial assets

We assume that there are two assets in which the agent can invest: a riskless asset with simple real return R_f, which we call *Treasury bills*, and a risky asset with simple real return R_t, which we call *stocks*. The excess return on the risky asset, $R_{t+1} - R_f$, is given by

$$R_{t+1} - R_f = \mu + \eta_{t+1}, \tag{7.7}$$

where η_{t+1}, the period $t+1$ innovation to excess returns, is assumed to be IID and normally distributed with mean zero and variance σ_η^2. We allow innovations to excess returns to be correlated with innovations to the aggregate component of permanent labor income, and we write the correlation coefficient as $\rho_{\xi\eta}$.

Retirement and liquid wealth

We model a system of mandatory saving for retirement in the following simple way. During working life the individual must save a fraction, θ, of current labor income as retirement wealth. Under this assumption, disposable labor income, L_{kt}^d, is given by

$$L_{kt}^d = (1 - \theta)L_{kt} \quad \text{for } t \leq S. \tag{7.8}$$

The amount θL_{kt} is added to retirement wealth, denoted by W_{kt}^R. During working life retirement wealth is illiquid; the individual cannot consume it or borrow against it. At age S retirement wealth is rolled into a riskless annuity, so that the individual receives in each of the retirement years the annuity value corresponding to W_{kS}^R. This assumption of riskless annuitization affects the portfolio choices of older investors. An interesting extension of this model would be to allow investors to choose between riskless and variable annuities.

We assume that the individual is forced to hold retirement wealth in riskless assets. This implies that $W_{kt}^R = B_{kt}^R$, where B_{kt}^R is the dollar amount of retirement wealth that investor k has in riskless assets. Campbell *et al.* (2001a) consider alternative systems in which retirement wealth is partially or fully invested in risky assets, but the allocation remains constant over time and is controlled by the government rather than the investor.

Investors also have liquid wealth outside their retirement accounts. We denote liquid wealth of investor k at date t by W_{kt}, with no superscript, and liquid holdings of bills and stocks by B_{kt} and S_{kt}, respectively. We assume that the investor faces the following borrowing and short-sales constraints:

$$B_{kt} \geq 0, \tag{7.9}$$

$$S_{kt} \geq 0. \tag{7.10}$$

The borrowing constraint (7.9) ensures that the investor's allocation to bills in both the liquid and retirement accounts is nonnegative at all dates. It prevents the investor from borrowing against future labor income or retirement wealth. The short-sales constraint (7.10) ensures that the investor's allocation to equities is non-negative at all dates.

The household's optimization problem

In each period of a household's working life ($t \leq S$) the timing of events is as follows. The investor starts the period with liquid wealth W_{kt} and retirement wealth W_{kt}^R. Then labor income L_{kt} is realized. Following Deaton (1991), we denote *cash on hand* in period t by

$$X_{kt} = W_{kt} + (1 - \theta)L_{kt}. \tag{7.11}$$

The investor must decide how much to consume, C_{kt}, and how to allocate the remaining cash on hand between stocks and bills. We denote the proportion of liquid wealth invested in stocks by α_{kt}.

Next-period liquid and retirement wealth are then given by

$$W_{k,t+1} = [1 + \alpha_{kt}R_{t+1} + (1 - \alpha_{kt})R_f][W_{kt} + (1 - \theta)L_{kt} - C_{kt}], \tag{7.12}$$

$$W_{kt+1}^R = (1 + R_f)[W_{kt}^R + \theta L_{kt}]. \tag{7.13}$$

After retirement ($t > S$), the problem takes the same form except that retirement wealth no longer accumulates. Instead, it is annuitized and provides riskless income $A(W_{ks}^R)$. After-tax labor income $(1 - \theta)L_{kt}$ in (7.11) and (7.12) is replaced by $A(W_{ks}^R)$.

The problem the investor faces is to maximize (7.3), subject to the working-life and retirement versions of (7.4)–(7.13), plus the constraints that consumption must be non-negative at all dates. The control variables of the problem are C_{kt} and α_{kt} at each date t. The state variables are time t (representing remaining age and the deterministic components of labor income), cash on hand X_{kt}, retirement wealth W_{kt}^R, and the permanent component of labor income υ_{kt}. The problem is to solve for the policy rules as functions of the state variables.

A slightly more complicated version of this model allows for a fixed cost F of stock market investment. We can define a binary variable f_{kt}, which equals zero until the investor pays the fixed cost of entering the stock market and equals one thereafter. The equity allocation α_{kt}^L is freely chosen when $f_{kt} = 1$, and equals zero when $f_{kt} = 0$. The budget constraint (7.12) contains an extra term $-(f_{kt} - f_{k,t-1})F$ to capture the one-time payment of the fixed cost. In this version of the model, f_{kt} becomes both an additional choice variable and a state variable.

Numerical solution
This problem cannot be solved analytically. CGM (1998) derive
the policy functions numerically by discretizing the state–space
and the variables over which the choices are made, and by using
Gaussian quadrature to approximate the distributions of the
innovations to the labor income process and risky asset returns
(Tauchen and Hussey 1991). The problem is then solved by using
backward induction. In period T, the investor consumes all his
wealth and the value function coincides with the instantaneous
utility. In every period t prior to T, and for each admissible
combination of the state variables, we compute the value associated with each level of consumption, decision to pay the fixed
cost of entering the stock market, and share of liquid wealth
invested in stocks. This value is equal to current utility plus the
expected discounted continuation value. To compute this continuation value for points that do not lie on the grid, we use cubic
spline interpolation. The combinations of the choice variables
ruled out by the constraints of the problem are given a very large
(negative) utility such that they are never optimal. We optimize
over the different choices using grid search.

When the fixed cost of equity market participation F is equal
to zero, we can simplify the solution by exploiting the scale
independence of the maximization problem and rewriting
all variables as ratios to the permanent component of labor
income.

7.2.2. Calibration

Time parameters and preferences
Adult age starts at age 20 for households without a college
degree, and at age 22 for households with a college degree. The
age of retirement is set to 65 for all households. The investor dies
with probaility one at age 100. Prior to this age we use the mortality tables of the National Center for Health Statistics to para-
meterize the conditional survival probabilities, p_j for $j = 1, \ldots, T$.
We set the discount factor δ to 0.96, and the coefficient of relative
risk aversion γ to 5. In variations of the benchmark case, we also
consider investors who are extremely impatient with $\delta = 0.80$,
comparatively risk-tolerant with $\gamma = 2$, and extremely risk-averse
with $\gamma = 10$.

The labor income process

Campbell *et al.* (2001a), following CGM (1998), use the PSID to estimate the labor income process. They use the family questionnaire of the PSID to estimate (7.4) and (7.5) which give labor income as a function of age and other characteristics. Families that are part of the Survey of Economic Opportunities subsample are dropped to obtain a random sample. Only households with a male head are used, as the age profile of income may differ across male- and female-headed households and relatively few observations are available for female-headed households. Retirees, non-respondents, students, homemakers, and household heads younger than 20 (22 for college-educated households) or older than 65 are also eliminated from the sample.

Like Storesletten, Telmer, and Yaron (1999), Campbell *et al.* (2001a) take a broad definition of labor income so as to implicitly allow for insurance mechanisms—other than asset accumulation—that households use to protect themselves against pure labor income risk. Such insurance mechanisms include welfare programs that effectively set a lower bound on the support of non-asset income, endogenous variation in the labor supply of both male and female household members, financial help from relatives and friends, and so on. Thus, we define labor income as total reported labor income plus unemployment compensation, workers' compensation, social security, supplemental social security, other welfare, child support, and total transfers (mainly help from relatives)—all this for both head of household and, if present, his spouse. Observations that still report zero for this broad income category are dropped. Labor income defined this way is deflated using the Consumer Price Index, with 1992 as the base year. The sample starts in 1970, so a household appears at most 24 times in the sample. Households with fewer observations are retained in the panel.

The estimation controls for family-specific fixed effects, and thus implicitly allows for cohort effects on the level of income. To control for education, the sample is split into three groups: households without high school education, those with high school education but without a college degree, and finally college graduates. This sample split is intended to accommodate the well-established finding that age profiles differ in shape across education groups (Attanasio 1995; Hubbard, Skinner, and Zeldes

1994). For each education group the function $f(t, Z_{kt})$ is assumed to be additively separable in t and Z_{kt}. The vector Z_{kt} of personal characteristics, other than age and the fixed household effect, includes marital status and household composition. Household composition equals the additional number of family members in the household besides the head and (if present) his spouse.

Ideally, one should also control for occupation. Using PSID data this is problematic, because from the 1975 wave onwards the majority of the unemployed report no occupation, and are categorized together with people who are not in the labor force. But modelling unemployment as a switch in occupation is inappropriate, as the possibility of unemployment through lay-off is one of the main sources of labor income risk. We explore this in greater detail in Section 7.2.4.

To obtain age profiles suitable for the simulation model of life-cycle portfolio choice, Campbell *et al.* (2001a) fit a third-order polynomial to the age dummies estimated from the PSID. The resulting income profiles are similar to those used in Attanasio (1995), Carroll and Summers (1991), and Gourinchas and Parker (2001). They are plotted in Figure 7.1 along with the underlying age dummies for each of the three education groups.

The method of Carroll and Samwick (1997) is used to estimate the variances of permanent and temporary shocks to labor income. Defining l_{kt}^* as

$$l_{kt}^* \equiv l_{kt} - \widehat{f}(t, Z_{kt}),$$ (7.14)

we have

$$\text{Var}(l_{k,t+d}^* - l_{kt}^*) = d\sigma_u^2 + 2\sigma_\varepsilon^2.$$ (7.15)

The parameters σ_u^2 and σ_ε^2 can be estimated by running an OLS regression of $\text{Var}(l_{k,t+d}^* - l_{kt}^*)$ on d and a constant term. Groups with less education tend to have more variable transitory income shocks, but less variable permanent shocks, than groups with a higher educational level. Table 7.1 reports these variances.

A similar procedure delivers estimates of the correlation between labor income shocks and stock returns, $\rho_{\xi\eta}$. The change in l_{kt}^* can be written as

$$\Delta l_{kt}^* = \xi_t + \omega_{kt} + \varepsilon_{kt} - \varepsilon_{k,t-1}.$$ (7.16)

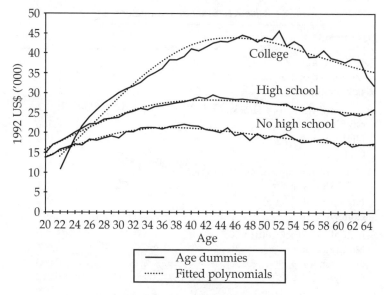

Figure 7.1. Labor income profiles.

Averaging across individuals gives

$$\overline{\Delta I_t^*} = \xi_t. \tag{7.17}$$

The correlation coefficient is then easily computed from the OLS regression of $\overline{\Delta I_t^*}$ on demeaned excess returns:

$$\overline{\Delta I_t^*} = \beta(R_{t+1} - \bar{R}_f - \mu) + \psi_t. \tag{7.18}$$

As an empirical measure for the excess return on our stylized risky asset, we use CRSP data on the New York Stock Exchange value-weighted stock return relative to the Treasury bill rate. For all education groups, the regression coefficients are strikingly low and insignificant. To allow for potential lags in the realization of labor income, we repeat the exercise with the excess stock return lagged one year. The relationship becomes much stronger: the regression coefficient now varies from 0.06 to 0.10, and the correlation coefficient from 0.32 to 0.52, as reported in Table 7.1. Interestingly, the correlation of labor income with the stock market is larger and more significant for households with higher education.

In our portfolio choice model, allowing for lags in the relationship between innovations in stock returns and permanent shocks to

Table 7.1. Baseline Parameters

Description	Parameter value
Retirement age (K)	65
Discount factor (δ)	0.96
Risk aversion (γ)	5
Variance of transitory shocks (σ_ε^2)	
No high school	0.106
High school	0.074
College	0.058
Variance of permanent shocks (σ_u^2)	
No high school	0.011
High school	0.011
College	0.017
Sensitivity to stock returns (β)	
No high school	0.096
High school	0.063
College	0.073
Correlation with stock returns ($\rho_{\xi\eta}$)	
No high school	0.328
High school	0.371
College	0.516
Riskless rate ($\bar{R}_F - 1$)	0.02
Mean excess return on stocks (μ)	0.04
Standard deviation of stock return (σ_η)	0.157
Fixed cost (F)	0 or 10,000
Social security tax rate (θ)	0.10

labor income unfortunately requires an additional state variable. We therefore assume that the correlation is contemporaneous. The model requires the variances of both ξ_t, the aggregate permanent labor income shock that is correlated with stock market risk, and ω_{kt}, the idiosyncratic permanent shock to labor income. The first variance is obtained immediately as the variance of $\overline{\Delta l}_t^*$. Subtracting this from the total variance of u_{kt} gives then the variance of ω_{kt}.

Other parameters
Our assumptions about asset returns are the same ones that we made in Chapter 6. We set the riskless real interest rate to 2% and

the simple equity premium μ to 4%. We set the standard deviation of innovations to the risky asset σ_η to 0.157. Recall that the classic formula for the risky asset portfolio share, under power utility with IID returns and no labor income, is $\mu/(\gamma\sigma_\eta^2)$. With these parameters the implied risky asset share would be about 1/3 at the benchmark risk aversion of 5; we find higher optimal shares in our model only because of the presence of labor income. We set the fixed cost of equity market participation to zero in the benchmark case, but we go on to consider a $10,000 fixed cost.

The social security tax rate θ is set equal to 10% of current labor income. With retirement wealth accumulating at the riskless interest rate, and annuitized at retirement to ensure zero balance of the system conditional on survival probabilities, this tax rate implies an average replacement ratio of 60% at age 65. Table 7.1 summarizes the parameters used in the baseline case.

7.2.3. Benchmark results

To study the behavior of the variables in the model, we calculate cross-sectional averages across 10,000 households receiving different draws of income and asset returns, and plot them against age. Figure 7.2 plots labor income net of social security contributions, consumption, liquid wealth, and retirement wealth for households with a high school degree. (The life-cycle patterns for other education groups are similar.)

The average consumer is borrowing-constrained early in life. Consumption tracks net income very closely, and little savings accumulate outside the retirement account until after age 40. These limited savings early in life are driven by the precautionary savings motive; thus, like Gourinchas and Parker (2001) we find that younger consumers are buffer-stock savers rather than life-cycle savers in the classic sense. Consumption rises with income early in life because of borrowing constraints, and falls later as increased mortality drives up the effective rate of time preference; thus, consumption profiles are hump-shaped over life, as found in the literature on life-cycle consumption behavior.[4]

---

[4] We could generate a more pronounced hump shape in consumption if we added age-specific preference shocks or subsistence levels to the model.

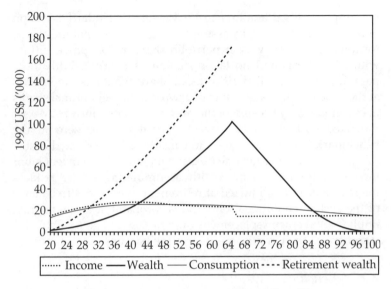

Figure 7.2. Consumption, income, and wealth

Figure 7.3 plots liquid wealth and liquid holdings of equities and bills over the life cycle. The borrowing constraint binds for young households; they would like to take more equity risk but are unable to do so. For approximately the first 20 years of life, they hold 100% of their portfolios in the form of equity. Households in mid life hold bills, but these holdings decrease again after retirement.

These results can be understood as follows. The crucial variables for portfolio composition are liquid wealth, retirement wealth, and future labor income. In the model future labor income, although risky, can be thought of as an implicit holding of a riskless asset. Innovations to labor income are positively correlated with innovations to stock returns, but this correlation is not sufficiently large for future labor income to resemble stocks more closely than bills. Since early in life the implicit holdings of the riskless asset in the form of future labor income are large, the investor wishes to invest what little liquid wealth he has fully into stocks. From age 40 onwards liquid wealth increases relative to future labor income and retirement wealth, so that implicit holdings of the riskless asset become less important. This induces a shift in the composition of

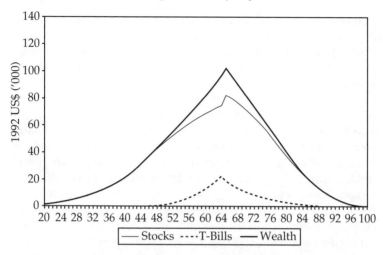

Figure 7.3. Liquid wealth, stocks, and Treasury bills.

liquid wealth towards bills. After retirement liquid wealth is run down more rapidly than the implicit annuitized holdings of the riskless asset. As this happens, the implicit holdings of the riskless asset become relatively more important, inducing a shift in portfolio composition back toward stocks.

One limitation of these results is that they counterfactually predict 100% stock market participation among younger investors. However, we can modify this prediction, with little effect on other aspects of the model, by adding a fixed cost of stock market participation. Campbell *et al.* (2001a) report results with a $10,000 fixed cost. With this level of fixed cost, all investors have paid the cost by age 30, and later in life the model behaves much as it did in the absence of the cost.

7.2.4. Heterogeneity

In the previous section we studied a representative household with a high school education but no college degree. Results are similar for representative households in the other two education groups. However, households may differ along other dimensions. For example, labor income processes may differ across households that work in different industries and for self-employed households. Also, some households may be more impatient or more risk-averse than others, as found by Barsky *et al.* (1997). These differences across households may have important effects on optimal investment strategies. In this section we consider this issue.

Measuring heterogeneity in labor income

The PSID can be used to measure variation in the stochastic structure of the labor income process across industries, and differences between self-employed and non-self-employed households. Campbell *et al.* (2001a) use the two-digit SIC classification to split households into 12 different industries. Starting in 1972, the PSID reports the current industry of the household head if currently working and the last industry if currently unemployed. This is the information we use. Three caveats apply, however. First, we ignore the industry of the spouse. This might be problematic, because the spouse's labor income is added to the head's labor income, yet it might have quite different risk characteristics. Second, on average, 16% of our respondents switch industries each year. Business cycle considerations (like the anticipation of a recession) might force people out of cyclical sectors and into less volatile industries. As we do not model the switching decision, our estimates of the sensitivities of labor income shocks to financial market risks for different industries might be biased. However, we did not find any significant effects when we regressed the number of industry switchers onto innovations in business cycle indicators. Third, there is a timing issue, because the labor income reported in the PSID is for the previous calendar year, while the industry concerns the current job.

Campbell *et al.* (2001a) report the number of household-year observations for each of the 36 different education–industry cells. There is tremendous variation across industries, with particularly small numbers in mining, personal services, and recreation. These industries are omitted from the tables. As a further cut-off, we drop cells in which any PSID wave contains fewer than 20 observations; these cells are left blank in the tables. We do however include observations in these small cells when estimating column and row totals, that is when reporting the results for a given industry across all education levels or for a given education group across all industries.

Table 7.2. Variance Decomposition of Labor Income

Industry	No high school		High school		College		All	
	Total	P/T	Total	P/T	Total	P/T	Total	P/T
Agriculture	—	—	0.31	0.14	—	—	0.32	0.08
Manufacturing	0.06	0.10	0.05	0.09	0.05	0.25	0.05	0.13
Construction	0.11	0.00	0.10	0.14	—	—	0.11	0.15
Transportation, communication	0.11	0.31	0.06	0.08	—	—	0.07	0.16
Trade	0.10	0.17	0.09	0.13	0.07	0.26	0.09	0.16
Financial, real estate, insurance	—	—	0.09	0.13	0.08	0.24	0.09	0.15
Business services	—	—	0.13	0.18	—	—	0.12	0.18
Professional services	—	—	0.07	0.12	0.07	0.20	0.08	0.15
Public administration	—	—	0.05	0.17	0.04	0.26	0.05	0.19
Self-employed	0.37	0.00	0.22	0.22	0.20	0.19	0.23	0.16
Non-self-employed	0.07	0.08	0.05	0.10	0.04	0.18	0.05	0.11
All	0.11	0.07	0.08	0.13	0.07	0.24	0.09	0.14

Notes: P/T = permanent/total.
All positive variances are significantly different from zero at the 0.1% level.
Two variances estimated to be negative have been set to zero.

Campbell *et al.* (2001a) re-estimate age profiles of labor income for the shorter PSID sample beginning in 1972, including industry dummies in the vector Z_{it} of personal characteristics. That is, industry is allowed to influence only the level and not the shape of the age profile for a household with a given amount of education. Campbell *et al.* then estimate the stochastic model of labor income separately for each education–industry cell.

Table 7.2 reports the total variance of income, and its decomposition into permanent and transitory components, for each different education–industry cell. Agriculture has by far the highest variance of labor income shocks; other industries subject to significant labor income shocks are construction and business services. The variance decomposition indicates that labor income shocks for construction workers without a high school degree are entirely temporary. At the other extreme, permanent income shocks are especially important for college graduates in public administration. As a general pattern, the relative importance of permanent shocks seems to increase with educational attainment. This was already documented for the column totals, but seems robust within individual industries.

The tenth and eleventh rows of Table 7.2 split the sample in a different way, by distinguishing self-employed from non-self-employed households. (We included both types of household in the industry analysis, since there are too few self-employed households to allow an industry decomposition.) Income variability is dramatically larger for self-employed households. Income shocks are entirely temporary for the self-employed without a high school degree, but are disproportionately permanent for the self-employed in the two higher education groups.

Table 7.3 considers heterogeneity in the sensitivity of different households' income shocks to lagged stock returns. Campbell *et al.* (2001a) repeat the exercise, replacing lagged stock returns with lagged returns on long-term government bonds. Unfortunately, the small cell sizes mean that the results are often statistically insignificant for individual industries, but there are many interesting patterns. Stock market risk seems especially relevant for people in manufacturing, construction, and public administration. Interest rate risk shows up for agriculture, professional services and finance, real estate, and insurance, in addition to the stock-market-sensitive sectors. Among college graduates, the self-employed are especially exposed to stock market risk, while interest rate risk is far more important for the non-self-employed. This finding supports the conclusion of Heaton and Lucas (2000) that privately owned business risk is an especially important substitute for stock market risk in the portfolios of many wealthy households.

Effects of heterogeneity on portfolio choice
In this section we illustrate the effects of investor heterogeneity on optimal consumption and portfolio choice. First, we consider the heterogeneity of preferences, calculating optimal behavior for highly risk-averse investors with $\gamma = 10$ and impatient investors

Table 7.3. Regression of Permanent Aggregate Shock on Lagged Excess Stock Returns

Industry	No high school		High school		College		All	
	β	ρ	β	ρ	β	ρ	β	ρ
Agriculture	—	—	0.33	0.35	—	—	0.18	0.22
Manufacturing	0.10	0.34	0.08	0.28	0.06	0.21	0.08[*]	0.35
Construction	0.32[**]	0.66	0.08	0.24	—	—	0.13[**]	0.55
Transportation, communication	−0.18	0.30	0.05	0.32	—	—	0.03	0.19
Trade	0.12	0.21	−0.01	0.02	−0.04	0.11	0.01	0.03
Financial, real estate, insurance	—	—	0.04	0.07	−0.01	0.02	0.05	0.13
Business services	—	—	−0.02	0.03	—	—	0.08	0.19
Professional services	—	—	0.03	0.09	0.06	0.35	0.05	0.26
Public administration	—	—	0.06	0.23	0.22[**]	0.51	0.11[**]	0.42
Self-employed	0.09	0.10	0.08	0.17	0.19[*]	0.42	0.11	0.32
Non-self-employed	0.10[*]	0.40	0.07[*]	0.41	0.05	0.30	0.07[**]	0.46
All	0.09	0.32	0.07[*]	0.38	0.07[**]	0.49	0.08[**]	0.46

[**]Significant at the 5% level; [*]significant at the 10% level.

with $\delta = 0.8$. Second, we consider differences in labor income risk of the sort illustrated in Tables 7.2 and 7.3. To highlight these differences, we simulate the behavior of households whose income is particularly risky and highly correlated with asset returns: self-employed college graduates.

Table 7.4 shows average consumption and liquid wealth (in thousands of dollars) and the share of liquid wealth invested in stocks for different age groups. This is a more compact way for us to summarize the information presented graphically in Figures 7.2 and 7.3. The first column of Table 7.4 uses the baseline parameters of the model.

The next column presents results for a higher risk aversion coefficient of 10 rather than 5. To understand the results for

Investing over the Life Cycle

Table 7.4. Life-Cycle Profiles

Age	Baseline	$\gamma = 10$	$\delta = 0.8$	Self-employed
Consumption				
20–35	20.22	20.13	20.53	25.09
36–50	25.48	25.12	26.50	38.39
51–65	24.61	24.23	23.94	35.23
66–80	22.43	22.65	15.95	32.67
81–100	16.98	19.04	14.27	27.26
Wealth				
20–35	5.94	8.20	3.39	12.84
36–50	29.34	39.28	7.25	65.75
51–65	75.77	100.16	10.23	173.70
66–80	77.28	105.50	5.71	159.76
81–100	13.60	30.85	0.11	46.75
Liquid portfolio share in stocks				
20–35	1.00	0.97	0.99	0.57
36–50	0.99	0.95	1.00	0.91
51–65	0.88	0.61	1.00	0.57
66–80	0.90	0.57	1.00	0.54
81–100	0.92	0.68	1.00	0.61

higher γ, it is important to recall that with isoelastic preferences this parameter measures both risk aversion and prudence (Kimball 1990). Greater prudence increases precautionary savings and explains why highly risk-averse investors consume less, and save more, until age 65. After this age the precautionary savings motive is reduced, since there is no labor income risk and retirement wealth is converted into a riskless annuity. Thus, highly risk-averse investors consume more after retirement.

Table 7.4 also shows that, as one would expect, highly risk-averse investors have a lower portfolio share in stocks. One interesting pattern that is not visible in the table is that, very early in life, these investors' equity portfolio share is increasing with age. This pattern does not show up for investors with $\gamma = 5$ because in early life these investors are constrained by their inability to borrow to finance equity investments. The reason for this increasing pattern is explained in CGM (1998). In the presence of an increasing labor income profile, the annuity value of future labor income, equivalent to implicit holdings of the risk-less asset, first increases with age as peak earnings years move closer in time. Investors respond to this increase by shifting liquid wealth toward risky financial assets. Later on, the annuity value of future labor income starts to decrease as peak earnings are realized and retirement approaches; investors respond by shifting out of stocks in middle age.

The next column of Table 7.4 shows optimal consumption, wealth, and portfolio allocation for impatient households with $\delta = 0.8$. These households consume more early in life (roughly up to age 50) and less later. They accumulate almost no wealth, never holding more than about $10,000 in liquid assets. What little wealth they do accumulate they hold in stocks; their exposure to the stock market is so small that they are extremely tolerant of equity risk.

The last column of Table 7.4 reports results for self-employed college-educated households. The preference parameters are the same as in the baseline case, but the results are quite different from the first column of the table which apply to households with only a high school education. The payroll tax rate is raised slightly to 10.50% to maintain the average replacement ratio for self-employed college-educated households at 60%. Looking at the share of liquid wealth invested in stocks, there are two distinctive features: first, the share invested in risky financial assets is much lower, and second, it exhibits a clear hump shape. The higher variance of labor income shocks and the large positive correlation between the latter and innovations to stock returns crowd out investment in risky financial assets. This effect is particularly strong early in life, when the self-employed investor has accumulated little liquid wealth.

7.3. CONCLUSION

In this chapter we have asked how working households should allocate their retirement savings. We have calibrated a life-cycle model to microeconomic US data and have solved the model numerically. Our main results are as follows.

First, risky investments should be extremely attractive to typical young households with many years until retirement and modest savings. Such households have large human wealth relative to financial wealth, and their human wealth is relatively safe; thus, they should be willing to tilt their financial portfolios strongly toward risky assets for reasons discussed in Chapter 6.

Second, the attractiveness of risky investments diminishes later in life as human wealth declines and financial assets accumulate. This is true even though our model assumes the existence of a retirement system that replaces labor income with a riskless real annuity in retirement. If households are constrained from borrowing to finance risky investments, they may remain with 100% risky portfolios for much of their working lives, but in late middle age most households should scale back their financial risks.

Third, there is considerable heterogeneity across households in their income processes and hence in their optimal investment strategies. Self-employed college graduates, for example, have riskier income that is more highly correlated with stock returns. These households own private businesses that are exposed to many of the same risks as publicly traded companies; they should scale back their financial risks accordingly.

Fourth, time preference and risk attitudes can have large effects on optimal portfolios. Households with high risk aversion, for example, are enthusiastic savers because they have a strong precautionary savings motive. Thus, they accumulate more financial wealth and are more exposed to financial risks in middle age. They should be cautious investors, both because of their high risk aversion and because of their greater financial wealth relative to their income. Impatient households, on the other hand, accumulate relatively little savings; financial risks are relatively unimportant for them compared with income risks, and thus they can afford to invest more aggressively.

It is interesting to compare these normative recommendations with the positive evidence on household portfolio allocation that we summarized in Section 7.1. Some of the qualitative patterns identified in the positive literature appear to match the recommendations of the life-cycle model in Section 7.2. The observed decline in risk-taking in late middle age and retirement, the heterogeneity in portfolio choice across households, and the tendency for households with private businesses to limit their equity exposure are all consistent with the model. Quantitatively, however, the match is quite imperfect. Much of the observed variation in risk-taking takes the form of discrete entry to or exit from the stock market, rather than variation in the portfolio allocation to equities. Also, very few households are as aggressive as would be recommended by our calibrated life-cycle model. Some of these inconsistencies no doubt arise from limitations of this particular model. We have assumed parameter values for average asset returns that we believe to be reasonable, but investors could certainly disagree with these assumptions and use alternative parameter values that would imply different portfolio allocations. We have also assumed that investors know parameter values with certainty; if instead they must learn about parameter values over time, this can have important effects on portfolio choice, as emphasized by Brennan (1998).

The model ignores both time variation in real interest rates and mean-reversion in stock returns, despite the important effects that these can have on optimal portfolios for long-term investors. Time variation in real interest rates is particularly interesting because it would introduce a distinction between short-term and long-term bonds. A safe stream of labor income is a substitute for the cash flows produced by a long-term inflation-indexed bond, so a model with time-varying real interest rates should imply that these bonds appeal to older households more than to younger ones.[5]

The model also ignores fixed commitments that households make during their lives. Most notably, the model ignores housing, which is an important asset for many households. Purchase of a house requires a stream of mortgage payments and is expensive to reverse if these payments become unaffordable. Expenses for private education of children can similarly be regarded as commitments that are costly to reverse. A model that incorporates fixed commitments will recommend more conservative investment strategies than the model solved in this chapter, along the lines of the subsistence–consumption model discussed in Section 6.1.3.[6]

A complete treatment of housing would need to capture several other interesting features of this asset. First, a house delivers

---

[5] Michaelides (2001) considers a model with both risky labor income and a predictable time-varying equity premium. However, he assumes a constant real interest rate.

[6] Cocco (1998) and Campbell and Cocco (2001) are preliminary attempts to integrate housing into a life-cycle model of portfolio choice.

a predictable stream of housing services and thus can be seen as a safe asset for a long-term investor who values those services, just as an inflation-indexed bond is a safe asset for a long-term investor who values consumption goods. This may help to explain why many investors place a large fraction of their wealth in an asset with an uncertain capital value. Second, housing receives special treatment from the tax authorities (through the deductibility of mortgage interest), from the legal system (housing wealth is often more readily sheltered from creditors in the event of bankruptcy), and even from college financial-aid offices. (Housing wealth is not counted when colleges offer reduced tuition to less wealthy families.)

Finally, we have omitted other relevant features of the tax code from our model. Dammon, Spatt, and Zhang (2001), for example, point out that the forgiveness of capital gains taxes at death makes equities particularly attractive investments for elderly investors. This effect works to reduce the shift out of equities predicted by the life-cycle model.

Despite these limitations of our normative analysis, it is likely also that many households fail to optimize their portfolios correctly. There is evidence that many households are inadequately diversified and are subject to behavioral biases such as those described by Kahneman and Tversky's (1979) prospect theory. It is our belief that financial economists will have an important role in providing scientifically grounded investment advice to help households overcome these problems.

The lessons of long-term portfolio choice theory
What are the lessons of portfolio choice theory for long-term investors? By considering a series of deliberately simplified models, we hope to have communicated the following important points.

First, Chapter 3 showed that Treasury bills and other money market investments are relatively safe for short-term investors but not for long-term investors. Long-term investors must roll over bills at uncertain future real interest rates. Just as long-term borrowers have come to understand the risk that short-term debt will have to be refinanced at high penalty rates, so long-term investors need to understand the risk that short-term assets will be reinvested at unattractively low interest rates. The safe asset for a long-term investor is not a Treasury bill but a long-term inflation-indexed bond; this asset provides a stable stream of real income, and therefore supports a stable stream of consumption, over the long term.

Second, nominal bonds share the attractive characteristics of inflation-indexed bonds when inflation risk is low. In an environment with uncertain inflation, however, nominal bonds are no longer safe long-term assets. Long-term investors can suffer large utility losses if inflation risk is high and inflation-indexed bonds are unavailable; in this sense, monetary policy and bond indexation are policy issues of first-order importance to investors. Chapter 3 showed that inflation risk has been relatively low in the USA since 1983 but was much higher earlier in the postwar period, while Chapter 4 confirmed the importance of inflation risk in postwar US data. Conservative long-term investors should be cautious about nominal bonds unless they are confident that the present regime of stable monetary policy will continue.

Third, Chapter 4 presented evidence for predictable components in excess returns on stocks and nominal bonds. The predictability of stock returns from dividend–price ratios implies that stocks are mean-reverting, with lower annualized risk at long horizons. This type of predictability creates positive intertemporal hedging demand for stocks by conservative investors. Such investors, with relative risk aversion greater than one, should be more enthusiastic buyers of equities than they would be if excess returns were unpredictable. Predictability also implies that all investors with constant relative risk aversion should be 'strategic market timers'; that is, they should adjust their portfolios gradually in response to the return signals provided by dividend–price ratios, yield spreads, and other information variables. It is not correct to adjust average holdings of long-term assets while maintaining a buy-and-hold strategy, as some authors have advocated.

Fourth, in Chapter 5 we explored two other effects that can reduce the demand for stocks by conservative long-term investors. Stock market volatility tends to increase, worsening investment opportunities, when stock prices fall. This creates negative intertemporal hedging demand for equities. Empirically, however, this effect is small relative to the mean-reversion in expected returns because volatility shocks tend to be transitory. Also, investors may be uncertain about long-term average stock returns. If they learn about average returns by observing realized returns, expected future returns will tend to increase when realized returns are high; this also creates negative intertemporal hedging demand for equities. The importance of this effect depends on the degree of uncertainty but will tend to diminish over time as investors become more confident of the process driving returns.

Fifth, labor income can have an enormous effect on strategic asset allocation. Chapter 6 showed that a riskless stream of labor income is equivalent to a large implicit holding of riskless assets; this strongly tilts the financial portfolio away from riskless assets and toward risky assets. Idiosyncratic risk in labor income diminishes but cannot reverse this tilt. Only if labor income is both sufficiently risky and sufficiently correlated with risky asset returns, as might be the case for an employee of a Wall Street firm, can the presence of labor income actually tilt the portfolio toward safe assets. Flexibility in labor supply—the ability to take on extra jobs, work extra hours, or delay retirement if necessary—also increases an investor's willingness to take on financial risk. Fixed commitments, on the other hand, act like negative labor income and tilt portfolios away from risky assets.

Sixth, these results have important consequences for investor behavior over the life cycle. A typical individual starts adult life with little financial wealth; initially, as labor income increases, human wealth may grow faster than financial wealth, but fairly early in adult life financial wealth starts to accumulate faster than the present value of remaining labor income. This implies that most younger investors with relatively safe labor income should concentrate their portfolios heavily in equities, and gradually shift toward fixed-income securities as they approach retirement.

These findings partially justify, but also clarify and qualify, the conventional wisdom of financial planners. The tendency of financial planners to recommend bonds to conservative investors is justifiable if the bonds are inflation-indexed or if inflation uncertainty is low, as it has been in the USA in recent years. Likewise, the tendency to recommend higher equity allocations to younger investors can be justified by mean-reversion in the stock market or by the typical pattern of labor income over the life cycle. Traditional financial planning advice, however, is rarely accompanied by an explicit statement of the beliefs that support the advice. Investors are likely to make better decisions if they understand what they must believe about the world in order to accept a recommended portfolio.

The practical implementation of strategic asset allocation is certainly not easy. To invest strategically, individuals and institutions must first think systematically about their preferences and about the constraints they face. They must form beliefs about the future—not just about average asset returns and the risks of these returns, but also about the dynamic processes that determine riskless interest rates and risk premia. Then they must combine preferences, constraints, and beliefs to form optimal portfolios along the lines described in this book. Finally, they must be willing to carry out their strategic plan without succumbing to psychological biases. One of the most interesting challenges of the twenty-first century will be the development of systems, combining the scientific knowledge of financial economists with information technology and the human expertise of financial planners, to help investors carry out the task of strategic asset allocation. Prototypes of such systems exist today, and writers on technology such as Dertouzos (1997) envision more advanced versions.[7] We hope that the ideas discussed in this book will have an important influence on the development of such financial planning systems.

---

[7] One example is the Financial Engines website (http://www.financialengines. com/), founded by William Sharpe. Dertouzos' vision of financial planning appears on pp. 134–6 of Dertouzos (1997).

References

Abel, Andrew B. (1990) 'Asset Prices under Habit Formation and Catching Up with the Joneses', *American Economic Review Papers and Proceedings* 80, 38–42.

Abowd, John M., and David Card (1989) 'On the Covariance Structure of Earnings and Hours Changes', *Econometrica* 57, 411–45.

Aït-Sahalia, Yacine, and Michael Brandt (2001) 'Variable Selection for Portfolio Choice', *Journal of Finance*, 56, 1297–351.

Ameriks, John, and Stephen Zeldes (2000) 'How Do Household Portfolio Shares Vary with Age?', unpublished paper, Columbia University.

Andersen, Torben, Luca Benzoni, and Jesper Lund (1998) 'Estimating Jump-Diffusions for Equity Returns', unpublished paper, Northwestern University.

Ang, Andrew, Geert Bekaert, and Jun Liu (2000) 'Why Stocks May Disappoint', unpublished paper, Columbia University.

Arrow, Kenneth (1970) *Essays in the Theory of Risk Bearing*, North-Holland, London.

Attanasio, Orazio (1995) 'The Intertemporal Allocation of Consumption: Theory and Evidence', *Carnegie–Rochester Conference Series on Public Policy*, pp. 39–89.

Balduzzi, Perluigi, and Anthony Lynch (1999) 'Transaction Costs and Predictability: Some Utility Cost Calculations', *Journal of Financial Economics* 52, 47–78.

Barberis, Nicholas C. (2000) 'Investing for the Long Run when Returns are Predictable', *Journal of Finance* 55, 225–64.

Barsky, Robert B., F. Thomas Juster, Miles S. Kimball, and Matthew D. Shapiro (1997) 'Preference Parameters and Behavioral Heterogeneity: An Experimental Approach in the Health and Retirement Study', *Quarterly Journal of Economics* 112, 537–79.

Basu, Susanto, and Miles S. Kimball (2000) 'Long-Run Labor Supply and the Elasticity of Intertemporal Substitution for Consumption', unpublished paper, University of Michigan.

Bawa, Vijay, Stephen Brown, and Roger Klein (1979) *Estimation Risk and Optimal Portfolio Choice*, North-Holland, Amsterdam.

Bekaert, Geert, Robert J. Hodrick, and David A. Marshall (1997a) 'On Biases in Tests of the Expectations Hypothesis of the Term Structure of Interest Rates', *Journal of Financial Economics* 44, 309–48.

Bekaert, Geert, Robert J. Hodrick, and David A. Marshall (1997b) 'The Implications of First Order Risk Aversion for Asset Market Risk Premiums', *Journal of Monetary Economics* 40, 3–39.

Benartzi, Shlomo (2001) 'Excessive Extrapolation and the Allocation of 401 (k) Accounts to Company Stock', *Journal of Finance* 56, 1747–64.

—— and Richard Thaler (2001) 'Naive Diversification Strategies in Defined Contribution Saving Plans', *American Economic Review* 91, 79–98.

Bernstein, Peter L. (1992) *Capital Ideas: The Improbable Origins of Modern Wall Street*, Free Press, New York.

Bertaut, Carol C., and Michael Haliassos (1995) 'Why Do So Few Hold Stocks?' *Economic Journal* 105, 1110–29.

—— and —— (1997) 'Precautionary Portfolio Behavior from a Life-Cycle Perspective', *Journal of Economic Dynamics and Control* 21, 1511–42.

Blanchard, Olivier J. (1985) 'Debt, Deficits, and Finite Horizons', *Journal of Political Economy* 93, 223–47.

—— (1993) 'Movements in the Equity Premium', *Brookings Papers on Economic Activity* 2, 75–118.

Bodie, Zvi, Robert C. Merton, and William Samuelson (1992) 'Labor Supply Flexibility and Portfolio Choice in a Life Cycle Model', *Journal of Economic Dynamics and Control* 16, 427–49.

Bollerslev, Tim, Ray Y. Chou and Kenneth Kroner (1992) 'ARCH Modeling in Finance', *Journal of Econometrics* 52, 5–59.

Bowman, David, Debby Minehart, and Matthew Rabin (1999) 'Loss Aversion in a Consumption–Savings Model', *Journal of Economic Behavior and Organization* 38, 155–78.

Brandt, Michael (1999) 'Estimating Portfolio and Consumption Choice: A Conditional Euler Equations Approach', *Journal of Finance* 54, 1609–45.

Breeden, Douglas (1979) 'An Intertemporal Asset Pricing Model with Stochastic Consumption and Investment Opportunities', *Journal of Financial Economics* 7, 265–96.

Brennan, Michael J. (1998) 'The Role of Learning in Dynamic Portfolio Decisions', *European Finance Review* 1, 295–306.

—— and Eduardo S. Schwartz (1988) 'Time Invariant Portfolio Insurance Strategies', *Journal of Finance* 43, 283–99.

—— —— and Ronald Lagnado (1997) 'Strategic Asset Allocation', *Journal of Economic Dynamics and Control* 21, 1377–1403.

—— —— and —— (1999) 'The Use of Treasury Bill Futures in Strategic Asset Allocation Programs', in William T. Ziemba and John M. Mulvey (eds), *World Wide Asset and Liability Modeling*, Cambridge University Press, Cambridge, pp. 205–28.

—— and Yihong Xia (2001) 'Dynamic Asset Allocation under Inflation', unpublished paper, UCLA and University of Pennsylvania.

Caballero, Ricardo J. (1990) 'Consumption Puzzles and Precautionary Savings', *Journal of Monetary Economics* 25, 113–36.

Campbell, John Y. (1987) 'Stock Returns and the Term Structure', *Journal of Financial Economics* 18, 373–99.

—— (1991) 'A Variance Decomposition for Stock Returns', *Economic Journal* 101, 157–79.

—— (1993) 'Intertemporal Asset Pricing without Consumption Data', *American Economic Review* 83, 487–512.

—— (1996) 'Understanding Risk and Return', *Journal of Political Economy* 104, 298–345.

—— (1999) 'Asset Prices, Consumption, and the Business Cycle', chapter 19 in John Taylor and Michael Woodford (eds), *Handbook of Macroeconomics*, Vol. 1, North-Holland, Amsterdam.

—— (2000) 'Asset Pricing at the Millennium', *Journal of Finance* 55, 1515–67.

—— Yeung Lewis Chan, and Luis M. Viceira (2001) 'A Multivariate Model of Strategic Asset Allocation', unpublished paper, Harvard University.

—— and João Cocco (2001) 'Household Risk Management and Optimal Mortgage Choice', unpublished paper, Harvard University and London Business School.

—— João Cocco, Francisco Gomes, and Pascal Maenhout, (2001a) 'Investing Retirement Wealth: A Life-Cycle Model', chapter 11 in John Y. Campbell and Martin Feldstein (eds), *Risk Aspects of Investment-Based Social Security Reform*, University of Chicago Press, Chicago, IL.

—————— and Luis Viceira (2001b) 'Stock Market Mean Reversion and the Optimal Equity Allocation of a Long-Lived Investor', *European Finance Review*, forthcoming.

—— and John H. Cochrane (1999) 'By Force of Habit: A Consumption-Based Explanation of Aggregate Stock Market Behavior', *Journal of Political Economy* 107, 205–51.

—— and Martin Feldstein (eds) (2001) *Risk Aspects of Investment-Based Social Security Reform*, University of Chicago Press, Chicago, IL.

—— and Ludger Hentschel (1992) 'No News is Good News: An Asymmetric Model of Changing Volatility in Stock Returns', *Journal of Financial Economics* 31, 281–318.

—— and Hyeng Keun Koo (1997) 'A Comparison of Numerical and Analytical Approximate Solutions to an Intertemporal Consumption Choice Problem', *Journal of Economic Dynamics and Control* 21, 273–95.

—— and Albert S. Kyle (1993) 'Smart Money, Noise Trading, and Stock Price Behavior', *Review of Economic Studies* 60, 1–34.

——Andrew W. Lo, and A. Craig MacKinlay (1997) *The Econometrics of Financial Markets*, Princeton University Press, Princeton, NJ.

——and Sydney Ludvigson (2001) 'Elasticities of Substitution in Real Business Cycle Models with Home Production', *Journal of Money, Credit, and Banking* 33, 847–75.

——and N. Gregory Mankiw (1989) 'Consumption, Income, and Interest Rates: Reinterpreting the Time Series Evidence', in Olivier J. Blanchard and Stanley Fischer (eds), *National Bureau of Economic Research Macroeconomics Annual 1989*, MIT Press, Cambridge, MA, pp. 185–216.

——and Robert J. Shiller (1988) 'The Dividend–Price Ratio and Expectations of Future Dividends and Discount Factors', *Review of Financial Studies* 1, 195–228.

——and——(1991) 'Yield Spreads and Interest Rates: A Bird's Eye View', *Review of Economic Studies* 58, 495–514.

——and——(1996) 'A Scorecard for Indexed Government Debt', in Ben S. Bernanke and Julio Rotemberg (eds), *National Bureau of Economic Research Macroeconomics Annual* Vol. 11, pp. 155–97.

——and——(2001) 'Valuation Ratios and the Long-Run Stock Market Outlook: An Update', NBER Working Paper No. 8221.

——and Luis M. Viceira (1999) 'Consumption and Portfolio Decisions when Expected Returns are Time Varying', *Quarterly Journal of Economics* 114, 433–95.

——and——(2000) 'Consumption and Portfolio Decisions when Expected Returns are Time Varying: Erratum', on http://kuznets.fas.harvard.edu/~campbell/papers.html

——and——(2001a) 'Who Should Buy Long-Term Bonds?', *American Economic Review* 91, 99–127.

——and——(2001b) Appendix to *Strategic Asset Allocation*, on http://kuznets.fas.harvard.edu/~campbell/papers.html.

Canner, Niko, N. Gregory Mankiw, and David N. Weil (1997) 'An Asset Allocation Puzzle', *American Economic Review* 87, 181–91.

Carroll, Christopher D. (1992) 'The Buffer-Stock Theory of Saving: Some Macroeconomic Evidence', *Brookings Papers on Economic Activity*, pp. 61–156.

——(1997) 'Buffer-Stock Saving and the Life Cycle–Permanent Income Hypothesis', *Quarterly Journal of Economics* 112, 1–55.

——(2001) 'Portfolios of the Rich', in Luigi Guiso, Michael Haliassos, and Tullio Jappelli (eds), *Household Portfolios: Theory and Evidence*, MIT Press, Cambridge, MA.

——and Miles S. Kimball (1996) 'On the Concavity of the Consumption Function', *Econometrica* 64, 981–92.

——and Andrew Samwick (1997) 'The Nature of Precautionary Wealth', *Journal of Monetary Economics* 40, 41–72.

Carroll, Christopher D, and Lawrence H. Summers (1991) 'Consumption Growth Parallels Income Growth: Some New Evidence', in B. D. Bernheim and John B. Shoven (eds), *National Savings and Economic Performance*, University of Chicago Press, Chicago, IL.

Chacko, George, and Luis M. Viceira (1998) 'Spectral GMM Estimation of Continuous-Time Processes', unpublished paper, Harvard University.

—— and —— (1999) 'Dynamic Consumption and Portfolio Choice with Stochastic Volatility in Incomplete Markets', NBER Working Paper No. 7377.

—— and —— (2000) 'Perturbation Methods for Dynamic Investment–Consumption Problems', unpublished paper, Harvard University.

Chamberlain, Gary, and Keisuke Hirano (1999) 'Predictive Distributions Based on Longitudinal Earnings Data', *Annales d'Economie et de Statistique* 55–6, 211–42.

Chan, Yeung Lewis (2000) *Essays on Financial Economics*, Ph.D. dissertation, Harvard University.

Clarida, Richard, Jordi Gali, and Mark Gertler (2000) 'Monetary Policy Rules and Macroeconomic Stability: Evidence and Some Theory', *Quarterly Journal of Economics* 115, 147–80.

Cocco, João (1998) 'Owner-Occupied Housing, Permanent Income, and Portfolio Choice', unpublished paper, Harvard University.

—— Francisco Gomes, and Pascal Maenhout (1998) 'Consumption and Portfolio Choice over the Life Cycle', unpublished paper, Harvard University.

Cochrane, John H. (2001) *Asset Pricing*, Princeton University Press, Princeton, NJ.

—— and Lars P. Hansen (1992) 'Asset Pricing Explorations for Macroeconomics', in Olivier J. Blanchard and Stanley Fischer (eds), *National Bureau of Economic Research Macroeconomics Annual*.

Comon, Etienne (2001) 'Extreme Events and the Role of Learning in Financial Markets', unpublished paper, Harvard University.

Constantinides, George M. (1983) 'Capital Market Equilibrium with Personal Tax', *Econometrica* 51, 611–36.

—— (1984) 'Optimal Stock Trading with Personal Taxes', *Journal of Financial Economics* 13, 65–89.

—— (1990) 'Habit Formation: A Resolution of the Equity Premium Puzzle', *Journal of Political Economy* 98, 519–43.

—— John B. Donaldson, and Rajnish Mehra (2001) 'Junior Can't Borrow: A New Perspective on the Equity Premium Puzzle', *Quarterly Journal of Economics*, forthcoming.

—— and Darrell Duffie (1996) 'Asset Pricing with Heterogeneous Consumers', *Journal of Political Economy* 104, 219–40.

Cox, John C., and Chi-fu Huang (1989) 'Optimal Consumption and Portfolio Policies when Asset Prices Follow a Diffusion Process', *Journal of Economic Theory* 39, 33–83.

—— and Hayne Leland (1982) 'Notes on Intertemporal Investment Policies', unpublished paper, Stanford University.

Cvitanić, J. and I. Karatzas (1992) 'Convex Duality in Constrained Portfolio Optimization', *Annals of Applied Probability*, 767–818.

Dammon, Robert M., Chester S. Spatt, and Harold H. Zhang (2001) 'Optimal Consumption and Investment with Capital Gains Taxes', *Review of Financial Studies* 14, 583–616.

Davis, Steven, and Paul Willen (2000) 'Occupation-Level Income Shocks and Asset Returns: Their Covariance and Implications for Portfolio Choice', NBER Working Paper No. 7905.

Deaton, Angus S. (1991) 'Savings and Liquidity Constraints', *Econometrica* 59, 1221–48.

Degeorge, Francois, Dirk Jenter, Alberto Moel, and Peter Tufano (2000) 'Selling Company Shares to Reluctant Employees: France Telecom's Experience', NBER Working Paper No. 7683.

Dertouzos, Michael (1997) *What Will Be: How the New World of Information Will Change Our Lives*, HarperCollins, New York.

Detemple, Jerome B. (1986) 'Asset Pricing in a Production Economy with Incomplete Information', *Journal of Finance* 41, 383–91.

Dothan, M., and David Feldman (1986) 'Equilibrium Interest Rates and Multiperiod Bonds in a Partially Observable Economy', *Journal of Finance* 41, 369–82.

Duesenberry, James S. (1949) *Income, Saving, and the Theory of Consumer Behavior*, Harvard University Press, Cambridge, MA.

Duffie, Darrell (1996) *Dynamic Asset Pricing Theory*, Princeton University Press, Princeton, NJ.

—— and Larry G. Epstein (1992a) 'Stochastic Differential Utility', *Econometrica* 60, 353–94.

—— and —— (1992b) 'Asset Pricing with Stochastic Differential Utility', *Review of Financial Studies* 5, 411–36.

Dybvig, Philip H. (1995) 'Duesenberry's Ratcheting of Consumption: Optimal Dynamic Consumption and Investment Policies given Intolerance for any Decline in Standard of Living', *Review of Economic Studies* 62, 287–313.

Eeckhoudt, Louis, Christian Gollier, and Harris Schlesinger (1996) 'Changes in Background Risk and Risk Taking Behavior', *Econometrica* 64, 1109–23.

Elmendorf, Douglas W., and Miles S. Kimball (2000) 'Taxation of Labor Income and the Demand for Risky Assets', *International Economic Review* 41, 801–32.

Elton, Edwin J., and Martin J. Gruber (2000) 'The Rationality of Asset Allocation Recommendations', *Journal of Financial and Quantitative Analysis* 35, 27–41.

Epstein, Lawrence, and Stanley Zin (1989) 'Substitution, Risk Aversion, and the Temporal Behavior of Consumption and Asset Returns: A Theoretical Framework', *Econometrica* 57, 937–69.

—— and Stanley Zin (1990) ' "First-Order" Risk Aversion and the Equity Premium Puzzle', *Journal of Monetary Economics* 26, 387–407.

—— and —— (1991) 'Substitution, Risk Aversion, and the Temporal Behavior of Consumption and Asset Returns: An Empirical Investigation', *Journal of Political Economy* 99, 263–86.

Fama, Eugene (1970) 'Multiperiod Consumption–Investment Decisions', *American Economic Review* 60, 163–74.

—— and Kenneth French (1988a) 'Dividend Yields and Expected Stock Returns', *Journal of Financial Economics* 22, 3–27.

—— and —— (1988b) 'Permanent and Temporary Components of Stock Prices', *Journal of Political Economy* 96, 246–73.

—— and —— (1989) 'Business Conditions and Expected Returns on Stocks and Bonds', *Journal of Financial Economics* 25, 23–49.

—— and —— (2000) 'The Equity Premium', unpublished paper, University of Chicago.

—— and G. William Schwert (1977a) 'Asset Returns and Inflation', *Journal of Financial Economics* 5, 115–30.

—— and —— (1977b) 'Human Capital and Capital Market Equilibrium', *Journal of Financial Economics* 5, 130–46.

Fischer, Stanley (1975) 'The Demand for Index Bonds', *Journal of Political Economy* 83, 509–34.

Fisher, Mark, and Christian Gilles (1998) 'Consumption and Asset Prices with Recursive Preferences', unpublished paper, Board of Governors of the Federal Reserve System.

French, Kenneth R., G. William Schwert, and Robert F. Stambaugh (1987) 'Expected Stock Returns and Volatility', *Journal of Financial Economics* 19, 3–29.

Gakidis, Harry (1997) 'Earnings Uncertainty and Life-Cycle Portfolio Choice', unpublished paper, MIT.

Gennotte, Gerard (1986) 'Optimal Portfolio Choice under Incomplete Information', *Journal of Finance* 41, 733–46.

Gertler, Mark (1999) 'Government Debt and Social Security in a Life-Cycle Economy', *Carnegie–Rochester Conference Series on Public Policy* 50, 61–110.

Ghysels, Eric, Andrew C. Harvey, and Eric Renault (1996) 'Stochastic Volatility', chapter 14 in G. S. Maddala and C. R. Rao (eds), *Handbook of Statistics*, Vol. 14, North-Holland, Amsterdam.

Giovannini, Alberto, and Philippe Weil (1989) 'Risk Aversion and Intertemporal Substitution in the Capital Asset Pricing Model', NBER Working Paper No. 2824, National Bureau of Economic Research, Cambridge, MA.

Glassman, James K., and Kevin A. Hassett (1999) *Dow 36,000: The New Strategy for Profiting from the Coming Rise in the Stock Market*, Times Books, New York.

Glosten, Lawrence R., Ravi Jagannathan, and David Runkle (1993) 'On the Relation between the Expected Value and the Volatility of the Nominal Excess Return on Stocks', *Journal of Finance* 48, 1779–801.

Goetzmann, William N., and Philippe Jorion (1993) 'Testing the Predictive Power of Dividend Yields', *Journal of Finance* 48, 663–79.

Gollier, Christian (2001) *The Economics of Risk and Time*, MIT Press, Cambridge, MA.

——and John W. Pratt (1996) 'Risk Vulnerability and the Tempering Effect of Background Risk', *Econometrica* 64, 1109–23.

——and Richard J. Zeckhauser (1997) 'Horizon Length and Portfolio Risk', NBER Technical Working Paper No. 216.

Gourinchas, Pierre-Olivier, and Jonathan Parker (2001) 'Consumption over the Life Cycle', *Econometrica*, forthcoming.

Green, Jerry, Michael Whinston, and Andreu Mas-Colell (1995) *Microeconomic Theory*, Oxford University Press, New York.

Grossman, Sanford J., and Robert J. Shiller (1981) 'The Determinants of the Variability of Stock Market Prices', *American Economic Review* 71, 222–7.

——and Zhongquan Zhou (1996) 'Equilibrium Analysis of Portfolio Insurance', *Journal of Finance* 51, 1379–403.

Guiso, Luigi, Michael Haliassos, and Tullio Jappelli (eds) (2001) *Household Portfolios: Theory and Evidence*, MIT Press, Cambridge, MA.

Gul, Faruk (1991) 'A Theory of Disappointment Aversion', *Econometrica* 59, 667–86.

Haliassos, Michael, and Carol Bertaut (1995) 'Why Do So Few Hold Stocks?', *Economic Journal* 105, 1110–29.

Hamilton, James D. (1994) *Time Series Analysis*, Princeton University Press, Princeton, NJ.

Hansen, Lars P., and Ravi Jagannathan (1991) 'Restrictions on Intertemporal Marginal Rates of Substitution Implied by Asset Returns', *Journal of Political Economy* 99, 225–62.

—— and Kenneth J. Singleton (1983) 'Stochastic Consumption, Risk Aversion, and the Temporal Behavior of Asset Returns', *Journal of Political Economy* 91, 249–68.

Harrison, J. Michael, and David M. Kreps (1979) 'Martingales and Arbitrage in Multiperiod Securities Markets', *Journal of Economic Theory* 20, 381–408.

Harvey, Campbell (1989) 'Time-Varying Conditional Covariances in Tests of Asset Pricing Models', *Journal of Financial Economics* 22, 305–34.

——(1991) 'The World Price of Covariance Risk', *Journal of Finance* 46, 111–57.

Heaton, John, and Deborah J. Lucas (1997) 'Market Frictions, Saving Behavior and Portfolio Choice', *Macroeconomic Dynamics* 1, 76–101.

—— and ——(2000) 'Portfolio Choice and Asset Prices: The Importance of Entrepeneurial Risk', *Journal of Finance* 55, 1163–98.

Hentschel, Ludger (1995) 'All in the Family: Nesting Symmetric and Asymmetric GARCH Models', *Journal of Financial Economics* 39, 71–104.

Hodrick, Robert J. (1992) 'Dividend Yields and Expected Stock Returns: Alternative Procedures for Inference and Measurement', *Review of Financial Studies* 5, 357–86.

Hubbard, Glenn, Jonathan S. Skinner, and Stephen Zeldes (1994) 'The Importance of Precautionary Motives for Explaining Individual and Aggregate Saving', *Carnegie–Rochester Conference Series on Public Policy* 40, 59–125.

Ingersoll, Jonathan E. Jr (1987) *Theory of Financial Decision Making*, Rowman & Littlefield, Totowa, NJ.

Jagannathan, Ravi, and Narayana R. Kocherlakota (1996) 'Why Should Older People Invest Less in Stocks than Younger People?', *Federal Reserve Bank of Minneapolis Quarterly Review*, pp. 11–23.

—— Ellen R. McGrattan, and Anna Scherbina (2001) 'The Declining US Equity Premium', NBER Working Paper No. 8172.

—— and Zhenyu Wang (1996) 'The Conditional CAPM and the Cross-Section of Expected Returns', *Journal of Finance* 51, 3–53.

Judd, Kenneth L. (1998) *Numerical Methods in Economics*, MIT Press, Cambridge, MA.

Kahneman, Daniel, and Amos Tversky (1979) 'Prospect Theory: An Analysis of Decision under Risk', *Econometrica* 46, 171–85.

Kandel, Shmuel, and Robert Stambaugh (1987) 'Long Horizon Returns and Short Horizon Models', CRSP Working Paper No. 222, University of Chicago.

—— and ——(1996) 'On the Predictability of Stock Returns: An Asset Allocation Perspective', *Journal of Finance* 51, 385–424.

Karatzas, Ioannis, J. Lehoczky, and Steven E. Shreve (1987) 'Optimal Portfolio and Consumption Decisions for a "Small Investor" on a Finite Horizon', *SIAM Journal of Control and Optimization* 25, 1557–86.

—— and Steven E. Shreve (1998) *Methods of Mathematical Finance*, Springer-Verlag, New York.

Keynes, John M. (1932) 'Economic Possibilities for our Grandchildren', in his *Essays in Persuasion*, Harcourt Brace, New York.

Kim, Tong Suk, and Edward Omberg (1996) 'Dynamic Nonmyopic Portfolio Behavior', *Review of Financial Studies* 9, 141–61.

Kimball, Miles S. (1990) 'Precautionary Saving in the Small and in the Large', *Econometrica* 58, 53–73.

—— (1993) 'Standard Risk Aversion', *Econometrica* 61, 589–611.

King, Robert G., Charles I. Plosser, and Sergio T. Rebelo (1988) 'Production, Growth, and Business Cycles, I: The Basic Neoclassical Model', *Journal of Monetary Economics* 21, 195–232.

Kocherlakota, Narayana (1996) 'The Equity Premium: It's Still a Puzzle', *Journal of Economic Literature* 34, 42–71.

Kogan, Leonid, and Raman Uppal (2000) 'Risk Aversion and Optimal Portfolio Policies in Partial and General Equilibrium Economies', unpublished paper, University of Pennsylvania (Wharton School) and London Business School.

Koo, Hyeng Keun (1998) 'Consumption and Portfolio Selection with Labor Income: A Continuous Time Approach', *Mathematical Finance* 8, 49–65.

—— (1999) 'Consumption and Portfolio Selection with Labor Income: A Discrete-Time Approach', *Mathematical Methods of Operations Research* 50, 219–43.

Kreps, David, and Edward Porteus (1978) 'Temporal Resolution of Uncertainty and Dynamic Choice Theory', *Econometrica* 46, 185–200.

Kritzman, Mark P. (2000) *Puzzles of Finance: Six Practical Problems and Their Remarkable Solutions*, John Wiley, New York.

Lax, Yoel (2000) 'Optimal Consumption and Portfolio Policies with Habit Formation and Subsistence Levels', unpublished paper, Wharton School, University of Pennsylvania.

Letendre, Marc-Andre, and Gregor Smith (2001) 'Precautionary Saving and Portfolio Allocation: DP by GMM', *Journal of Monetary Economics* 48, 197–215.

Lewis, Karen (1999) 'Trying to Explain Home Bias in Equities and Consumption', *Journal of Economic Literature* 37, 571–608.

Liptser, Robert S., and Albert N. Shiryaev (2001) *Statistics of Random Processes, II, Applications*, 2nd edn, Springer-Verlag, Berlin.

Liu, Jun (2001) 'Portfolio Choice in Stochastic Environments', unpublished paper, UCLA.

Lucas, Robert E. Jr (1978) 'Asset Prices in an Exchange Economy', *Econometrica* 46, 1429–46.

Lynch, Anthony W. (2001) 'Portfolio Choice and Equity Characteristics: Characterizing the Hedging Demands Induced by Return Predictability', *Journal of Financial Economics* 62, 67–130.

MaCurdy, Thomas E. (1982) 'The Use of Time Series Processes to Model the Error Structure of Earnings in a Longitudinal Data Analysis', *Journal of Econometrics* 18, 83–134.

Mankiw, N. Gregory (1986) 'The Equity Premium and the Concentration of Aggregate Shocks', *Journal of Financial Economics* 17, 211–19.

—— and Stephen P. Zeldes (1991) 'The Consumption of Stockholders and Nonstockholders', *Journal of Financial Economics* 29, 97–112.

Markowitz, Harry (1952) 'Portfolio Selection', *Journal of Finance* 7, 77–91.

Mayers, David (1972) 'Nonmarketable Assets and Capital Market Equilibrium under Uncertainty', in Michael C. Jensen (ed.), *Studies in the Theory of Capital Markets*, Praeger, New York.

McCulloch, J. Huston, and Heon-Chul Kwon (1993) 'US Term Structure Data 1947–1991', Working Paper No. 93–6, Ohio State University.

Mehra, Rajnish, and Edward C. Prescott (1985) 'The Equity Premium: A Puzzle', *Journal of Monetary Economics* 15, 145–61.

Merton, Robert C. (1969) 'Lifetime Portfolio Selection under Uncertainty: The Continuous Time Case', *Review of Economics and Statistics* 51, 247–57.

—— (1971) 'Optimum Consumption and Portfolio Rules in a Continuous-Time Model', *Journal of Economic Theory* 3, 373–413.

—— (1973) 'An Intertemporal Capital Asset Pricing Model', *Econometrica* 41, 867–87.

—— (1980) 'On Estimating the Expected Return on the Market: An Exploratory Investigation', *Journal of Financial Economics* 8, 323–61.

—— (1990) *Continuous Time Finance*, Basil Blackwell, Cambridge, MA.

Michaelides, Alexander (2001) 'Portfolio Choice, Liquidity Constraints, and Stock Market Mean Reversion', unpublished paper, University of Cyprus.

Modigliani, Franco, and Richard Sutch (1966) 'Innovations in Interest Rate Policy', *American Economic Review* 56, 178–97.

Mossin, Jan (1968) 'Optimal Multiperiod Portfolio Policies', *Journal of Business* 41, 205–25.

Muirhead, Robb J. (1982) *Aspects of Multivariate Statistical Theory*, John Wiley, New York.

Neftci, Salih N. (1996) *An Introduction to the Mathematics of Financial Derivatives*, Academic Press, San Diego, CA.

Nelson, Charles R., and Myung J. Kim (1993) 'Predictable Stock Returns: The Role of Small Sample Bias', *Journal of Finance* 48, 641–61.

Nelson, Daniel B., and Dean P. Foster (1994) 'Asymptotic Filtering Theory for Univariate ARCH Models', *Econometrica* 62, 1–41.

Nielsen, Lars Tyge, and Maria Vassalou (2000) 'Portfolio Selection with Randomly Time-Varying Moments: The Role of the Instantaneous Capital Market Line', unpublished paper, INSEAD and Columbia University.

Pastor, Lubos (2000) 'Portfolio Selection and Asset Pricing Models', *Journal of Finance* 55, 179–223.

Pischke, Jörn-Steffen (1995) 'Individual Income, Incomplete Information, and Aggregate Consumption', *Econometrica* 63, 805–40.

Pliska, S. (1986) 'A Stochastic Calculus Model of Continuous Trading: Optimal Portfolios', *Mathematics of Operations Research*, 11, 371–82.

Polyanin, Andrei D., and Valentin F. Zaitsev (1995) *Handbook of Exact Solutions for Ordinary Differential Equations*, CRC Press, Boca Raton, FL.

Poterba, James M. (2001) 'Taxation and Portfolio Structure: Issues and Implications', NBER Working Paper No. 8223.

——— and Andrew Samwick (2001) 'Household Portfolio Allocation over the Lifecycle', in S. Ogura, T. Tachibanaki, and D. Wise (eds), *Aging Issues in the US and Japan*, University of Chicago Press, Chicago, IL.

——— and Lawrence H. Summers (1988) 'Mean Reversion in Stock Returns: Evidence and Implications', *Journal of Financial Economics* 22, 27–60.

Pratt, John W. (1964) 'Risk Aversion in the Small and in the Large', *Econometrica* 32, 122–36.

——— and Richard J. Zeckhauser (1987) 'Proper Risk Aversion', *Econometrica* 55, 143–54.

Restoy, Fernando (1992) 'Optimal Portfolio Policies under Time-Dependent Returns', Bank of Spain Working Paper No. 9207, Madrid.

Rogers, Chris G. and Denis Talay (eds) (1997) *Numerical Methods in Finance*, Cambridge University Press, Cambridge, UK.

Ross, Stephen A. (1999) 'Samuelson's Fallacy of Large Numbers Revisited', *Journal of Financial and Quantitative Analysis* 34, 323–39.

Rubinstein, Mark (1976a) 'The Strong Case for the Generalized Logarithmic Utility Model as the Premier Model of Financial Markets', *Journal of Finance* 31, 551–71.

——— (1976b) 'The Valuation of Uncertain Income Streams and the Pricing of Options', *Bell Journal of Economics* 7, 407–25.

Ryder, Harl E. Jr, and Geoffrey M. Heal (1973) 'Optimum Growth with Intertemporally Dependent Preferences', *Review of Economic Studies* 40, 1–33.

Samuelson, Paul A. (1963) 'Risk and Uncertainty: A Fallacy of Large Numbers', *Scientia* 1–6.

——— (1969) 'Lifetime Portfolio Selection by Dynamic Stochastic Programming', *Review of Economics and Statistics* 51, 239–46.

Samuelson, Paul A. (1979) 'Why We Should Not Make Mean Log of Wealth Big though Years to Act Are Long', *Journal of Banking and Finance* 3, 305–7.

—— (1989) 'A Case at Last for Age-Phased Reductions in Equity', *Proceedings of the National Academy of Sciences* 86, 9048–51.

—— (1991) 'Long-run Risk Tolerance when Equity Returns are Mean Regressing: Pseudoparadoxes and Vindication of a "Businessman's Risk"', in William C. Brainard, William D. Nordhaus, and Harold W. Watts (eds), *Money, Macroeconomics, and Economic Policy: Essays in Honor of James Tobin*, MIT Press, Cambridge, MA, pp. 181–200.

Schroder, Mark, and Costis Skiadas (1999) 'Optimal Consumption and Portfolio Selection with Stochastic Differential Utility', *Journal of Economic Theory* 89, 68–126.

Sharpe, William F. (1964) 'Capital Asset Prices: A Theory of Market Equilibrium under Conditions of Risk', *Journal of Finance* 19, 425–42.

—— (1966) 'Mutual Fund Performance', *Journal of Business*, 119–38.

Shiller, Robert J. (1979) 'The Volatility of Long-Term Interest Rates and Expectations Models of the Term Structure', *Journal of Political Economy* 87, 1190–219.

—— (1982) 'Consumption, Asset Markets, and Macroeconomic Fluctuations', *Carnegie Mellon Conference Series on Public Policy* 17, 203–38.

—— (1989) *Market Volatility*, MIT Press, Cambridge, MA.

—— (1999) 'Human Behavior and the Efficiency of the Financial System', in John Taylor and Michael Woodford (eds), *Handbook of Macroeconomics*, Vol. 1, North-Holland, Amsterdam.

—— John Y. Campbell, and Kermit L. Schoenholtz (1983) 'Forward Rates and Future Policy: Interpreting the Term Structure of Interest Rates', *Brookings Papers on Economic Activity* 1, 173–217.

Shore, Stephen, and Joshua White (2001) 'External Habit Formation and the Home Bias Puzzle', unpublished paper, Harvard University.

Siegel, Jeremy (1994) *Stocks for the Long Run*, McGraw-Hill, New York.

Singleton, Kenneth J. (1990) 'Specification and Estimation of Intertemporal Asset Pricing Models', in Ben Friedman and Frank Hahn (eds), *Handbook of Monetary Economics*, North-Holland, Amsterdam.

—— (2001) 'Estimation of Affine Asset Pricing Models Using the Empirical Characteristic Function', *Journal of Econometrics* 102, 111–41.

Stambaugh, Robert F. (1999) 'Predictive Regressions', *Journal of Financial Economics* 54, 375–421.

Stiglitz, Joseph E. (1970) 'A Consumption-Oriented Theory of the Demand for Financial Assets and the Term Structure of Interest Rates', *Review of Economic Studies* 37, 321–51.

Storesletten, Kjetil, Chris I. Telmer, and Amir Yaron (1999) 'The Risk Sharing Implications of Alternative Social Security Arrangements', *Carnegie–Rochester Conference Series on Public Policy* 50.

Sundaresan, Suresh M. (1989) 'Intertemporally Dependent Preferences and the Volatility of Consumption and Wealth', *Review of Financial Studies* 2, 73–89.

Svensson, Lars E. O. (1989) 'Portfolio Choice with Non-expected Utility in Continuous Time', *Economics Letters* 30, 313–17.

——and Ingrid M. Werner (1993) 'Nontraded Assets in Incomplete Markets: Pricing and Portfolio Choice', *European Economic Review* 37, 1149–68.

Tauchen, George, and R. Hussey (1991) 'Quadrature-Based Methods for Obtaining Approximate Solutions to Nonlinear Asset Pricing Models', *Econometrica* 59, 371–96.

Teplá, Lucie (2000) 'Optimal Portfolio Policies with Borrowing and Short-sale Constraints', *Journal of Economic Dynamics and Control* 24, 1623–39.

Thaler, Richard (1985) 'Mental Accounting and Consumer Choice', *Marketing Science* 4, 199–214.

Tobin, James (1958) 'Liquidity Preference as Behavior towards Risk', *Review of Economic Studies* 25, 68–85.

Vasicek, Oldrich (1977) 'An Equilibrium Characterization of the Term Structure', *Journal of Financial Economics* 5, 177–88.

Viard, Alan D. (1993) 'The Welfare Gain from the Introduction of Indexed Bonds', *Journal of Money, Credit, and Banking* 25, 612–28.

Viceira, Luis M. (1998) *Optimal Consumption and Portfolio Choice for Long-Horizon Investors*, Ph.D. thesis, Harvard University.

——(2001) 'Optimal Portfolio Choice for Long-Horizon Investors with Nontradable Labor Income', *Journal of Finance* 56, 433–70.

Vissing-Jorgensen, Annette (1999) 'Limited Stock Market Participation and the Equity Premium Puzzle', unpublished paper, University of Chicago.

Wachter, Jessica (2000) 'Risk Aversion and Allocation to Long-Term Bonds', Chapter 2 in *Essays in Financial Economics*, PhD dissertation, Harvard University.

——(2002) 'Portfolio and Consumption Decisions under Mean-Reverting Returns: An Exact Solution', forthcoming *Journal of Financial and Quantitative Analysis*.

Weil, Philippe (1989) 'The Equity Premium Puzzle and the Risk-Free Rate Puzzle', *Journal of Monetary Economics* 24, 401–21.

Williams, Joseph (1977) 'Capital Asset Prices with Heterogeneous Beliefs', *Journal of Financial Economics* 5, 219–39.

Xia, Yihong (2001) 'Learning about Predictability: The Effects of Parameter Uncertainty on Dynamic Asset Allocation', *Journal of Finance* 56, 205–46.

Author Index

Abel, Andrew B. 177, 181
Abowd, John M., with
  D. Card 182
Ait-Sahalia, Yacine with
  M. Brandt 154
Ameriks, John, with S. Zeldes 199,
  200, 201
Andersen, Torben, with L. Benzoni
  and J. Lund 149
Ang, Andrew, with G. Bekaert
  and J. Liu $9n$
Arrow, Kenneth $22n$
Attanasio, Orazio 207

Balduzzi, Perluigi, with
  A. Lynch $7n$
Barberis, Nicholas C. $7n$, $33n$, 89,
  110, $155n$
Barsky, Robert B., with F. T. Juster,
  M. S. Kimball and
  M. D. Shapiro 214
Basu, Susanto, with
  M. S. Kimball $175n$
Bawa, Vijay, with S. Brown and
  R. Klein $155n$
Bekaert, Geert
  with J. Liu and A. Andrew
  $9n$
  with R. J. Hodrick and
  D. A. Marshall $9n$, 107
Benartzi, Shlomo 199
  with R. Thaler 199
Benzoni, Luca, with J. Lund and
  T. Andersen 149
Bernstein, P. 3

Bertaut, Carol C., with
  M. Haliassos 198
Blanchard, Olivier J. 11, 182
Bodie, Zvi, with R. C. Merton and
  W. Samuelson 15, 162–3, 165,
  $171n$, 174
Bollerslev, Tim, with R. Y. Chou
  and K. Kroner 147
Bowman, David, with D. Minehart
  and M. Rabin $9n$
Brandt, Michael, with
  Y. Ait-Sahalia 154
Breeden, Douglas 7, 11, 40, 57
Brennan, Michael J. 121, 154,
  158, 221
  with E. S. Schwartz 179
  with E. S. Schwartz and
  R. Lagnado $7n$
  with Y. Xia 121, 126
Brown, Stephen, with R. Klein
  and V. Bawa $155n$

Caballero, Ricardo J. 166, 194
Campbell, John Y. 11, $11n$, 39, 41,
  49, 51, 53, 55, 63, 69, 89,
  91, 96, 102, 106, 133, 154,
  203
  with Y. L. Chan and
  L. M. Viceira 90, 93, 101, 106,
  115, 116
  with J. Cocco $221n$
  with J. Cocco, F. Gomes and
  P. Maenhout 196, 197, 202,
  204, 207, 208, 213, 214, 215,
  216

Campbell, John Y. (*cont.*):
  with J. Cocco, F. Gomes,
  P. Maenhout and
  L. M. Viceira 94, 118n
  with J. H. Cochrane 119, 177
  with M. Feldstein 196n
  with L. Hentschel 149
  with H. K. Koo 93
  with A. S. Kyle 167
  with A. W. Lo and
    A. C. MacKinlay 59, 63, 96,
    103, 143, 147
  with S. Ludvigson 174
  with N. G. Mankiw 203
  with K. L. Schoenholtz and
    R. J. Shiller 143
  with R. J. Shiller 11, 53, 73,
    97, 115, 116, 187
  with L. M. Viceira 8, 28, 51, 62,
    64, 68, 70, 89, 93, 94–5, 97–8,
    100, 101, 106, 112, 126, 133,
    145, 150, 184, 186
Canner, Niko N., with
  G. Mankiw and D. N. Weil 4,
  5, 45, 79–80, 82, 222
Card, David, with
  J. M. Abowd 182
Carroll, Christopher D. 183,
  187n, 199
  with M. S. Kimball 169n
  with A. Samwick 187n, 208
  with L. H. Summers 208
Chacko, George, with
  L. M. Viceira 91, 120, 126, 147,
  148–50, 152
Chamberlain, Gary, with
  K. Hirano 187n
Chan, Yeung Lewis 175n
  with L. M. Viceira and
  J. Y. Campbell 90, 93, 101, 106,
  115, 116
Chou, Ray Y., with K. Kroner
  and T. Bollerslev 147

Clarida, Richard, with J. Gali
  and M. Gertler 70, 78
Cocco, João 221n
  with J. Y. Campbell 221n
  with F. Gomes and
  P. Maenhout 7n, 197, 202,
  206, 218
  with F. Gomes, P. Maenhout
    and J. Y. Campbell 196, 197,
    202, 204, 207, 208, 213, 214,
    215, 216
  with F. Gomes, P. Maenhout,
    L. M. Viceira and
    J. Y. Campbell 94, 118n
Cochrane, John H. 39
  with J. Y. Campbell 119, 177
  with L. P. Hansen 39
Comon, Etienne 155n
Constantinides, George M. 13n,
  177, 180
Cox, John C.
  with C. Haung 133, 137, 140
  with H. Leland 133, 179
Cvitanić, J., with I. Karatzas 61

Dammon, Robert M., with
  C. S. Spatt and
  H. H. Zhang 13n, 222
Davis, Steven, with P. Willen
  166, 194
Deaton, Angus S. 205
Degeorge, Francois, with D. Jenter,
  A. Moel and P. Tufano 198n
Dertouzos, Michael 225
Detemple, Jerome B. 154
Dothan, M., with D. Feldman 154
Duesenberry, James S. 177n
Duffie, Darrell 120
  with L. G. Epstein 144
Dybvig, Philip H. 180n

Eeckhoudt, Louis, with C. Gollier
  and H. Schlesinger 171n, 173n

Elmendorf, Douglas W., with
  M. S. Kimball 171n, 192
Elton, Edwin J., with
  M. J. Grubber 5n
Epstein, Larry G., with D. Duffie
  144
Epstein, Lawrence, with S. Zin
  8n, 9n, 43, 46

Fama, Eugene 6, 76n
  with K. French 11, 96, 97, 110
  with G. W. Schwert 7, 102, 203
Feldman, David, with
  M. Dothan 154
Feldstein, Martin, with
  J. Y. Campbell 196n
Fischer, Stanley 85n
Fisher, Mark, with C. Gilles 144
Foster, Dean P., with
  D. B. Nelson 155
French, Kenneth R.
  with E. Fama 11, 97
  with G. W. Schwert and
  R. F. Stambaugh 149

Gali, Jordi, with M. Gertler and
  R. Clarida 70, 78
Gennotte, Gerard 154, 156
Gertler, Mark 182
  with R. Clarida and J. Gali
  70, 78
Ghysels, Eric, with A. C. Harvey
  and E. Renault 147
Gilles, Christian, with
  M. Fisher 144
Giovannini, Alberto, with
  P. Weil 46
Glassman, James, with
  K. Hassett 117
Glosten, Lawrence R., with
  R. Jagannathan and
  D. Runkle 91, 102, 154

Goetzman, William N., with
  P. Jorion 107
Gollier, Christian 22n
  with J. W. Pratt 171n, 173n
  with H. Schlesinger and
  L. Eeckhoudt 171n, 173n
  with R. J. Zeckhauser 8n
Gomes, Francisco
  with P. Maenhout, J. Y. Campbell
  and J. Cocco 196, 197, 202,
  204, 207, 208, 213, 214, 215,
  216
  with P. Maenhout and J. Cocco
  7n, 197, 202, 206, 218
  with P. Maenhout, L. M. Viceira
  J. Y. Campbell and J. Cocco
  94
Gourinchas, Pierre-Olivier, with
  J. Parker 208, 211
Green, Jerry, with M. Whinston
  and A. Mas-Colell 22n
Greenspan, Alan 70
Grossman, Sanford J.
  with R. J. Shiller 7, 11, 39, 102
  with Z. Zhou, subsistence
  179
Grubber, Martin J., with
  E. J. Elton 5n
Guiso, Luigi, with M. Haliassos
  and T. Jappelli 198n
Gul, Faruk 9n

Haliassos, Michael
  with C. C. Bertaut 198
  with T. Jappelli and
  L. Guiso 198n
Hamilton, James D.,
  Kalman filter 70
Hansen, Lars P.
  with J. H. Cochrane 39
  with R. Jagannathan 39, 72
  with K. J. Singleton 7, 39, 40

Harrison, J. Michael, with
  D. M. Kreps 134
Harvey, Andrew C., with
  E. Renault and
  E. Ghysels 147
Harvey, Campbell 91, 154
Hassett, Kevin, with
  J. Glassman 117
Heal, Geoffrey M., with
  H. E. Ryder Jr 177n
Heaton, John, with D. J. Lucas
  162n, 164, 198, 199, 200,
  201, 216
Hentschel, Ludger 147
  with J. Y. Campbell 149
Hirano, Keisuke, with
  G. Chamberlain 187n
Hodrick, Robert J. 89, 102, 107
  with D. A. Marshall and
  G. Bekaert 9n, 107
Huang, Chi-fu, with J. C. Cox
  133, 137, 140
Hubbard, Glenn, with
  J. S. Skinner and
  S. Zeldes 202, 207

Ingersoll, Jonathan E. Jr 22n

Jagannathan, Ravi
  with L. P. Hansen 39, 72
  with E. R. McGrattan and
  A. Scherbina 11, 187
  with D. Runkle and
  L. R. Glosten 91, 102, 154
  with Z. Wang 203
Jappelli, Tullio, with L. Guiso and
  M. Haliassos 198n
Jenter, Dirk, with A. Moel,
  P. Tufano and F. Degeorge
  198n
Jorion, Philippe, with
  W. M. Goetzman 107
Judd, Kenneth L. 125

Juster, F. Thomas, with
  M. S. Kimball, M. D. Shapiro
  and R. B. Barsky 214

Kahneman, Daniel, with
  A. Tversky 9, 222
Kandel, Shmuel, with
  R. Stambaugh 89, 155n
Karatzas, Ioannis
  with J. Cvitanić 61
  with J. Lehoczky and
  S. E. Shreve 133
  with S. E. Shreve 120, 123n
Kim, Myung J., with
  C. R. Nelson 107
Kim, Tong Suk, with E. Omberg
  89, 93, 97, 99n, 113, 125
Kimball, Miles S. 171n, 173n, 190
  with S. Basu 175n
  with C. D. Carroll 169n
  with D. W. Elmendorf 171n, 192
  with M. D. Shapiro, R. B. Barsky
  and F. T. Juster 214
King, Robert G., with C. I. Plosser
  and S. T. Rebelo 174
Klein, Roger, with V. Bawa and
  S. Brown 155n
Kocherlakota, Narayana 11n
Kogan, Leonid, with R. Uppal 132
Koo, Hyeng Keun 164, 169n, 171n,
  189, 192
  with J. Y. Campbell 93
Kreps, David M.
  with J. M. Harrison 134
  with E. Porteus 43
Kritzman, Mark P. 35, 36
Kroner, Kenneth, with
  T. Bollerslev and R. Y. Chou
  147
Kwon, Heon-Chul, with
  H. J. McCulloch 69
Kyle, Albert S., with
  J. Y. Campbell 167

Lagnado, Ronald, with
  M. J. Brennan and
  E. S. Schwartz 7n
Lax, Yoel 180, 181
Lehoczky, J., with S. E. Shreve
  and I. Karatzas 133
Leland, Hayne, with
  J. C. Cox 133, 179
Letendre, Marc-Andre, with
  G. Smith 183
Lewis, Karen 199
Lipster, Robert S., with
  A. N. Shiryaev 156
Liu, Jun 126, 127
  with A. Andrew and
  G. Bekaert 9n
Lo, Andrew W., with
  A. C. MacKinlay and
  J. Y. Campbell 59, 63, 96,
  103, 143, 147
Lucas, Deborah J., with
  J. Heaton 162n, 164, 198,
  199, 200, 201, 216
Lucas, Robert E. Jr 7, 11, 53
Ludvigson, Sydney, with
  J. Y. Campbell 174
Lund, Jesper, with T. Andersen
  and L. Benzoni 149
Lynch, Anthony W. 7n
  with P. Balduzzi 7n

McCulloch, J. Huston, with
  H.-C. Kwon 69
McGrattan, Ellen R., with
  A. Scherbina and
  R. Jagannathan 11, 187
MacKinlay, A. Craig, with
  J. Y. Campbell and A. W. Lo
  59, 63, 96, 103, 143, 147
MaCurdy, Thomas E. 182
Maenhout, Pascal
  with J. Y. Campbell, J. Cocco
  and F. Gomes 196, 197, 202,

204, 207, 208, 213, 214, 215,
  216
  with J. Cocco and F. Gomes
  7n, 197, 202, 206, 218
  with L. M. Viceira,
  J. Y. Campbell, J. Cocco
  and F. Gomes 94, 118n
Mankiw, N. Gregory
  with J. Y. Campbell 203
  with D. N. Weil and
  N. N. Canner 4, 5, 79–80,
  82
  with S. P. Zeldes 198
Markowitz, Harry 1–2, 17
Marshall, David A., with
  G. Bekaert and
  R. J. Hodrick 9n, 107
Mas-Colell, Andreu, with J. Green
  and M. Whinston 22n
Mayers, David 7
Mehra, Rajnish, with E. C. Prescott
  7, 11, 53, 73
Merton, Robert C. 6, 7, 14, 15, 33,
  50, 57, 89, 120, 121, 123n,
  124, 125, 155
  with W. Samuelson and
  Z. Bodie 15, 162–3, 165, 171n,
  174
Michaelides, Alexander 221n
Minehart, Debby, with M. Rabin
  and D. Bowman 9n
Modigliani, Franco, with
  R. Sutch 6, 58
Moel, Alberto, with P. Tufano,
  F. Degeorge and D. Jenter
  198n
Mossin, Jan 6

Neftci, Salih N. 121
Nelson, Charles R., with
  M. J. Kim 107
Nelson, Daniel B., with
  D. P. Foster 155

Nielsen, Lars Tyge, with
    M. Vassalou 138

Omberg, Edward
    with T. S. Kim 89, 93, 97, 99n,
    113
    with T. S. Suk 125

Parker, Jonathan, with
    P.-O. Gourinchas 208, 211
Pastor, Lubos 155n
Pischke, Jörn-Steffen 203
Pliska, S. 133
Plosser, Charles I., with
    S. T. Rebelo and R. G. King
    174
Polyanin, Andrei D., with
    V. F. Zaitsev 125, 129
Porteus, Edward, with
    D. Kreps 43
Poterba, James M. 199
    with L. H. Summers 96, 110
Pratt, John W. 23
    with C. Gollier 171n, 173n
    with R. J. Zeckhauser 171n, 173n
Prescott, Edward C., with
    R. Mehra 7, 11, 53, 73

Quinn, J. B. 4, 5

Rabin, Matthew, with D. Bowman
    and D. Minehart 9n
Rebelo, S. T., with R. G. King
    and C. I. Plosser 174
Renault, Eric, with E. Ghysels
    and A. C. Harvey 147
Restoy, Fernando 56–7
Rogers, L., with D. Talay 125
Ross, Stephen A. 8n
Rubinstein, Mark 6–7, 11, 39,
    57, 58, 166, 177
Runkle, David, with L. R. Glosten
    and R. Jagannathan 91, 102,
    154

Ryder, Harl E. Jr, with
    G. M. Heal 177n

Samuelson, Paul A. 6, 14, 33,
    36, 89, 181
Samuelson, William, with
    Z. Bodie and R. C. Merton 15,
    162–3, 165, 171n, 174
Samwick, Andrew, with
    C. D. Carroll 187n, 208
Scherbina, Anna, with
    R. Jagannathan and
    E. R. McGrattan 11, 187
Schlesinger, Harris, with
    L. Eeckhoudt and
    C. Gollier 171n, 173n
Schoenholtz, Kermit L., with
    R. J. Shiller and
    J. Y. Campbell 143
Schroder, Mark, with
    C. Skiadas 46, 126, 127
Schwartz, Eduardo S.
    with M. J. Brennan 179
    with R. Lagnado and
    M. J. Brennan 7n
Schwert, G. William
    with E. Fama 7, 102, 203
    with R. F. Stambaugh and
    K. R. French 149
Shapiro, Matthew D., with
    R. B. Barsky, F. T. Juster and
    M. S. Kimball 214
Sharpe, William F. 20, 225n
Shiller, Robert J. 7, 9, 39, 103,
    149n
    with J. Y. Campbell 11, 53, 73,
    97, 115, 116, 187
    with J. Y. Campbell and
    K. L. Schoenholtz 143
    with S. J. Grossman 7, 11, 39, 102
Shiryaev, Albert N., with
    R. S. Lipster 156
Shore, Stephen, with J. White 181

Shreve, Steven E.
  with I. Karatzas 120, 123n
  with I. Karatzas and
    J. Lehoczky 133
Siegel, Jeremy 88–9, 100–1, 108,
    110–11, 117, 118
Singleton, Kenneth J. 149n
  with L. P. Hansen 7, 39, 40
Skiadas, Costis, with
    M. Schroder 46, 126, 127
Skinner, Jonathan S., with
    S. Zeldes and G. Hubbard
    202, 207
Smith, Gregor, with
    M.-A. Letrendre 183
Spatt, Chester S., with H. H. Zhang
    and R. M. Dammon 13n, 222
Stambaugh, Robert F. 106, 107
  with K. R. French and
    G. W. Schwert, volatility
    149
  with S. Kandel 89, 155n
Stiglitz, Joseph E. 6–7, 58
Storesletten, Kjetil, with
    C. I. Telmer and A. Yaron 207
Summers, Lawrence H.
  with C. D. Carroll 208
  with J. M. Poterba 96, 110
Sundaresan, Suresh M. 177
Sutch, Richard, with
    F. Modigliani 6, 58
Svensson, Lars E. O. 144
  with I. M. Werner 125n, 166, 194

Talay, Denis, with L. Rogers 125
Telmer, Chris I., with A. Yaron
    and K. Storesletten 207
Teplá, Lucie 61
Thaler, Richard 9
  with S. Benartzi 199
Tobin, James 3, 21, 30
Tufano, Peter, with F. Degeorge,
    D. Jenter and A. Moel 198n

Tversky, Amos, with
    D. Kahneman 9, 222

Uppal, Raman, with
    L. Kogan 132

Vasicek, Oldrich 62, 127, 128
Vassalou, Maria, with
    L. T. Nielsen 138
Viceira, Luis M. 164, 182, 183,
    185
  with J. Y. Campbell 8, 28, 51, 62,
    64, 68, 70, 89, 93, 94–5, 97–8,
    100, 101, 112, 126, 133, 145,
    150, 184, 186
  with J. Y. Campbell and
    Y. L. Chan 90, 93, 101, 115,
    116
  with J. Y. Campbell, J. Cocco,
    F. Gomes and P. Maenhout
    94, 118n
  with G. Chacko 91, 120, 126,
    147, 148–50, 152
Volcker, Paul A. 70

Wachter, Jessica 126, 141, 142–3
Wang, Zhenyu, with
    R. Jagannathan 203
Weil, David N., with N. N. Canner
    and G. Mankiw 4, 5, 79–80,
    82
Weil, Philippe 43
  with A. Giovannini 46
Werner, Ingrid M., with
    L. E. O. Svensson 125n, 166,
    194
Whinston, Michael, with
    A. Mas-Colell and J. Green
    22n
White, Joshua, with S. Shore 181
Willen, Paul, with S. Davis 166,
    194
Williams, Joseph 154

Xia, Yihong 158–60
  with M. J. Brennan 121, 126

Yaron, Amir, with K. Storesletten
  and C. I. Telmer 207

Zaitsev, Valentin F., with
  A. D. Polyanin 125, 129
Zeckhauser, Richard J.
  with C. Gollier 8n
  with J. W. Pratt 171n, 173n

Zeldes, Stephen
  with J. Ameriks 199, 200, 201
  with G. Hubbard and
    J. S. Skinner 202, 207
  with N. G. Mankiw 198
Zhang, Harold H., with
  R. M. Dammon and
  C. S. Spatt 13n, 222
Zhou, Zhongwuan, with
  S. J. Grossman 179
Zin, Stanley, with L. Epstein 8n,
  9n, 43, 46

Subject Index

absolute risk aversion 23, 24,
    166–7
    see also risk aversion;
    exponential utility
absolute risk tolerance 23
    see also risk tolerance
affine term structure model *see*
    term structure model
age
    effect on consumption 211–12,
        217–18
    effect on portfolio choice 164,
        181, 195, 199–202, 219–20
    and subsistence levels 181
    see also horizon effects; pension
        plans; retirement; life-cycle
agriculture 215
American Stock Exchange
    (AMEX) 69
annualized return 31
    see also K-period return
annuity value of wealth 46
approximate analytical solution
        to intertemporal portfolio
        choice problems 7–8
    continuous time framework
        129–33, 143, 145–6
    discrete time framework 62, 66,
        91–8, 167–77, 183–6
AR (autoregressive) process 95
    see also mean-reversion;
        VAR system
asset allocation puzzle 4–5, 79–83
asymptotic tests of
        predictability 107

background risk 171
balanced growth 174, 176n

bankruptcy, log portfolio
    return 28–9
Bayesian rule 156, 159
behavioral finance 9–10
Bellman optimality principle
    121–7, 144–5, 150
benchmark asset 21
bills 203, 213
    asset allocation puzzle 5
    in long-term portfolios 6
    mean–variance analysis 2–3
    nominal yield 103–4
    risk in USA 101–16
    volatility 108
bond–stock ratio 2, 4–5
bonds 1
    asset allocation puzzle 4–5
    bond market risk in USA
        101–16
    consol bonds 50, 59–62, 67, 79
    coupon bonds 59, 64, 68, 79,
        82, 86
    duration 103
    indexed bonds *see*
        inflation-indexed bonds
    inflation-indexed bonds 1, 6,
        14, 48–9, 62–7, 74, 79–80,
        115–16
    loglinear approximation to
        coupon-bond return 59, 103
    long-term portfolios 6
    mean–variance analysis 2–3
    model with constant variances
        and risk premia 50–62
    nominal bonds 12, 14, 48, 62,
        67–9, 74, 80–3, 104
    real bonds *see* inflation-indexed
        bonds

bonds (*cont.*):
  risk premium 65, 68, 72–4, 104
  see also bills; term structure of
    interest rates
borrowing constraint 50, 61, 62,
  78, 82n, 204
budget constraint *see*
  intertemporal budget
  constraint
buffer-stock savers 198, 211

capital asset pricing model
  (CAPM) 45
capital gains, forgiveness at
  death 222
  see also taxation
CAPM *see* capital asset pricing
  model
CARA *see* constant absolute risk
  aversion
cash *see* bills
cash on hand 205
CCAPM *see* consumption capital
  asset pricing model
Center for Research in Security
  Prices (CRSP) 69, 103, 104
coefficient of relative prudence
  see prudence
coefficient of risk aversion *see*
  risk aversion
coefficient of risk tolerance *see*
  risk tolerance
cohort effects 200–1
complete markets 91
conditional variances 96
consol bonds 50, 59–62, 67, 79
consol return 59
constant absolute risk aversion
  (CARA) 166–7
  see also risk aversion;
    exponential utility
constant relative risk aversion
  (CRRA) 24, 42–4

see also risk aversion; power
  utility; Epstein–Zin utility
constraint *see* borrowing
  constraint; intertemporal
  budget constraint;
  short-sales constraint
consumption 8
  and age 212, 218
  and bond indexation 85
  constant consumption–wealth
    ratio 40–2, 85
  consumption capital asset
    pricing model (CCAPM) 40
  as dividend on optimally
    invested wealth 136
  and labor income 184–6
  in life-cycle model 212
  and long-term portfolio choice
    in a VAR model 90–4
  substituting consumption out of
    the consumption-based
    model 53–5
  utility of consumption 37–46
  see also Epstein–Zin utility;
    intertemporal budget
    constraint; power utility;
    precautionary savings;
    subsistence
consumption capital asset pricing
  model (CCAPM) 40
continuation value 206
continuous-time framework 62,
  160–1
  dynamic programming
    approach 121–33
  hedging of volatility risk
    147–54
  martingale approach
    133–43
  parameter uncertainty 154–60
  recursive utility 143–6
continuously compounded
  portfolio return 26

contrarian investment
    strategy 164
corporate bond yield 103
coupon bond 59, 64, 68, 79, 82, 86
covariance, conditional and
    unconditional 96
Cox–Huang solution method
    see martingale method
CREF *see* TIAA-CREF
CRRA *see* constant relative
    risk aversion
CRSP *see* Center for Research
    in Security Prices

decision theory 9n
defined-benefit pension plans 1
defined-contribution pension
    plans 198–9, 201
dentists vi
Depression 104
discrete-state approximations 7
diversification 12, 199, 222
dividend–price ratio 106, 107,
    112n, 114–15
dividend yield *see* dividend–price
    ratio
duration 103
dynamic budget constraint
    see intertemporal budget
    constraint
dynamic programming
    approach 34, 43, 121–33

education, and labor income
    process 207–10, 215, 217
efficient frontier, *see*
    mean–standard deviation
    diagram; mean–variance
    analysis
elasticity of intertemporal
    substitution in consumption
    (EIS) 18, 39–40, 42–6, 166, 190
elasticity of labor supply 175–7

envelope condition 124, 130,
    145–6, 176
Epstein–Zin utility 18, 42–6, 143
    see also power utility
equities *see* stocks
equity premium *see* risk premia
equity premium puzzle 10–11
Euler equations 38–40, 43–5,
    53, 184
expectations hypothesis of the
    term structure of interest
    rates 64–5, 68
exponential utility 24–5
external habit formation *see*
    habit formation

fallacies of long-term portfolio
    choice 35–6
Federal Reserve Treasury
    Accord 70, 103
Fidelity, recommended asset
    allocation 4–5
Financial Engines website 225n
financial planners 3–5, 224–5
fixed costs of equity
    investment 197

Gaussian quadrature 206
general equilibrium 118
growth-optimal portfolio 27, 36,
    137–8

habit formation 119, 177
habitat 58
hedging
    income hedging demand 188–9
    intertemporal hedging demand
    12, 15, 50, 57–8, 98–100,
    151–4, 158, 160
    US stock and bond market
    risk 112–16
heterogeneity of households,
    life-cycle portfolio choice
    213–19

homoskedasticity 91
horizon effects 14
  see also age; retirement
household asset allocation
  197–202
housing 13, 221–2
human capital *see* human wealth
human wealth 6, 15, 162–94,
  195
  see also labor income

idiosyncratic labor income
  risk 186–9
  see also labor income risk
IID *see* independently and
  identically distributed returns
income *see* labor income
income effect, on
  consumption–wealth ratio 42
independent and identically
  distributed (IID) returns 18,
  32–3, 35, 42, 89
indexation, benefits 83–6
indexed bonds *see*
  inflation-indexed bonds
individual investors 12
individual retirement accounts
  (IRAs) 199
inflation 48, 67–72, 76–8, 102,
  104, 108
inflation risk 48, 67–8, 71–3,
  87, 115–17, 223–4
inflation-indexed bonds 1, 6, 14,
  48–9, 62–7, 72–4, 79–80,
  115–16
institutional investors 1, 7, 13,
  162n
insurance 207
  see also portfolio insurance
interest rate 48, 58, 187, 210
  risk *see* interest rate risk
  stability of 47

and the stochastic discount
  factor 135, 141
in term structure models 63,
  71–2, 127
in a VAR model 101–4
  see also inflation; term structure
  of interest rates; yield
interest rate risk 48–9, 58,
  86–7, 107–10, 112–14,
  116, 117
interior decorator fallacy 4
internal habit formation *see*
  habit formation
intertemporal budget
  constraint 37, 40, 43,
  50–3, 122, 136, 183
  see also liquid wealth; retirement
  wealth
intertemporal hedging
  demand 12, 15, 50, 57–8,
  98–100, 151–4, 158, 160
  US stock and bond market
  risk 112–16
intertemporal substitution *see*
  elasticity of intertemporal
  substitution of consumption
investment horizon 107–10
  see also age; retirement
investment opportunity set 98
isoelastic utility *see* power utility
Itô's Lemma 28, 121, 123, 139

Jane Bryant Quinn, recommended
  asset allocation 4–5
Jensen's inequality 72, 104

Kalman filter 70
Kamakura Risk Information
  Services 69
K-period return 31, 96
  return volatility at short and
  long horizons 107–10

labor income 6, 162, 193–4
  analogy between labor income
    and subsistence needs 177–9
  education 215
  fixed labor supply 167–73
  flexible labor supply 174–7
  human wealth 163
  life-cycle portfolio choice 202–3
  measuring heterogeneity
    214–16
  permanent shocks to 182–3,
    203, 208–10, 215–16
  portfolio choice with riskless
    labor income 162–4
  portfolio choice with risky labor
    income 188, 190
  precautionary savings 182–93
  private businesses 162*n*
  risk *see* labor income risk
  transitory shocks to 182–3, 203,
    208–10, 215–16
  see also human wealth
labor income risk 171–3, 186–9,
    191–3
  correlated 189
  idiosyncratic 186–9
  mean-preserving increase
    in 173
labor supply 15, 194
  fixed 167–81
  flexible 174
learning 12
  impact on portfolio choice
    154–60
  about predictability of
    returns 158–60
leisure 174
leveraged position 28
life-cycle model 13*n*, 16, 166,
    182, 183
life-cycle portfolio choice 195–7,
    202–19
  see also age; pensions; retirement

liquid wealth 204–6, 211–13,
    217, 219
log utility 18, 24, 27, 42–4, 46
  long-term portfolio choice 35–6
  see also Epstein–Zin utility;
    power utility
loglinear approximation
  to coupon bond return 59, 103
  to intertemporal portfolio choice
    problems *see* approximate
    analytical solution to
    intertemporal portfolio
    choice problems
  to portfolio return 27–30
lognormal returns 25
  consumption-based model
    39–40
  power utility 25–30
long-horizon portfolio choice 4,
    6–8, 163, 181
  and labor income risk 191–3
long-horizon return *see* K-period
    return

market timing 101, 117
martingale approach 121, 133–43
mean-preserving increase in labor
    income risk 173
mean aversion 108
  see also mean reversion
mean reversion 7*n*, 15, 89, 95–7
  stock returns in USA 107–10
  see also K-period returns
mean–standard deviation
    diagram 2
mean–variance analysis 1–3, 7,
    12, 14, 18–21, 86
  and bonds 86
  with many risky assets 20
  with no riskless asset 21
mental accounting 9
Merrill Lynch, recommended asset
    allocation 4–5

monetary policy 70, 103, 223
Monte Carlo analysis 107
Moody's 103
moral hazard 162
multi-period return *see*
    K-period return
mutual fund theorem 3, 21, 30
myopic portfolio choice 14
    long-term 31–46
    short-term 18–30

NASDAQ (National Association
    of Securities Dealers
    Automated Quotation
    service) 69
National Center for Health
    Statistics 206
New York Stock Exchange
    (NYSE) 69
New York Times, recommended
    asset allocation 4–5
nominal bonds 12, 14, 48, 62,
    67–9, 72–4, 80–3, 104
    see also term structure of
        interest rates
non-tradable assets 163, 164
non-tradable labor income 6, 162
    see also labor income

ordinary differential equation
    (ODE) 125, 129–30, 145–6
Ornstein–Uhlenbeck process 7*n*,
    97, 159

PaineWebber, advertisement 4*n*
Panel Study of Income Dynamics
    (PSID) 197–8, 207, 208, 214
parameter uncertainty 154–60,
    161
partial differential equation
    (PDE) 125
partial equilibrium model 118
pension plans 1, 198–9
    defined-benefit 1

defined-contribution 198–9,
    201
    see also age; retirement
portfolio
    insurance 179
    loglinear approximation of
        return 27–30
    long-term 6–8
    myopic long-term 31–46
    myopic short-term 18–30
power utility 7*n*, 18, 24
    of consumption, long-term
        portfolio choice 37–42
    and Epstein–Zin utility 42–3
    and exponential utility 24–5
    of wealth, long-term portfolio
        choice 31–5
    of wealth, short-term portfolio
        choice 25–30
    see also utility function
precautionary savings 40, 44,
    183, 190–1
predictability
    asymptotic tests of 107
    learning about 158–60
    of stock and bond returns in
        USA 101–10
    see also *K*-period return; mean
        reversion
pricing kernel 134
    see also stochastic discount factor
private businesses 201, 202, 216,
    220
    and household asset
        allocation 198–9
    and human wealth 162*n*
private equity, *see* private
    businesses
proprietorial income, *see*
    private businesses
prospect theory 9
prudence 191
Puzzles of Finance (Kritzman) 35

quadratic utility 24
quadrature, Gaussian 206

real bonds *see* inflation-indexed
 bonds
real interest rate *see*
 inflation-indexed bonds;
 interest rate
recursive utility, *see* Epstein–Zin
 utility
relative prudence 191
relative risk aversion 23, 24, 42–4
 see also risk aversion
retirement 1, 12, 16, 162, 182
 and liquid wealth 204–5
 and portfolio choice 186–9
 and savings 190–1
 individual retirement accounts
  (IRAs) 199
 retired investors 184–5, 188
 retirement wealth 204–5,
  211–12, 219
 see also age; pension plans
return
 asymptotic tests of
  predictability 107
 independent and identically
  distributed (IID)
  returns 32–3, 35, 42, 89
 loglinear approximation to
  coupon bond return 103
 loglinear approximation to
  portfolio return 27–30
 lognormal returns 25–30,
  39–40
 see also K-period return; mean
  reversion; VAR system
risk
 fallacies of long-term
  portfolio choice 35–7
 time-varying risk 147–54
 stock and bond market risk
  in USA 101–16

see also inflation risk; interest
 rate risk; labor income risk;
 mean-variance analysis;
 risk aversion; risk premia;
 risk tolerance; riskless
 asset; volatility
risk aversion 23
 absolute risk aversion 23–4,
  166–7
 and myopic portfolio
  choice 25–35
 and portfolio choice over the
  life-cycle 211–13, 216–19
 and portfolio choice with
  interest rate risk 78–86
 and portfolio choice with
  labor income risk 186–9,
  191–3
 and portfolio choice with
  time-varying risk premia
  98–101, 110–13, 115–16
 and portfolio choice with
  volatility risk 147–54
 constant absolute risk aversion
  (CARA) 166–7
 constant relative risk aversion
  (CRRA) 24, 42–4
 relative risk aversion 23, 24,
  42–4
 see also risk; risk tolerance; utility
  function
risk premia 14
 with Epstein–Zin utility 45,
  54–5
 on inflation-indexed bonds 65,
  72–4
 on nominal bonds 68, 72–4,
  104
 with power utility of
  consumption 40
 predictability of 89, 105–6
 on stocks 69, 74, 76, 104, 187,
  210–11

risk premia (*cont.*):
  see also Epstein–Zin utility;
    equity premium puzzle;
    power utility
risk tolerance 23–5
  see also risk; risk aversion;
    utility function
riskless asset 18–19, 27, 58–60,
    222–3
riskless interest rate *see* interest
    rate; riskless asset

S & P 500 Index 102
safe asset *see* riskless asset
savings, *see* consumption;
    precautionary savings
scale-independent utility
    functions 17
Sharpe ratio 20, 35–6, 73–5, 79,
    84, 105, 112, 116, 138, 147–8
short position 28
short-sales constraints 50, 61–2,
    78, 82*n*, 204
short-term portfolio choice 18–30
social security 196
Spectral Generalized Method of
    Moments 149*n*
Standard & Poor's 500
    Index 102
state–price density 134
stochastic discount factor
    (SDF) 38–9, 62–9, 133–5
  see also martingale approach
stochastic volatility *see* volatility
stocks
  asset allocation puzzle 5, 79–83
  and bonds, optimal
    allocations 78, 80–3, 110–16
  equity premium puzzle 10–11
  and labor income risk 186–9,
    191–3
  and life-cycle portfolio
    choice 211–13, 216–19

in long-term portfolios 6
  mean reversion of 94–101
  mean–variance analysis 2–3
  predictability of stock returns in
    a VAR model 104–7
  risk premium 69, 74, 76, 104,
    187, 210–11
  stock and bond market risk in
    USA 107–10
  see also bond–stock ratio
Stocks for the Long Run (Siegel)
    88–9
strategic asset allocation viii,
    13, 99, 117, 223, 225
subsistence
  and asset allocation 177–81
  see also consumption
substitution effect, on
    consumption–wealth ratio 42
surplus consumption 178–80
Survey of Consumer Finances
    (SCF) 197–8
Survey of Financial Characteristics
    of Consumers 197

tactical asset allocation viii, 99, 117
taxation 3, 13
  capital gains, forgiveness at
    death 222
  deductibility of mortgage
    interest 222
  tax incentives 199
Taylor approximation 27
term structure of interest rates
  affine model 10, 62–86
  continuous-time Vasicek
    model 127–8
  in USA 69–78
TIAA–CREF 1
time discount factor 37, 39
time effects 199–201
time-separable power utility
    37, 43

time-varying expected
  returns 138, 157
time-varying risk *see* risk
transaction costs 13
Treasury bills *see* bills

unconditional variances 96
universities 162n
updating rule 155
USA
  household asset allocation
    197
  inflation risk 71–3, 87, 115–16,
    223–4
  labor income risk 207–10
  monetary policy 70, 103, 223
  pensions 1
  social security 196
  stochastic volatility 148–9,
    160
  stock and bond market risk 86,
    101–16
  term structure of interest
    rates 69–78
utility function 8–10, 22–5
  see also Epstein–Zin utility;
    exponential utility;
    log utility; power utility

value function 97
VAR (vector autoregressive)
  system 89
  long-term portfolio choice
    90–101
  stock and bond market risk in
    USA 101–2, 104–16

variance
  conditional and
    unconditional 96
  model with constant variances
    and risk premia 50–62
  variance decomposition 215–16
variance ratio 96
Vasicek model 62, 127–8
volatility
  hedging 147–54
  stochastic volatility 10, 148
  US stock and bond market
    risk 107–10
  volatility risk 11, 154, 160

Wall Street 224
wealth 4, 13–15
  and risk tolerance 23–4
  liquid wealth 205, 206, 211–13,
    217, 219
  power utility of 31–5
  retirement wealth 204–5,
    211–12, 219
  see also consumption-wealth
    ratio; wealth–income ratio
wealth elasticity of consumption
  170, 172, 185, 187, 190
wealth–income ratio 190–1, 193
Wiener process 157
World War II 104

yield 59, 63–4, 68, 102–7
  spread 102–7, 113–15
  see also dividend yield;
    interest rate; term structure
    of interest rates